10/26/15
42.00

'At a time when reporting on the Israeli-Palestinian conflict is under unprecedented scrutiny, James Rodgers provides an essential and insightful historical perspective on the long "war of words" behind a major conflict of our time. Rodgers' book is essential reading for those seeking a greater understanding of the difficult dynamics behind reporting – and resolving conflicts.'

Lyse Doucet, Chief International Correspondent, BBC News

'*Headlines from the Holy Land* is an impressively, innovative form of history as media history, looking at one of the most complex stories of our age through the imperfect, shifting but revelatory perspectives of the many journalists who covered this often compelling tale as it unfolded, from its 1946 roots through the various wars and propaganda battles fought in the streets of Gaza or the networks of social media. James Rodgers offers an insightful, empathetic, and rigorous guide to how journalism struggled – often heroically – to tell one of the most brutal and difficult of international stories.'

Charlie Beckett, Director, Polis, Department of Media and Communications, London School of Economics, UK

'James Rodgers is honestly direct about the challenges and pressures that make reporting on the Israeli-Palestinian conflict unique among the myriad of crises faced by international journalists, something he was uniquely placed to do as the only Western correspondent based in the Gaza Strip in the tumultuous years immediately after 9/11. But what makes this book so refreshing and incisive is that this account of reporting on this most intractable yet consequential conflict is the work of someone with the benefit of having been an experienced foreign correspondent but who now writes with the rigour of an academic's eye on how our world is reported. In doing so, Rodgers leaves very few stones unturned, from the war over terminology and language to the increasing role of religion in a crisis centred on a small area brimful of contested holy sites, and he has framed it in a way that has context, careful analysis and is accessible to all those who either want to understand how this war which continues to have a major international impact is reported or to those who want to report it themselves.'

Rageh Omaar, International Affairs Editor, ITV News

'Reporting on the Israeli-Palestinian conflict often generates as much controversy as the issue itself. James Rodgers' book is rare for approaching the subject of how the story has been told by Western journalists over the decades with an open mind and academic rigour. It combines detailed research and candid insights from many of the region's seasoned correspondents with an accessible style that keeps the pages turning. With so many thoroughly biased self-appointed media watchdogs out there, it is refreshing to read something that genuinely attempts to tackle the job of reporting on the Israeli-Palestinian conflict with intelligent thoughtfulness.'

Paul Danahar, Author of *The New Middle East: The World after the Arab Spring*

'The conflict between Israelis and Palestinians has been more intensively covered by the media, and for a longer period, than any other in recent times. In this fascinating book, James Rodgers tells us the story of the story. He shows how, as the struggle came to be as much about meaning, language, and perception as about bullets, bombs, or negotiations, reporters were under constant pressure from the two sides seeking to control the narrative to their own advantage. He shows, too, how they brought their own prejudices and national viewpoints to the story and how, nevertheless, good reporting did emerge and was, as it remains, vital in sustaining what informed public opinion there is on the dire state of affairs in the Holy Land of the title.'

Martin Woollacott, commentator on international affairs and
former foreign editor, *The Guardian*

'An important and necessary book.'

Patrick Cockburn, *The Independent*

Headlines from the Holy Land

Reporting the Israeli-Palestinian Conflict

James Rodgers
City University London, UK

First published 2015 by
PALGRAVE MACMILLAN

Palgrave Macmillan in the UK is an imprint of Macmillan Publishers Limited, registered in England, company number 785998, of Houndmills, Basingstoke, Hampshire RG21 6XS.

Palgrave Macmillan in the US is a division of St Martin's Press LLC, 175 Fifth Avenue, New York, NY 10010.

Palgrave Macmillan is the global academic imprint of the above companies and has companies and representatives throughout the world.

Palgrave® and Macmillan® are registered trademarks in the United States, the United Kingdom, Europe and other countries.

ISBN 978–1–137–39512–2

This book is printed on paper suitable for recycling and made from fully managed and sustained forest sources. Logging, pulping and manufacturing processes are expected to conform to the environmental regulations of the country of origin.

A catalogue record for this book is available from the British Library.

A catalog record for this book is available from the Library of Congress.

Dedicated to the memory of my father,
Ian MacDonald Rodgers, 1938–2013.
Our last conversation was about my plans for this book.

Contents

Foreword

This exploration of the challenges facing journalists whose task it has been to report on developments in the Israeli-Palestinian conflict is refreshingly direct and engaging. Tackling his subject from the perspective of the men and women appointed by various media organizations to report the news first hand from 'the Holy Land', James Rodgers draws both on his own experiences as the only foreign correspondent based inside the Gaza Strip between 2002 and 2004 and on the insights and accounts of many other fellow journalists who have covered the conflict over the years.

His approach is that of the professional correspondent turned academic, forensically seeking out evidence to substantiate his every point. As a result, he passes no judgement on the rights and wrongs of the protagonists, simply reporting the lengths to which they are prepared to go to try to shape how events are covered in the international media. In so doing, Rodgers identifies the structures and methods used by the contending parties to facilitate or deny access to different locations and people 'on the ground'.

In the course of the book Rodgers reveals the relative advantages of foreign correspondents, compared with diplomats, in terms of their freedom of movement around the West Bank and Gaza Strip, occupied by Israel since the Six-Day War of 1967. Indeed, the restrictions placed on foreign diplomats by the Israeli authorities to prevent them roaming at will around these areas and seeing for themselves what life is like for ordinary Palestinians under occupation in the West Bank or under the blockade in Gaza have increased in recent years.

An example is recounted by Dan Kurtzer, former US ambassador to Israel, in an interview with Rodgers. Whereas Kurtzer was able to explore by himself the Gaza Strip and the West Bank in the 1980s, when he was serving on the staff at the US Embassy in Tel Aviv, by the time he returned as ambassador such access was impossible, even for more junior officials. Security concerns are cited as the justification for the constraints, yet intrepid reporters can still report from around the occupied territories, if they are so minded.

What distinguishes different journalists in terms of whether they take the risks entailed in going 'to see for themselves' has to do with their own sense of responsibility. On this Rodgers is forthright: the real professionals know that they owe it to their audiences to rise to the challenge. After all, if even the foreign diplomats are increasingly obliged to rely on journalists for their information – a point which Rodgers makes compellingly – then those journalists must take their fact-finding mission seriously. The prospects of conflict resolution depend on it.

Interestingly, Rodgers reveals, every ambitious journalist, himself included, sees the challenge of covering the Israeli-Palestinian conflict as a potentially career enhancing test of their skills – and one to be embraced. Similarly, he says, senior diplomats regard trying their hand at conflict mediation in the Israeli-Palestinian context as a way to prove themselves, literally *because* so many before them have tried and failed to achieve a breakthrough.

It is in this respect, among others, that Rodgers deems the Israeli-Palestinian conflict as unique. The stakes are especially high because the land and sites in contention are holy to each of the three great monotheistic faiths and thence of concern to Jews, Muslims, and Christians around the world. On which note, Rodgers documents the increasing role of religion in defining the positions of the protagonists and concludes that this is rendering the parties even less amenable to accepting a compromise solution than seemingly they were in earlier decades.

Another respect in which covering the Israeli-Palestinian conflict poses a uniquely testing challenge for journalists has to do with terminology. Both the Israelis and the Palestinians are deeply invested in influencing, if not controlling, the way their conflict is depicted in the media. Various examples of how this plays out are discussed in this work, including whether or not a journalist describes the West Bank and Gaza as 'disputed' or 'occupied' territories; if they include the actual names of individuals killed in conflict or not; and whether or not the word 'settlement' adequately conveys the presence of some of the large conurbations in the West Bank inhabited by Jewish Israelis.

Particularly vexed is use of the term 'terrorist' as a descriptor. In which connection, one of the distinguishing features of this book is the inclusion of a detailed discussion of how journalists reported events which occurred in the last days of British Mandate in Palestine, in particular the bombing of the King David Hotel, headquarters of the British authorities, in 1947. Rodgers' research on newspaper coverage of that episode makes fascinating reading and reveals that reporters on the scene at the time were so much less constrained in their use of terminology than their contemporary counterparts.

At the time, press coverage was monitored by officials in the Zionist movement and supporters of their cause overseas, and remonstrations –

letters to the editor – were made in many cases. However, as Rodgers discusses, there was nothing akin to the sophisticated and comprehensive monitoring operation that currently exists and which both journalists and diplomats keep constantly in mind as they frame their despatches. Diplomats also have to be aware of the likelihood of leaks and misrepresentations.

To compound the difficulties faced by journalists, meanwhile, the advent of social media poses new challenges. On the surface, it would appear that the role of the professional correspondents has been overtaken by citizen journalists, and the former must be tweeting responses to social media posts 24/7, even before they have had a chance to 'see for themselves', interview witnesses and report 'the facts'.

In concluding, however, James Rodgers succeeds in making the case for on-the-spot correspondents, trained and practised in compiling first-hand accounts backed up by evidence, for whom there is still no replacement. By tackling his subject in that same vein, Rodgers provides his readers with a particularly engaging account of what it is like to file the headlines from the Holy Land.

Rosemary Hollis, Professor of Middle East Policy Studies,
City University London

Acknowledgements

I am grateful to all my contributors for the time which they have given me out of their busy schedules. Fayruz Rajpar's assistance with archive research and transcribing interview material has been invaluable. Glenys Sugarman of the Foreign Press Association in Israel was extremely helpful both with contacts and information. Maya Morav, guest relations manager of the King David Hotel, kindly showed me around and helped with my questions about the hotel's history. I am also grateful to Felicity Plester and Sneha Kamat Bhavnani at Palgrave Macmillan. My employers at City University London were kind enough to contribute funding towards the costs of my research.

My mother's house was the perfect place to finish the manuscript – my thanks to her now, and always. My thanks also go to my wife, Mette Jørgensen Rodgers, and our daughters, Freya and Sophia, for their love, support, and interest in my work.

Introduction

The Israeli-Palestinian conflict is the ultimate challenge for an international correspondent. Covering other major stories may demand resourcefulness, knowledge of history, politics, culture, and faith, judgement, bravery. Reporting on the Israeli-Palestinian conflict can demand all of those qualities. It usually demands all of them at the same time. For that reason, it has, at one time or another, drawn many of the greatest journalists working in international news. The conflict has so far defied a solution. The world's interest, while it flags from time to time, has never gone away. Diplomats, too, are drawn to it: tempted, perhaps, by the hope of succeeding where none has previously managed.

Part of the focus of this book is the relationship between journalism and diplomacy. Its main purpose, though, is to explain the task facing journalists who choose to cover the Israeli-Palestinian conflict: why that task is unique, how it has changed, and continues to change. For while millions of words have been written about the struggle for the land between the River Jordan and the Mediterranean Sea, the way that the journalism covering it has evolved has not received the attention it deserves. Why does this matter? It matters because for the vast majority of people with any interest in the Israeli-Palestinian conflict – from casual news consumers to policy makers – some, or all, of the information from which they form their views comes from journalists. Some might argue that the journalism of the conflict is so riddled with omissions and inaccuracies, so generally flawed, that it is all but worthless. Certainly, that often seems to be the view of anyone who has a strong opinion in favour of one side or the other. The head of Israel's Government Press Office, for example, speaking in an interview for this book, said of the international correspondents under his oversight, 'the majority of them are lazy'. Support groups for both Israel and the Palestinians around the world regularly express dismay at the way the conflict is covered. Letter-writing campaigns have given way to email campaigns which in turn have given way to bombardments on social media. As almost anyone who has written or spoken in public about the conflict knows, to do so is to invite scorn, ridicule, abuse, or insult. Telling a colleague at a leading British university one day of my plans for this book prompted the response, 'You do realize everyone will hate it, don't you?'

Why take on the task, then? Journalists covering the Israeli-Palestinian conflict have a rare perspective which informs the views of countless others right up to policy makers, prime ministers, and presidents. It has often been repeated that journalism is the first draft of history. In the case of the Israeli-Palestinian conflict, I would argue that journalists are also privileged to have a more complete picture than almost anyone else. With a seemingly ever-diminishing number of exceptions, journalists are among the few people who are able to travel widely throughout the land which is so bitterly contested. Israelis rarely venture into Gaza or the West Bank unless they are armed, or in uniform, or residents of settlements which stand as symbols of Israel's power over the Palestinians, or all of those things. Palestinians, especially those living in the cramped towns and concrete 'refugee camps' of Gaza, have rarely seen an Israeli unless it is during a military incursion. It was not always so. When I, then in my mid-thirties, lived in the territory from 2002 to 2004 many Gazans of my age, and a bit younger, had met Israelis because they had had casual jobs in Israel. That kind of contact stopped during the second intifada, and did not resume after it. In consequence, the mutual fear and suspicion between Israelis and Palestinians has only increased. Where conditions exist for mistrust and hatred, ignorance can help them to spread. In a time when there is almost no contact between Israelis and Palestinians which might be considered normal interaction between two neighbours not at war, the relationship between them is more poisoned than ever. In September 2014, even the veteran Israeli correspondent Amira Hass, best known outside Israel for her book *Drinking the Sea at Gaza* (an account of her time reporting from the territory), was asked to leave Birzeit University on the West Bank – despite the fact that she had been asked there to deliver a lecture.[1] International journalists covering the conflict, while they may well face restrictions on their access to certain people and places, do so in individual cases, and not as a general rule. As such, they have a wider view of the whole situation – or at least the opportunity to have one. This, of course, is not an opportunity always taken.

Almost without exception, international correspondents are resident in Israel rather than the Palestinian territories. The degree to which they choose to cross over to cover the other side of the line varies, sometimes to the dismay even of their own colleagues. Nevertheless, journalists have opportunities to travel, and to talk to people, largely denied both to Israelis and Palestinians, and to many others. Diplomats from the European Union and the United States are not able to talk to representatives of Hamas; journalists can. How can anyone build up a picture of what is happening in the region without the ability to discuss opinions, motives, and strategy with the group which runs the Gaza Strip, and which is seen as the focus of Palestinian armed opposition to Israel?

Journalists themselves have not always excelled at seeking out sources such as these. The newspaper reporting of the bombing of the King David Hotel in July 1946, and the 'manhunt' which followed (and which today would no doubt be called an anti-terror operation) does not generally seek to go into the wider context of the bombers' possible motives. The British newspaper reports stuck loyally to the line that any attack on the British political or military authorities was to be condemned. The American newspapers reporting the same story seemed more even handed. The contrast was greater when the Mandate came to an end. British readers were treated to an account of the closing of a glorious chapter of imperial history; the *New York Times* wrote of Britain's relief. These reports read like what they are: a draft of history which has now itself become history. Today we are in a different world. There is some continuity amid the change. The reporters of the 1940s knew what their later counterparts would recognize: censorship of sensitive military operation; the wiles of public relations officers (today we would call it 'spin'); and pressure from the parties to the conflict. They also experienced the deaths of some of their colleagues. These have all continued. When I lived in Gaza, the British cameraman James Miller, gathering material of house demolitions in the bullet-ridden refugee areas at the southern edge of the Gaza Strip (the demolitions were carried out by the Israeli Army with the stated aim of depriving their enemies of firing positions and cover; the properties demolished were often family homes) was shot and killed by Israeli fire. Yet while there are common characteristics of journalists' working lives right from the 1940s to the present, there are other aspects which have been completely transformed. Reporters may still come under pressure from what their Mandate-era counterparts termed 'public relations officials', but they are also likely to encounter extreme pressure, and even abuse, on social media – a phenomenon not even imagined then.

In that respect, reporting the Israeli-Palestinian conflict has much in common with controversial stories around the world. In other respects, it is unique – and herein lies the fascination for both journalists and diplomats. In this book, I have sought to define that uniqueness, considering the combination of history and policy which makes Israel-Palestine a priority for correspondents. Then there is faith: ever present, and increasingly important in a conflict where secular politics and conventional diplomacy have failed to deliver the elusive solution which would offer justice and peace for all. This idea that the land is God given, and cannot be given away at any price, meaning that the 'ceding of western Palestine to Israel was therefore an irreligious act'[2] in the view of Hamas, is an extremely powerful one on both sides of the conflict. It is held no less fervently by settlers on the West Bank carrying out 'price tag' attacks on their Palestinian neighbours, simply because the latter have had the impudence to live there, than by the Hamas fighter born in a refugee camp in Gaza, and dreaming of an ancestral home he has never known. Covering the conflict as a correspondent myself in the second intifada, I came to see it as existing on at least two levels: the day-to-day one of attack and counterattack which we wrote about for the radio, and the one you came across whenever you came to ask a contributor more than a few questions. This second one concerned the land not just as an agricultural or economic commodity, a resource – significant factor in the conflict though this is – but also as a spiritual one. On one of my visits to Jerusalem to conduct research for the book, I had dinner with Robbie Gringras, a university friend now living in Israel, where he works as Creative Director of Makom. He drew my attention to a cartoon drawn by two artists on either end of the Israeli political spectrum: Uri Fink and Shay Charka, the latter a religious settler living on the West Bank. Each had tried to draw the other with the trappings of views they rejected: Fink appeared with a skullcap and a rifle; Charka with a T-shirt bearing the peace sign. As Gringras explained in an article for The Forward's website, in the final version of the cartoon, Charka appears with lines, symbolizing the land, under his feet. 'He can no more delete the lines indicating the land on which he stands than he can delete the lines of his nose. Land is part of his identity. It is part of who he is.'[3] This is a sentiment which countless Palestinian refugees and their descendants would also recognize, and one which attempts to solve the conflict have failed adequately to address. This is an idea which I explored to some extent in my earlier book *No Road Home: Fighting for Land and Faith in Gaza*, an account of the people to whom I spoke when I lived in and reported from the territory. I return to it here in greater detail, convinced of the need to discuss the challenges it represents for people seeking to report on the Israeli-Palestinian conflict.

I was duly warned by the colleague whom I cite above that my book would be vulnerable to criticism, and, in anticipation that he will be proved right, I should explain some of the decisions behind the way I have selected my material. Even from the outset, I was convinced that no single volume could adequately address the subject I had chosen. I took the decision, therefore, to limit my focus to the journalism and the diplomacy of the conflict between the Israelis and the Palestinians, and that part of the conflict which has taken place on the territory between the River Jordan and the Mediterranean Sea: modern-day Israel, the West Bank, and Gaza. In consequence, there is no consideration here of the reporting of Israel's wars in Lebanon, or of the Suez crisis. This is not because I consider them insignificant. The reporting of the 1973 Arab-Israeli War, on the other hand, is discussed mainly for the way it seems to represent an evolution in the way that western reporters looked at Israel as a fighting force. No longer the terrorists of the 1940s, there is a hard-won respect for the Israeli Army – alongside others chronicling the civilian casualties of their air raids on Egyptian villages. The journalism of 1967, from the war which gave the region today's de facto borders, is considered at greater length and I was fortunate, in David Hirst and David Rubinger, to speak to two veteran reporters who covered that conflict. The other correspondents I approached are almost all from the British or American media. I accept that this means that my account lacks the perspectives of other countries, but the choice was made on the grounds that in the 1940s, where my account begins, the British were the dominant outside power in the region. Since then, of course, the United States has taken on that mantle, or shouldered that burden, depending upon which metaphor you consider more accurate. With few exceptions, the contributors I approached agreed to talk to me, most of them on the record. There are subjects here which are absent. While I consider the use of language at some length, I do not address the fact that relatively few correspondents who cover the conflict speak either of the main languages. They rely therefore on fixers and translators who have, of course, their own stakes and loyalties in the conflict. Both of these are important issues, but they will be for other books. Nor have I considered in detail here the role of Palestinian and Israeli journalists working for international news organizations. Again, this is only because the scope of this particular volume was not planned to include it. I did, though, in *Reporting Conflict* (2012), write about Palestinians working for international media in Gaza during 'Operation Cast Lead' in 2008–2009, and would refer interested readers to chapter 6 of that book.

While selecting what I would have to omit from the book was difficult, the starting point was not. The bombing of the King David Hotel in the summer of 1946 was covered in great detail – although the absence of bylines, especially from broadsheet papers, was frustrating – and provides a perfect starting point. There are echoes of the Israeli-Palestinian conflict today, and also, from the journalist's point of view, of the US-led invasions of Iraq and Afghanistan. There too journalists have been close to military and political power as it struggled against forces it would eventually prove incapable of controlling. It is to situate the Israeli-Palestinian conflict in the wider context of today's world, though, that after the first two chapters which deal with the way that the conflict was reported historically, the book's main focus is on the years since 11 September 2001.

Following the opening chapters on the reporting of the last years of the British Mandate, and the wars of 1967 and 1973, Chapter 3 discusses why the conflict has received, and continues to receive, the media attention which it does. Chapter 4 considers the coverage of the presentation in 2003 of the Roadmap. This has been chosen because the plan presented then included many of the elements also present in those which came before, and since: principally, the idea of two states, Israel and Palestine. Chapter 5, 'Going Back Two Thousand Years All the Time', considers the particular challenges for journalists of satisfying the need for context in reporting a conflict where history and ancient religions have huge influence on day-to-day life. Chapter 6 discusses ideas of access: key to any good reporting, and an area in which, in this conflict journalists often have the edge over diplomats. This chapter includes interviews with former British and American ambassadors to Israel, as well as other senior figures in Middle Eastern diplomacy. No contemporary assessment of international reporting can be complete without a consideration of the effect which changing technology, especially social media, has had on newsgathering and distribution – so Chapter 7 looks at these phenomena, with particular reference to Israel's 'Operation Protective Edge' carried out in Gaza in the summer of 2014. The book's concluding chapter looks at the reasons for the greater prominence of religion in both Israeli and Palestinian politics, and discusses the difficulties this represents for both diplomacy and journalism. Both are being changed and challenged by the increasing unpredictability of the wider region, and the way in which technological change is altering the way that diplomats and journalists work.

The reporting of the Israeli-Palestinian conflict is not perfect. It includes many errors and omissions. One of my motives for writing this book is to point out that, for all those shortcomings, it is of immense importance. Journalists strive to do what others cannot, or will not. Their work is essential to everyone's understanding. The reader of the greatest book, written by the most learned expert on the Israeli-Palestinian conflict, would still need news reporting in order to use the knowledge they had acquired. Since leaving full-time journalism, I have come to appreciate this even more. In my country, the United Kingdom, journalism is these days often looked down upon because of the phone-hacking scandals which have come to light in recent years (the fact that other journalists played the biggest role in bringing this to public attention does not always receive the recognition it should). Internationally, reporters are targets as never before – killed for what they write, what they know, even now, it seems, just for being journalists. In however small a way, this book aims to fight back against that by showing just how valuable journalism can be.

1

Reporting from the Ruins

The End of the British Mandate and the Creation of the State of Israel

The heat and harsh light of the Holy Land – especially when the sun is high in the summer sky – can make covering difficult and dangerous stories particularly hard. The reflected glare of the sun's rays at midday make you squint, closing one eye to a tiny slit if you are not wearing sunglasses; the sun's heat – beating down from above, and bouncing back up from stone below – soon becomes uncomfortable; mouths and throats crave cool water. Proximity to death makes all these symptoms worse, and yet more easily ignored: drowned out by the thrill of being in the centre of a major story, a thrill that, at that moment, makes many journalists forget everything except their desire to tell that story. Reflection, and perhaps realization that they could themselves have been among the dead or wounded, often only comes later.

22 July 1946 seems to have been just such a day. To tell the story of the way that the Israeli-Palestinian conflict has seemed to those who have written and broadcast about it, this seems the place to start. The experience of the journalists then, and in the days that followed, is both telling of its time, and an experience in which some of their counterparts in our time would recognize parts of their own. They would know the same sense of urgency; pressure of competition; struggle to make sense of sudden, violent events; fear of danger. At 12.37 pm local time, as hotel residents, British colonial officials, and, probably, some reporters, were having a pre-lunch drink in the bar, a huge explosion destroyed part of the King David Hotel in Jerusalem. It is hard to imagine now what a blow this must have been, what a show of strength by the bombers and the cause that they served. For the hotel housed the headquarters of the British Administration which was the government of the country then still known as Palestine. Not only that, it was the main meeting place

for the international press corps. One reporter, Barbara Board, whose fate we will learn shortly, was on her way there to consult the 'Reuter's board'. Today, reporters and officials may meet in certain hotels and other places to exchange information – to question, to spin, to mislead, to assist each other – but rarely is their activity as concentrated as it seems to have been in the King David Hotel: a seat of government, a military headquarters, an international press centre, and the residence of many of those involved in all those activities, and others beside. It is the equivalent in the early years of this century of an attack causing scores of casualties in the Green Zone of Kabul or Baghdad. For that reason – that shock – it seems a good starting point for an account of the way that the Israeli-Palestinian conflict has been reported. For the journalists then in Jerusalem, it was a massive news story combining scores of deaths, politics, foreign policy, and personal good fortune.

The King David Hotel had officially opened in 1931, more than a decade after Britain had, in the aftermath of the First World War, been 'mandated' by the League of Nations to administer Palestine. Palestine had for centuries been part of the Ottoman Empire – one of the vast political power blocs, along with Tsarist Russia, which did not survive the early 20th century's first experience of mass, mechanized warfare. As Britain's time in charge of Palestine went on, the country became increasingly unstable. Jewish immigration was at first tolerated, even encouraged, by the country that had produced the Balfour Declaration – a British pledge made in 1917, 'incautiously and ambiguously', to 'establish a "national home" for the Jews' in Palestine.[1] Jewish immigration had then increased dramatically during the Holocaust, and continued after the Second World War. By 1946, the British found themselves between belligerents divided by tradition, culture (many of the more recent Jewish arrivals were from Europe, and must have understood little of the lives of some of their co-religionists, never mind their Arab neighbours), desire for land, and faith. Far from succeeding in satisfying the needs of the different inhabitants of Palestine, old and new, the British Administration satisfied very few. It may have been an impossible task. It certainly seems to have been an ill-defined one. As Naomi Shepherd wrote in her account of British rule in the Holy Land, 'The purpose of the Mandate was never entirely clear to those serving in Palestine.'[2] In any case, the bombing of the King David Hotel convinced one correspondent, Clare Hollingworth, of the nature of the determination of some of the Jews then in Palestine to have the land for their state. She wrote later of the attack, and Menachem Begin, the future Israeli prime minister who was one of those behind it, 'It was, in fact, a diabolical statement by the terrorist leader that the fight was on again and the State of Israel would be created out of blood if necessary.'[3]

Hollingworth may by then have been writing with the benefit of hindsight – the quotation above comes from a book published in 1990 – but her disgust did not diminish with the years. Her account concludes, 'When Begin rose to power in the late 1970s I often found myself in his presence. But I never greeted him. I would not shake a hand with so much blood on it.'[4] Perhaps her enduring enmity was prompted in part by her own proximity to the bombing. At the time, she was talking in a car about 300 yards away but, as a resident of the hotel, she could just as well have been inside it. Barbara Board, who was working for the *Daily Mirror*, just about was. Her front-page story the following day, 23 July, was headlined, '50 die as Jews blow up our Palestine H.Q.: digging goes on'. It began:

> I owe my life, and the fact that I am able to write this story of the bloodiest terrorist outrage, to the cool courage of a British military policeman. When a great charge of dynamite blew up the Palestine Government Secretariat in the King David Hotel, a few moments ago, I was walking into the hotel entrance.
>
> As the thunderous boom roared out and the five-storey building col-lapsed like a pack of cards with 200 British, Arabs, and Jews inside, one military policeman on guard at the entrance threw me onto the ground and shielded me with his body.[5]

Hollingworth and Board were lucky – and their writing shows that they both understood that. In her 1990 account, Hollingworth puts the num-ber killed at, 'Over a hundred – Britons, Arabs, and Jews.'[6] Other sources give 91.[7] Still, the competitive journalistic instinct kicked in. Had the *Daily Mail* news desk perhaps read an early edition of Board's dramatic account of her near miss when they headlined their story, '3 am News: 50 still missing in "King David" ruins. Hotel Ghq death-roll may be over 90'[8]? Their '3am News' seems like an attempt to trump her eyewitness story by bringing their readers later developments. A. Gordon, the *Daily Mail*'s special correspondent, was also on hand to witness a moment of drama, one without a happy ending.

> This morning, as cranes and bulldozers and Arab labourers still tear at the wreckage, it is feared that the death toll in the King David Hotel bomb outrage in Jerusalem may exceed 90 [...].

I have just seen a paratrooper dig his way under a two-ton ceiling to reach a corporal.

But when the man was brought out he was dead.[9]

In newsreel footage from the time, British servicemen, shirtless and in shorts, some with cigarettes hanging from their lips, toil away in the Middle Eastern midsummer heat. Even in black and white, perhaps especially in black and white, the daylight seems strikingly bright. There is no natural sound on the film, which has been overlaid with funereal music, and a voiceover in the kind of mid-20th-century British accent which is heard no more, clipped vowels its characteristic. The newsreel begins with the caption 'Tragedy in Jerusalem'[10] and shows soldiers shifting rubble by hand, occasionally a crane lifting larger pieces of wreckage, bodies covered by blankets carried away on stretchers. 'In broad daylight, dozens of Jews, Arabs, and Britishers, were murdered in cold blood by the notorious Jewish terrorist organization, Irgun Zvai Leumi'[11] the voiceover, credited to Flight Sergeant Flitchen, tells the viewer. 'Words cannot express the stark tragedy of this ghastly incident.'[12] In the newspaper coverage, the solemn, condemnatory tone is also present – the attackers are everywhere referred to as 'terrorists' – but combined with breathless eyewitness accounts like Board's close escape, and, in the following days, excitement about the 'manhunt' which is launched to find the killers.

In the *Daily Express*, Peter Duffield, who was staying in the hotel at the time, could not quite compete with Board's being shielded by a policeman – but his colleagues in London made the most of his presence.

> The *Daily Express* reporter was sitting in his room, No 105, on the second floor of the King David Hotel at noon yesterday when terrorists blew one-eighth of the hotel skyhigh.
>
> The reporter was typing a feature requested by the *Daily Express* called 'Date Line King David'.[13]

The introduction to the feature in question concludes with Duffield's allowing himself a little journalistic joke – in questionable taste. 'Hours later he cabled, "A lot of the hotel I was writing about is not standing now – but maybe the feature will stand up." '[14] The article, most of which was obviously written before the bombing, is a description of life inside the building which was the centre of political and military power in

Mandate Palestine. It includes a glimpse of the daily routine of Sir John Shaw, then chief secretary (second in command) of the British Administration. It was a routine which would not last much longer: as Motti Golani notes in his introduction to the diary of Sir Henry Gurney, Shaw's successor, Shaw left Palestine later that year, 1946, 'unable to continue in office because he was under certain threat of assassination.'[15] Sir John Shaw, it seems, hardly felt safe then. Duffield describes the numerous security checks to which he is subject before being admitted to Shaw's office. Prior to describing the maps which hang on the walls, Duffield cannot resist falling back on an old British journalistic way of conveying the size of a country or territory. The only surprise here is that it was considered worn-out even as far back as the first half of the last century. 'The geographic cliché about Palestine is that it is the size of Wales,'[16] he explains. It is in this office that Shaw tries to deal with the claim and counterclaim on property and territory which make fulfilling the British Mandate an increasingly impossible task. Under the crosshead 'Propaganda', Duffield explains the wider situation which makes Shaw's role so difficult, and dangerous. 'That Palestine scene – with its fierce hatreds, its distortions and mutilations of the truth – is visible in Shaw's wastepaper basket. Into it each day, after perusal, go thousands of words of propaganda, pleading, demands and threats.'[17] This image of the 'thousands of words' which end up in the wastepaper basket is understandable, if, at this distance a little unsettling – especially as one aspect of the bombing upon which opinions seem to differ even today is whether warnings of the bombing were adequately given, or acted upon. Could there have been some vital piece of intelligence among the 'propaganda, pleading, demands, and threats'?

With the eyewitness reports of the 'bloodiest terrorist outrage' came attempts to piece together what had happened, and predict the response that would follow. A 'staff reporter' for the *Daily Express* reported in that newspaper's front-page story that, 'The bombs were planted in the basement by Jewish terrorists, dressed as Arab milkmen, and carrying the bombs in churns.'[18] The *Times*, whose Special Correspondent seems not to have joined his or her mid-market colleagues either in narrowly missing death, or in watching the rescue operation among the rubble, does judge that 'the outrage was planned with fresh ingenuity and cold-bloodedness',[19] and does seem to have spoken to the 'Arab servants' in an attempt to work out how the attack had been carried out:

> several men dressed as Beduin began to unload milk churns, and one, it is reported, carried a sack. Five went farther into the kitchens of

the cabaret restaurant called La Régence, situated next to the hotel kitchens. Here, according to the story of the Arab servants, the men held up the kitchen staff of the restaurant and apparently set to work to lay the bomb.[20]

The *Manchester Guardian* (as the forerunner of today's *Guardian* was then known) offers a fuller account, although the correspondent who sent it was not identified in that day's paper. The report appeared under the byline 'From Our Special Correspondent', and, at the end of the article, added ' "The Times" & "Manchester Guardian" Service'. This detailed and well-written account described how 'several men dressed as Bedouins began unloading milk churns', before going on to report the first, smaller, explosion, in the street outside, which was designed to distract attention from those disguised bombers who had entered the hotel itself.

Meantime outside in the street a small bomb exploded 100 yards away; it had been placed in a box under a tree. No one was seriously injured. Firing began at various points. The first shot was fired when a British officer emerged from a military telephone exchange at the basement entrance while the 'milk churns were being unloaded.'[21]

The *Manchester Guardian* correspondent seems to have been able to get a lot of detail which eluded competitors, and his or her account stands up to scrutiny even today. With their target in mind, the bombers, 'Irgun members disguised as Arabs',[22] as the hotel's own account has it,[23] set about their task. Today, even as the Israeli-Palestinian conflict continues, it is hard to imagine that the King David Hotel was a war zone. The lobby is a picture of luxury, where guests chat quietly, or tap away at tablet computers or smartphones. The chairs are deep and comfortable, the ceilings high. The odd, overheard, snatch of conversation gives away the fact that, as well as casual glancing at news headlines or social media, there is serious business in hand here. Where once the King David was home to British diplomatic and military power, it is now home from home for the global political and business elite when they visit Jerusalem. One corridor leading away from the reception area has the signatures of prestigious guests petrified for posterity among the marble floor tiles. Beneath here, though, are places which allow today's visitor to try to picture what the place must have been like the day the attackers struck. Having decided to plant their explosives in a kitchen which was located in the basement of the hotel's south wing, the Irgun attackers made their way along a subterranean passage, running beneath the corridor tiled with the autographs of presidents and prime ministers. Today the passage still leads to the kitchen (although it is not in exactly the same place as the one which was blown up and buried that day, but en route), and you can imagine the bombers carefully dragging their deadly delivery – the hotel's history suggests there were 350 kg of explosives[24] – along it. Perhaps uncomfortable in the unfamiliar clothes which were their disguises, presumably nervous that they might be caught, and with their eyes struggling to adjust from the blinding light of noon at high summer outside to the murkier glow of underground artificial light, they made their way along the passage. They hit their target with merciless efficiency: so merciless, in fact, that even today there are attempts to suggest that the bombers did not intend to kill so many people. A plaque attached to the hotel's fence near the wing which was destroyed explains, 'Warning phone calls has [*sic*] been made, to the hotel's despatch, the "Palestine Post" and the French Consulate, urging the hotel's occupants to leave immediately. The hotel was not evacuated, and after 25 minutes, the bombs exploded.' The account concludes, 'to the Irgun's regret 92 persons were killed'.[25] The hotel's own account also seems to seek to shift the blame from the bombers, saying, 'Today no single explanation is accepted as to why the British did not act on the warning.'[26] Certainly, the warnings form part of the story of that day.[27] Whatever the intention, whoever was at fault, and however many were killed, the attack was a massive news story – especially as the bombers got away, prompting a massive security operation to try to track them down. The *Manchester Guardian* piece also offers an account of how the bombers made their escape. As the shooting, described in the extract above, continued, it seems, 'Five men in Arab dress then came running out of the hotel. In all there were some 14 to 15 terrorists and they all got away in the confusion.'[28] In the adjacent column, the *Manchester Guardian* also carries a more factual account of the attack, sent by the Reuters News Agency, and based largely on 'An official statement from British Military Headquarters late last night.' It concludes with the detail, 'Several newspaper men were either inside the hotel or a few yards away at the time.'[29] This betrays an interesting period detail. Although both Board and Hollingworth gave eyewitness accounts of their proximity to the explosion, it is still the newspaper *men* whose closeness to danger is considered newsworthy. Perhaps accepting the way that things were, Board had already published a memoir called *Newsgirl in Palestine*.[30] The preface describes the book as 'a record of things I have seen and heard as a newsgirl in Palestine'[31] and, despite her readiness to describe herself as a girl amongst men, offers an account of the Holy Land at that time which few men could have written. Board's gender gives her access to female society which would have been largely off limits to men and she makes the most of that access.[32]

It was Board, too, who could claim something of a scoop as far as the angle of the telephone warning went. Her story from 23 July directly challenges the sequence of events given by the King David Hotel plaque, and apparently widely accepted in Israel today. At the end of the article which begins with her being saved by the military policeman, she says that she has spoken to Emil Christian, an 'Arab telephone operator', at the hotel, 'who received a telephone message from one of the girl terrorists a few moments before the explosion.'[33] Board's piece continues, 'A voice suddenly came on the line saying, "The building has been mined. You have four minutes to escape," Emil told me.'[34] The question of how and when the warning was given is differently interpreted by the *New York Times*, which, although it does question it, gives much more weight to the Irgun's version of events than the British press does. Its front-page story from 24 July is headlined, 'ZIONIST TERRORISTS SAY THEY SET BOMB; DENOUNCE BRITISH.'[35] The article which follows – 'By Clifton Daniel. By wireless to the New York Times' (the news media, then, as always, loved to boast of their use of the latest technology) – begins with a top paragraph that gives much more prominence to the Irgun's version of events than any account in the British papers.

> Irgun Zvai Leumi, an extremist Zionist organization, announced that it had been responsible for the bombing of the British headquarters here in a communiqué issued tonight in Tel Aviv but blamed the 'British Tyrants themselves' for the loss of life.[36]

Although the article does use the word 'claimed' (often, of course, journalistic code to qualify as debatable or even difficult to believe the words to which it is attached), and it does challenge part of the account (specifically, that there was some kind of 'consultation with military experts' which might have led to the bombs being made safe before they exploded) it is much more detached than some of the up-close eyewitness material sent by the British correspondents. On the basis of his report, it is hard to imagine Clifton Daniel scrabbling about in the rubble as some of his transatlantic counterparts did – nor would Board have had any time for his reporting of the Irgun's claims that its 'telephoned warnings to the King David Hotel's switchboard had given the Government twenty-two minutes – between 12:15 and 12:37 P.M. – to evacuate civilian personnel.'[37] The *Daily Mirror* does run the story – 'Jew terror army admits outrage'[38] – but not without this damning dismissal, which appears in bold type in the original. 'But Barbara Board, Daily Mirror correspondent who was entering the hotel as the explosion occurred cables: "This is a gross untruth. The telephone operator at the hotel had only four minutes" warning.'[39] In the original, the words appear in bold type.

Long before her 1990 account, Hollingworth would have been aware that Menachem Begin was one of those suspected of being behind the attack: he was listed among those wanted even then. The coverage from the days that followed seem, even now, to speak of excitement, fear, and, probably, intense journalistic competition. Today, international TV news channels would have set up live positions as close as the res-cuers and investigators would have allowed; they would have broadcast updates around the clock as the operation to save anyone trapped under the rubble continued. Then, the newspapers had no such possibilities – but their coverage shows what a huge story this must have been, and suggests that the correspondents covering it among the danger and destruction of the recently bombed hotel were under great pressure to 'take the story on', as journalistic slang describes the successful search for a new angle. On page 2, the *Daily Express* reproduced a wanted poster then circulated throughout British Mandate Palestine. Begin's was among those faces which appeared under the headline, 'The types behind the terror'. The coverage in the days which followed, as British forces sought to hunt down those 'types', tells a story of a stated aim to hit back at the insurgents – as similar attackers would no doubt have been labelled in reports from Iraq or Afghanistan in recent years – and of the difficulties of achieving that aim. In terms of the history of journal-ism, it shows a time when access to facts and events was difficult, and, as the attack itself had shown, potentially dangerous. In consequence, there seems to have been a huge reliance on official sources – and all the correspondents, obviously, had the same ones. There is little or no attempt to offer context, or explanation, of the motive for the bombing. The newsreel voiceover describes the dead as 'innocent people, victims of a terrible outrage – an outrage solemnly condemned by sane peo-ple the world over'[40] and this assessment is shared by the coverage as a whole.

Two days after the *Daily Express* identified 'the types behind the ter-ror', the *Daily Mail* warned them what was to come. 'Palestine army to crush terrorists',[41] ran the headline to the front-page story from O'Dowd Gallagher, 'Daily Mail Special Correspondent', whose opening lines,

> The biggest military operation in the history of Britain's 23-year-old Palestine Mandate is being planned tonight on the top floor of the bomb-blasted King David Hotel. Object of the operation will be to wipe out the Jewish terrorist organisation indicated in the British Government's White Paper.

suggested he had been charged with trying to match the scale of the initial story. What followed makes, in places, uncomfortable reading today. That 'biggest military operation' in the history of the Mandate involved sending thousands of troops – Barbara Board gives the number as 13,000 – to Tel Aviv in an attempt to capture the King David Hotel bombers and their leaders. Board, perhaps still shaken from the moment her life was saved by the military policeman's quick thinking, proved herself capable of matching – even exceeding – Gallagher's sense of unprecedented events as she described what unfolded. She describes 'Army X-ray operators' who were checking anyone in hospital with a plaster-cast, 'looking for gunshot cases masquerading as victims of accidents.' The troops carried out a huge operation as they sought to track down the bombers:

> The search began at dawn, when hundreds of Jewish men in pyjamas, and women and girls in nightdresses, were brought into the streets and lined up in barbed-wire cages for questioning.[42]

For the *Daily Mail*, Gallagher was not far behind. That paper's edition from the same day, 31 July 1946, headlined his story '143 JEWS HELD IN TEL-AVIV CAGES'. Gallagher reported that

> Many of those arrested are suspected of being members of Irgun Zvai Leumi, but the chief quarry, Menahem [*sic*] Begin 'commander' of Irgun, has so far evaded arrest.

> A strict curfew was imposed, and troops had orders to shoot on sight anyone breaking it.[43]

Any sense of outrage on behalf of, or even pity for, victims of genuine accidents, who found themselves caught up in the 'world's greatest manhunt', is absent. The image of 'Jewish men in pyjamas [...] lined up in barbed-wire cages,' may, in our time, seem troubling. Even the *New York Times* seems to choose not to stress what amounts to collective punishment. It headlines its story, 'BRITISH SEIZE 376 IN PALESTINE DRIVE'[44] and offers some diplomatic background, too: with the news that neither Arabs nor Jews seem likely to accept a British invitation to hold talks – 'consultations', as Daniel calls them – in London. Is it too much of a stretch of the imagination to think that some of these 'Jewish men in pyjamas', given the time and the place, had themselves survived the death camps of Europe, which had their own barbed-wire cages, and their own uniforms, which resembled pyjamas? If so, the newspaper reporters of the time choose not to reflect on this in their articles. Instead, the coverage suggests a journalistic culture which was uncritical of the political and military approach taken by the Mandate Authorities. Jewish fighters – they would probably be described as 'insurgents' today – were fighting against forces whose role in the region seems not to have been questioned. This may of course be a consequence of the time. It was, after all, a year after the end of the Second World War, a conflict during which journalistic ideas of balance or impartiality had largely been suspended in the English-speaking world as reporters and editors identified themselves as part of the war effort. In *The Media at War*, Susan Carruthers describes the Second World War as a time when 'political leaders were gratified by how uncomplainingly editors, reporters and film-makers lent their talents to the war effort'.[45] It may be that the Mandate authorities benefited, in terms of press coverage, from this factor: both journalists and their audiences were accustomed to supportive coverage of British military operations overseas, and, presumably, of Britain's role as an imperial power, of which the Mandate was itself an example. If it is true, as Shepherd suggested, that the purpose of the Mandate was unclear to those serving in Palestine, then the correspondents must have known this from their conversations off, if not on, the record. In the aftermath of the bombing of the King David Hotel, however, any such doubts appear absent. The sense that the perpetrators must, and will, be punished seems to grow stronger as coverage continues. Today, the language seems to echo that used by the United States and its allies in the 'war on terror' which followed the attacks of 11 September 2001: those engaged in fighting Mandate troops are 'terrorists' whom the army will 'crush'. There is one interesting distinction which emerges from a reading of some of the articles. Where the administration of President George W. Bush sought to make the distinction between 'terrorists' and Muslims (especially after Mr Bush's use, on 16 September 2001, of the word 'crusade' to describe the 'war on terrorism'[46]), the Mandate authorities, enraged by the loss of life and challenge to their power, had no such scruples. The *Daily Mail* of 29 July 1946 carries an account of 'unconfirmed reports' about the contents of a letter which the British Commander in Palestine, Lieutenant General Sir Evelyn Barker, had apparently addressed to his troops. According to the article, the letter said that:

> The Jewish community in Palestine cannot be absolved of responsibility for a long series of outrages culminating in the blowing-up of a large part of the Government offices in the King David Hotel, causing grievous loss of life…without the support of the general Jewish public the terrorist gangs who carry out these acts would soon be unearthed, and in this measure the Jews of the country are accomplices and bear a share of the guilt.[47]

There are echoes here of some of the debates which followed the killings at the French magazine *Charlie Hebdo* and the Kosher supermarket in Paris in January 2015 – with some, including the newspaper proprietor, Rupert Murdoch, suggesting that the Muslim attackers' co-religionists should share some of the blame for the deaths.[48] When Barker wrote his letter, because Israel had not to come into existence, the language did not yet exist for soldiers, diplomats, or journalists to identify the 'general Jewish public' otherwise than by their faith. Still, the identification of 'the Jews of the country' as giving 'support' to 'terrorist gangs' tars all of that faith with the same brush. Such thinking presumably made it easier for acts of collective punishment, such as rounding up civilians in their nightclothes and enclosing them in barbed-wire cages, if the logic ran that they were all helping the bombers anyway. British correspondents seem not to have challenged this approach. As the search for suspects continued in Tel Aviv, the *Daily Mail* and the *Daily Express* both reported on the discovery of an arms cache. 'ARMY FIND ARSENAL IN SYNAGOGUE,' was the *Express*'s headline.[49] The paper went on to explain, 'Paratroop padre, the Rev. Harry Hyde, from Hersham, Surrey, led a search party of Sixth Airborne men today into Tel Aviv's Great Synagogue – the biggest in Palestine – and found a secret arsenal.'[50] The *Express*'s correspondent, Peter Duffield, may have been pleased with his piece. He may also have been on the receiving end of a sharp message from his newsdesk in London. His rival at the *Daily Mail*, O'Dowd Gallagher, seemed to have got more detail. The *Mail*'s headline, 'Terrorist HQ found in Great Synagogue'[51] suggests that the find was of greater significance than the discovery of an arms cache alone might have been. Gallagher also makes the bold connection, without really standing it up, as journalists say, between the 'Terrorist HQ'; the bombing of the King David Hotel and another recent attack on British Army personnel:

> British troops searching the vaults of the Great Synagogue in Tel-Aviv today found that it was the 'operations room' of the hooded men who recently kidnapped three British officers, and possibly the same men who blew up the King David Hotel headquarters [...].

Gallagher is especially keen to highlight the discovery of 'a soft cloth cap on which was sewn a black hood, with slits cut for eyeholes' – apparently the kind of headgear worn by one of the officers' captors.[52]

Gallagher adds to the superior detail of his piece with a line about fake uniforms, apparently sewn, as he puts it by 'terrorists' tailors'. They have erred in their attempt to copy Paratroops' uniforms by 'sewing paratroopers wings on both sleeves of their jackets. Paratroopers carry their wings only on the right sleeve.'[53] This element of the story was also picked up by that morning's *Daily Mirror*, which reported, under the headline 'Stolen British Uniforms found in synagogue':

> British Navy, Army, and Air Force uniforms, 'Airborne' berets, 'booby trap' mines, ammunition, and firearms were found yesterday hidden in Palestine's largest synagogue in Tel Aviv.
>
> Hats of the Palestine Police, a woman's police dress, bales of forged bonds of the Palestine Government and a radio transmitter were also found hidden in a basement.[54]

The *Manchester Guardian*, which earlier in the week had offered a mournful account of the burial of some of those killed in the King David Hotel bombing – 'Jerusalem was a city of gloom as the funeral processions of some of the dead wound their way towards the Protestant, Catholic, Jewish, and Moslem cemeteries'[55] – now attempted to convey the scale of the search which police and troops undertook as they searched for suspects. Under the headline 'SEARCH FOR TERRORISTS IN PALESTINE Progress of Operations in Tel Aviv' the newspaper tried to convey the scale of what Barbara Board had called 'the world's greatest manhunt'. 'The area, in which nearly 200,000 persons live, is to be searched room by room, and every one of these inhabitants is to be questioned. That is the object of this gigantic undertaking.'

Studying these accounts almost 70 years later, and even discounting the advantage of knowing what was to come, the reader is struck by a sense of coming disaster for the British Mandate. For there seems to be little they can do to contain the challenge to their power. There is evidence of division among the elite. The letter in which Sir Evelyn Barker had accused the Jewish community in Palestine of being 'accomplices and bear(ing) a share of the guilt' for the attack on the King David was clearly controversial. Sir Evelyn's political masters in London soon distanced themselves from the sentiments his letter contained. The same day that the *Daily Mail* carried Gallagher's dramatic and detailed account of the discovery of the 'Terrorist HQ', it reported that Herbert Morrison, deputizing for the Prime Minister, Clement Attlee, had told the House of Commons that, 'The Chief of the Imperial General Staff (was) now dealing with the matter.' In other words, there seemed to be an expectation that Sir Evelyn would be asked, or told, to soften the tone of his language in future. Mr Morrison explained:

> making all allowances for the provocation to which our forces are exposed – and in view of the fact that it was written soon after the King David Hotel outrage – the Government feel they must dissociate themselves from the actual terms in which it was couched.[56]

There are hints at this time too of the challenges which the Mandate Authorities faced in controlling Jewish immigration: boatloads of destitute, desperate, and traumatized refugees from the horrors of the Holocaust and post-war Europe making their way to Palestine. At the end of its report on the arms find in the synagogue, the *Daily Mirror* included the following line, *'Illegal immigrant ship, third in three days, was reported off Haifa last night with 2,000 aboard'* (italics in original). A few days later, the *Manchester Guardian* described a 'VISIT TO ILLEGAL IMMIGRANTS AT HAIFA – A Vast Organisation at Work – SHIPS IN HARBOUR, WAITING AT SEA, AND LOADING IN ITALY'.[57] The overall impression is of a project – the British Mandate itself – which can no longer succeed. The British Authorities are unable to contain the population which they have been asked to govern, and that population is growing with successive waves of immigration. Faced with the increasing violence, and casualties among their administrative and military personnel, the British elite is showing signs of disunity. There is no obvious solution, and no end in sight. It was in this time of terror and uncertainty, after the bombing of the King David Hotel, that Sir John Shaw, as noted above, decided he had had enough. 'He left Palestine secretly on September 13th'[58] to be replaced by Sir Henry Gurney. Gurney was to be the last to hold the post of chief secretary in the Mandate Administration, which, at the time of his appointment, was to last under than two more years. His diary gives fascinating insights into the way that the correspondents who covered the end of the mandate operated: glimpses of their relationships with each other, their approach to the story, their relationship with political power. Then, as now, the media operation runs alongside the military and political one, in the shape of the Principal Information Office, or P.I.O. Even in the final weeks of his authority, before the outbreak of war in 1948, Gurney seems to have a care for the way in which the British presence in Palestine is being portrayed. He is pleased to note, in his diary entry of 5 April that the *Times* is to do an article on a new book, published by the British Government's Stationery Office, which has 'admirable pictures and photographs' of 'the Holy City under British care.'[59] Peter Duffield of the *Daily Express* merits a mention – his competitive streak shown by his disdain for what he saw as the excessive the help that his fellow reporters were getting. Duffield, Gurney tells us, has complained that the P.I.O. is so 'helpful that all journalists were reduced to the same level by being able to get all they want merely by sitting in the press room'.[60] Then, as now, the civil servants and soldiers charged with running a war zone, seem to feel a mixture of muted disdain and fascination for the reporters who follow their actions. 'The American press go about in pink baseball caps and white jeeps: *"The Times"* in a Wolseley: the rest in anything they can get, labeled [*sic*] largely "Press", which of course entitles them to intervene anywhere.'[61] We learn from Gurney's mention of a meeting with Dick Stubbs, the Public Information Officer (and the person responsible for the press room that was, in Duffield's view, making lazy reporters' lives too easy) that there are '120 Palestine newspapers' and, in addition, 'about 70 foreign correspondents who send out a continual stream of facts or misstatements, according to whom they get it from.'[62] What would he have made of 24-hour news channels, and their 'continual streams', let alone social media? Still, perhaps in a reflection of his own difficulty in understanding fully what was happening around him (remember Sir John Shaw's wastepaper basket, filled and perhaps overflowing with 'thousands of words of propaganda'), Gurney seems to have had some admiration for the work the press were doing. 'It's not easy to follow what's going on,' he admits, 'even when you have access to all the information there is, but these fellows have to go out and get it for themselves.'[63] In a foretaste of covering the Israeli-Palestinian conflict of later years, this was not always easy, or safe. On 3 December 1947, the *Daily Express* reported, 'Transjordan has warned the U.S. government that no visas will be given to American correspondents because it cannot be responsible for their safety.'[64]

For the territory was becoming increasingly ungovernable. Newspaper reports from late 1947 paint a picture of growing lawlessness across the region. As the British Mandate entered its last sixth months, Palestine's Arab and Jewish population fought each other with the British caught between them. Sometimes, it seemed a better idea just to stay out of it. Following the United Nations' decision in late 1947 to partition Palestine, the *Daily Express* reported that the Jewish population of Tel Aviv were dancing in the streets, but added, 'Street fights started in Jerusalem among hundreds of Jews celebrating partition and Arabs protesting against it. British troops were confined inside their barbed wire security zones.'[65] The Jewish population of the Holy Land had the opposite idea. Both the *Express* and the *Daily Mirror* reported on 1 December that the Haganah, the Zionist military organization which was later to become a core part of the Israeli Army, had 'ordered all Jews between 17 and 25 to register for "national service" today'.[66] . The *Express* two days later carried a despatch from Eric Grey in Jerusalem in which he reported that a 'Council of Learned Men' at Al-Azhar University in Cairo had, 'declared a Holy War in defence of Palestine' and that 'whoever neglects it is a sinner'.[67] Whether this was a retaliatory or parallel measure to the Haganah 'order' does not seem to have preoccupied correspondents at that time. Rather, it seemed to contribute to a growing sense of doom prior to departure. In December, the *Daily Express* reported, 'American oil experts' had been flown to Haifa from their camp in the Transjordan desert after an attack by Arabs: ' "They even tore up our wives' photographs," said one', the paper reported.[68] The day after the oil experts' evacuation was covered, the *Express* carried the story of fighting in Tel Aviv and Haifa – the place to which the oil men had apparently been flown for their safety. 'Two new battles raged tonight in Tel Aviv and Haifa, in the Mufti's week old campaign of murder and violence. Two Britons, a soldier and a policeman, and ten Jews were killed by Arabs today.'[69] In the Mandate's violent final phase, military personnel felt unsafe even in their quarters. 'When we went to bed, we handcuffed a Sten gun to our wrists,' remembers Peter Tooley, a Londoner who was serving in the British Army in Gaza, 'because we didn't know what was going to happen during the night.'[70] Donald Christie, a British national serviceman who arrived in Palestine in October 1946 to join the Mandate Police Force, recalled something slightly different in a memoir written decades later:

we were issued uniforms, rifles and a pistol – also most importantly an ancient pair of handcuffs – this latter item was not for securing prisoners but were used to handcuff our rifles to the metal frames of our beds to prevent them from being stolen. Later I was to learn that a.303 S.M.L.E[71] rifle was worth at least 50 pounds on the black market, a lot of money in those days.[72]

The threat was real. Christie later relates the story of another British constable who 'went to pick up a suit from an Arab tailor in the Souk – carrying his rifle for protection and was shot dead by an Arab who stole his rifle.'[73] Christie also gives some grim insights into the way the Mandate forces sometimes operated. In the summer of 1947, after two British Army sergeants had been killed by the Irgun, in retaliation for the execution of Dov Gruner, an Irgun fighter, Christie is made aware of a plan to 'terrorize' a Jewish area 'shooting anyone moving and blasting shop windows.'[74] Christie concludes, 'I recognized that I was being asked to take part in a pogrom.'[75] He writes that he refused to get involved, and dissuaded the two men under his command from doing so either. While it appears clear from Christie's account that this was a plan without official backing, it is nevertheless apparently tolerated. Those who did take part 'cleaned their guns and oiled them and the authorities did nothing about it. They needed those ten A/Cars'[76] – i.e. the armoured cars which had been used in the 'pogrom'.

These kind of details seem absent from contemporary accounts. Journalism's strength can be its immediacy, its weakness the pressure under which it can find itself in war zones – fuller accounts only emerging years later, sometimes prompted by guilt, or an urge for self-justification. At the time, there is an increasing sense of instability, uncertainty, and peril. Eric Grey's story from the *Daily Express* on 1 December 1947 also includes colourful detail from the Mandate's last months. Telephone contact between Tel Aviv and Jerusalem is lost; British troops barricade the King David Hotel. Both those developments would presumably have made correspondents' lives more difficult, whether they were looking for information, or just for a gin and tonic. The Palestine Police 'fought it out' with Arabs whom they were trying to keep from entering Jewish Areas. Perhaps Constable Christie was among them. Perhaps he was already counting the days until he would leave. Certainly, departure for all Mandate personnel was in the offing. Also on 1 December, the *Mirror*, under the headline, 'We begin to quit in Jan' outlined provisional plans for the pull-out, although it cautioned, 'It is estimated that to remove all our troops, stores and equipment within six months would require hundreds more ships than are available.' In a line which might have interested Constable Christie, the next day's *Express* reported that, 'The price of a rifle has increased from £10 to £25 since UNO partitioned the country 48 hours ago.'[77] The price was not the £50 he had heard earlier, but any the change in the price of weapons in the region has long been a sign either of new supply, or increased demand. As a correspondent in Gaza in the summer of 2003, I remember one Israeli source explaining that when their informants in the territory told them that the price of ammunition had fallen, they knew that more must have been smuggled in.

The belligerents then were getting weapons, too – whether or not British service personnel chained their rifles to their wrists as they slept. When, in the spring of 1948, Sir Henry Gurney is making ready to leave Palestine, information comes through of the large-scale killing of Arab civilians in the village of Deir Yassin, outside Jerusalem. In his diary, Gurney describes this 'massacre of innocent women and children' as 'one of the worst things the Irgun and Stern[78] have done'.[79] The journalists for whom Gurney has previously expressed his grudging admiration find it a hard story to cover. The *Times* correspondent, Gurney writes, was unable to get through to the village, 'stopped by the Haganah' – a situation instantly recognizable to correspondents of later eras who have been similarly obstructed by the Haganah of later eras: the Israeli Army. Deir Yassin is remembered by Palestinians as the 'best-known and perhaps bloodiest atrocity of the war'.[80] Some 250 people were killed there[81] on 9 April 1948 as Palestine became increasingly violent and ungovernable as the British Mandate drew to a close. It shocked even some of those who fervently supported the cause of Jewish statehood. Harry Levin, a journalist working for Haganah's illegal radio station, refers in his diary to 'appalling accounts' of 'indiscriminate killing of men, women, and children.'[82]

When Israeli independence came, the month after the massacre at Deir Yassin, Clare Hollingworth seems to have had a remarkably prescient sense of what the future held. She writes with dismay of the commercial cost which Britain was poised to pay as a result of the end of the Mandate, describing:

the rather shameful scurry of British commercial firms – a scurry to be blamed on the Government rather than on individual firms – to get out of Palestine during the last two months, without doing more, in some cases, than withdrawing any loose cash and then shutting the doors and departing, has done infinite harm to our formerly predominant commercial position in Palestine.[83]

Of particular relevance to her and her fellow correspondents is the news that,

> Cable and Wireless has shut down in its Jerusalem station which in April handled over 1,200,000 words. This left the capital without any communications with the outside world. As, further, the Jerusalem high-speed transmitter carried a great deal of traffic from other parts of the country its withdrawal was felt all over Palestine.[84]

The report from which these extracts come is datelined 'Jerusalem. By Air Mail. May 14'. It is hard for us to imagine today what a colossal headache this must have been for journalists then. Whatever challenges may be involved in covering the Israeli-Palestinian conflict now, being left incommunicado is almost never among them. Hollingworth's predicament is reminiscent of that faced by correspondents covering the Russian revolution of 1917 – they too experienced a huge moment in history, and no telegraph to send stories about it – and belongs very much to the journalistic era of the last century. Hollingworth uses Cable and Wireless's departure very cleverly in her report. She notes that 'a large team' of American technicians has arrived, setting up their own operation, 'Before Cable and Wireless had actually pulled out'. Her report concludes by, in effect, correctly predicting the wider significance of one company's decision to close its operations as Israel came into being.

> It is unlikely that Cable and Wireless will again be able to get a foothold in Palestine – they have shifted to Amman, where, in fact, they are not really wanted – and so an important British interest has been needlessly sacrificed. There is little doubt that the Jewish State will build itself up commercially at considerable speed and provide the United States with a firm foothold in the Middle East.

The establishment of the office of the Radio Corporation of America, although, 'Ostensibly this transmitter is worked by and the property of the American State Department', as Hollingworth says, seems an echo of British diplomatic and military decline in the Middle East – preparing the world for an era in which the United States would be the dominant power broker in the region.

As the Mandate came to an end, foreign correspondents found themselves chroniclers of the year that was to shape the modern Middle East. While attempts over the last few years at making peace have focused on solutions based on the borders as they were in 1967, it is 1948 which looms largest in the stories that the two peoples – the Israelis and the Palestinians – tell of themselves. The year is a starting point in two sharply contrasting national narratives, the existence of which makes reporting this conflict so complex. For Israelis, 1948 is the year of independence, of statehood at last, of the realization of a goal which had been so long in the achieving. For the Palestinians, it is the year of death, terror, and dispossession: remembered as Al-Nakba, 'the catastrophe'. The way this year is celebrated or mourned by the people who dwell between the River Jordan and the Mediterranean symbolizes all that divides them. For the Palestinians, the day is often marked by demonstrations. When I was based in Gaza in 2003, for example, a crowd gathered in the city's main square to hear Yasser Arafat, then under siege in his compound in Ramallah on the West Bank, speak to them of their history, and all that had befallen them since the year Israel came into being. Some demonstrators carried outsized cardboard keys marked with the words 'Right of Return', and symbolizing the properties they had lost when driven from their farms and villages by the armed forces of the nascent Jewish state.[85] Some then were old enough to remember life before 1948, although with each year since they have grown fewer in number. Souvenirs and countless stories ensure that younger generations feel a longing for a home they have never actually known. On the Israeli side of the line, there are barbecues and picnics, and stories of statehood hard won. The correspondents covering the events that are now remembered so differently in Israel and the Palestinian Territories knew they had a huge story on their hands. For the British reporters, as might be expected, much of the focus of their reporting on the events of May 1948 is the fate of British interests in the region. Hollingworth's despatch describing the departure of Cable and Wireless is an example. There are attempts to assess the Mandate, and to present it in a positive light. The *New York Times* and Associated Press are more circumspect. The American media, after all, were working in a very different political environment. As Colin Shindler has pointed out, when writing of the United States' rapid recognition of the new State of Israel, 'Whereas the United States had taken eleven minutes after the end of the Mandate to accord de facto recognition, Britain took over eight months.'[86] Nor did the speed of recognition mean that it was an easy, uncontroversial one. Opinion was in fact divided among the United States' political elite. As the veteran US diplomat, the late Richard Holbrooke, wrote in 2008, President Truman's decision was, 'opposed by almost the entire foreign policy establishment.'[87] The division in Washington was prompted not least by the State Department's 'suspicion that any takeover by left-wing Zionists would provide a base for Soviet influence in the Middle East.'[88] What a contrast with today when identification with, and support for, Israel have come almost to be a *sine qua non* for success in American politics, especially on the right.

On 14 May 1948, the *Daily Mirror* marked the last day of the Mandate by reporting a series of statistics apparently designed to persuade that British rule in Palestine had not been a complete failure. The article, headlined 'Palestine – last appeal as we quit', reads today very much like the statements of government ministers maintaining that the invasion and occupation of Afghanistan from 2001 onwards was a success – even if some of the language is a little more direct than that which might be considered appropriate today.

> When British rule began, says the Colonial Office, Palestine was primitive and underdeveloped. The population of 750,000 were disease-ridden and poor. But new methods of farming were introduced, medical services provided, roads and railways built, water supplies improved, malaria wiped out.[89]

This was not, of course, the full story. Violence against British service personnel and officials, and fighting between the two peoples living in Palestine, still dominate the news agenda. In *Disenchantment*, her account of the *Guardian*'s changing relationship with Israel, Daphna Baram describes the paper as 'having a forgiving attitude towards the Jewish violence in Palestine in the late 1940s'.[90] She quotes a *Guardian* editorial following mass arrests of Jews on 'Black Sabbath' (29 June 1946), in which the paper accuses the government of having, 'blundered into one of those campaigns of suppression, all too common in our history, which are always abhorrent and nearly always unsuccessful'.[91] This kind of analysis is absent from the news coverage of the bombing, less than a month later, of the King David Hotel, and the 'manhunt' which followed. The editorial goes on to talk of 'the very Jews whom we placed in Palestine to escape from persecution in Europe'.[92] As with the *Mirror* article quoted above, the combined, and sometimes conflicting, senses of involvement and responsibility are factors which seem to influence reporters and their newspapers. As the end approached, though, there were few illusions. Clare Hollingworth had suggested in the *Observer* a couple of weeks earlier that 'it now appears likely that the British administration in Palestine will have collapsed before May 15'.[93] Hollingworth's reporting in the *Observer* does not share the *Guardian*'s 'forgiving attitude to Jewish violence'. Reporting, in the same article, on recent fighting she says:

> The Jewish action at Haifa, and their previous actions at Deir Yassin, Tiberias, and other places where superior strength and fire-power was ruthlessly employed, was in calculated execution of a policy of terror, a policy they learned while they suffered from the Germans.[94]

However notorious a case Deir Yassin remains now, Hollingworth's comparison seems somewhat striking today. An equating of tactics employed by Jewish fighters to those used by Nazi Germany would be far less likely to make it into the mainstream news media. Indeed, perhaps not surprisingly, in the following week's *Observer*, Hollingworth's article is the subject of a complaint from the Jewish Agency. Surprisingly, the complaint is not specifically about the implication that the Jewish forces in Palestine had adapted a Nazi 'policy of terror'. In response, Lucien Harris, from the Information Department of the Jewish Agency for Palestine, writes:

> This statement does not square with the report cabled to the Colonial Secretary by the High Commissioner Sir Alan Cunningham. Sir Alan emphasised that there was 'no massacre' at Haifa, and stated 'The battle was the direct consequence of continued Arab attacks on Jews during the past four days. The Arabs themselves were responsible for the outbreak, despite repeated warnings.'[95]

Hollingworth seems to have fallen victim, perhaps rightly on this occasion, to a phenomenon familiar to any journalist covering the Middle East then, and in the decades since: a highly efficient monitoring of the reporting of the conflict with a view to putting pressure on journalists. More modern forms of this will be discussed in later chapters, but it is interesting to note this antagonism between the authorities and foreign reporters seems to pre-date even the founding of the State of Israel. Was Hollingworth still infuriated by her own relatively close escape from the carnage at the King David Hotel? The enduring anger she expresses in her 1990 memoir – almost half a century later – leads one to suspect that her resentment may have been even greater then, less than two years after the explosion. Certainly, Hollingworth is not shy of condemning the Jewish Agency itself in her stories – especially where she sees attempts to mislead reporters. Her story for the *Observer* on 11 April 1948 suggests that she may have had something of a running battle with the Agency – perhaps even with the letter-writing Lucien Harris himself. This piece gives us an insight into the way that reporters then must have seen the sources of information available to them:

> There is no longer the slightest reliance to be placed in Jewish reports. Their Press is under strict censorship, imposed and enforced by the Jewish Agency, and its misrepresentations and distortions are reaching astonishing heights. There is indeed an atmosphere of quite unbelievable reality in the Jewish approach to the situation.[96]

We might wonder now if such cutting criticism was what prompted the Agency's decision to complain about her report two weeks later. In any case, it seems now the forerunner of future disputes between the Israeli authorities and those who arrive to report on the country. Hollingworth, whatever her reason for deciding to use part of her story to highlight the Jewish Agency's 'misrepresentations and distortions', does not spare the other parties to the conflict in this respect. Her piece continues:

> On the Arab side the Press indulges in childish boasting and highly-coloured accounts of Arab victories while what must be termed 'official Arab sources' simply do not know what is happening, as their means of communication and collection and collation of data are hopelessly inadequate.[97]

Hollingworth, one imagines, would be a spin doctor's nightmare today. Having excoriated the Jewish and Arab sources, she then turns her attention to the British officials. Where Sir Henry Gurney was expressing a sort of sympathy for the correspondents, one of their number was not so understanding of officials. As sources, Hollingworth seems to have found them almost as 'hopelessly inadequate' as the Arab press:

> Unfortunately, the British authorities, police and military, who might be expected to provide at least a check upon the prevailing exaggerations, appear usually to be in the position of having to obtain their information from the Press. They never know anything more.[98]

As will be discussed in Chapter 6, this is a situation which, many contemporary correspondents argue, continues today.

Hollingworth's judgements give us an understanding of how hard it must have been to find reliable information. Still, after the Israeli declaration of statehood was made on the afternoon of 14 May 1948, the correspondents covering what came next were often in a position to make up for what they could not know at a distance with what they saw before them. Reporting for the *Daily Express*'s edition of 17 May 1948, Sydney Smith described what was happening around him. His despatch is datelined 'in Jerusalem (under Jewish censorship)' – in other words, the authorities of the nascent state seem to have moved quickly to extend their control beyond the Jewish press to include the international news media, too.

> Shells from Arab 75s fell all day in the main streets. Mortar bombs exploded in the Old City as the Jews launched attacks on the Arabs surrounding them. The Jews have not yet opened the road from Tel Aviv. Truce negotiations are held up because of the difficulty in contacting the outside world. Jerusalem is virtually isolated.[99]

One wonders what he might have been able to tell without the censorship. His report seems remarkably matter-of-fact and lacking in colour. If Jerusalem was indeed 'virtually isolated', then perhaps he had the potential for a scoop – a potential that ended with the censor. It is interesting, though, to note that Smith feels able to refer to 'Arab 75s' without further explanation. I suppose, after checking, that he means 75mm artillery shells. He obviously felt able to assume a much larger military knowledge on the part of his audience a large proportion, perhaps even a majority, of whom would have served in the Second World War, and some of whom would have fought in the First World War. No correspondent of the early 21st century could make a similar assumption unless they were writing for a military publication. A few days earlier, as statehood was declared, Smith seems not to have been subject to restrictions when he 'cabled' from Jerusalem:

> The ceasefire collapsed and battle was joined for the City before Britain's High Commissioner, Sir Alan Cunningham, left for Haifa and home.

> From 4 am mortar-bomb explosions and machine guns were heard. But there was a lull in the fighting when Sir Alan and his staff with a six mile long cover of British troops drove out of Jerusalem at 8 a.m. Above circled eight Spitfires and four Lancasters.[100]

The apparently tireless Peter Duffield was still working hard, too – also for the *Express*. Sir Alan Cunningham, having reached Haifa, he sails 'at one second after midnight', reported Duffield in the same edition which carried Smith's report of Cunningham's departure from Jerusalem. Readers might almost get the impression that Duffield had sailed with Cunningham, for he tells his readers, 'the ship's band struck up and the sound of guns ashore faded.'[101] This seems unlikely, as Tuesday's *Express* credits him with a Haifa dateline. By Monday, as the fighting for Jerusalem and other strategic points rages, the journalists covering it are increasingly subject to censorship from the combatants. If Hollingworth's assessment of the month before is to be trusted, correspondents must have struggled both to get reliable information and distribute it. The newspapers from these days, depending on the dateline, are peppered with 'under Jewish censorship' or 'censored by the Arabs'. As Hollingworth's caustic verdict on the relative merits of the combatants as sources of information suggests, the beginning of the shooting war between Israel and the Arabs seems also to have been the beginning of some of the propaganda techniques – cruder, yes, than now – which have their contemporary counterparts. Hollingworth's judgement that the Jewish news media possessed, 'the determination to maintain at all costs the illusion that it is impossible for Jews to lose in any encounter with Arabs' shows the importance they placed on positive news for consumption by their own community. The split opinion among Washington's foreign policy elite on the merits or otherwise of Israel's cause shows that they must have been acutely aware of the need to garner international support, too. As any fledgling state seeking recognition knows, a just cause may be strengthened by a willingness for its supporters to fight for it, and win. O'Dowd Gallagher, of the *Daily Mail*, was in Jerusalem as the first days of Israel's history unfolded in war. He reports that 'Palestinian Arab guerrillas…smashed the resistance of about 800 Jewish fighters in the Jewish quarter of the Old City and gave them the choice of surrendering, starving or being systematically wiped out by a creeping barrage from mortars.'[102] Although the Old City today often feels tense – whether for political reasons, or because tempers can fray as shopkeepers try to force heavily-laden hand-carts of goods through narrow alleyways already filled with crowds – the image of being faced with a choice of dying from hunger or explosives is something altogether different. Israeli police, and sometimes soldiers, are never far away – but it is hard to imagine these pedestrian streets, thronged with shoppers, traders, tourists, and pilgrims, as a war zone. Yet the streets are ranged around the world's closest collection of sacred sites, sites which are the focus for the reason that this city has been fought over for centuries, and is still fought over today. In May 1948, it must have been a terrifying place to live – and a very dangerous place to report from. On Tuesday 20 May, both the *Mail* and the *Express* reported the death of Richard Wyndham, a British journalist. The *Express*, which calls him a correspondent for Kemsley Newspapers, says he 'was hit by a burst of machine gun fire when taking pictures of the fight for Sheikh Jarrah'.[103] Sheikh Jarrah, a residential district, lies to the north of the Old City, and guards its approaches. In the last few years, it has been in the news because of the influx of Jewish settlers. In some cases, Palestinian families have been driven from homes they have lived in for decades, ostensibly on the basis that they could not prove ownership of the property.[104] The settlers' houses are easily distinguished by the Israeli flags which fly from their rooftops in an area of the city inhabited overwhelmingly by Palestinians.

The Mandate Authorities, as Duffield's report, above, makes clear, left literally the moment they could. The focus of some of the reporting, therefore, switches to London – where, the *Daily Mail* reported on 16 May, the arrival of the flag which had flown over the King David Hotel as a symbol of British power in Palestine was itself seen as newsworthy. 'The weather-beaten, sun-dried Union Jack which was lowered for the last time from British Headquarters in the King David Hotel in Jerusalem early yesterday was carried in the airways terminal building at Victoria, S.W. at 12.45 am today.'[105] Sir Henry Gurney led the group of officials who brought the flag. They were themselves, presumably, 'weather-beaten', 'sun-dried' too – as well as exhausted. Despite the tone of disappointment, the reporting of these final moments of the Mandate retains an air of respect for imperial ceremony. The same *Daily Mail* story reports that 'as General Sir Alan Cunningham, last High Commissioner, left Jerusalem a solitary piper played on the roof of Government House.' For reporters such as Board, Duffield, Gallagher, and Hollingworth who had narrowly missed the carnage in the King David, and who had covered its bloody consequences, the final abandonment of the hotel by the British must have been a moment of major reflection.

For correspondents from the United States, the story was different. Despite the differences of opinion which existed among the political elite, Washington had declared its view, and already recognized the fledgling Jewish state. Clifton Daniel, who had covered the bombing of the King David Hotel in Jerusalem almost two years before, was now reporting from London for the *New York Times*. There are no accounts of lone pipers or sun-bleached Union flags for him. His story, datelined 14 May, begins, 'With obvious relief Britain turned her back on Palestine today.'[106] For a correspondent in London for one of the United States' leading newspapers, his focus is the diplomatic angle. While the United

States has surged ahead, Britain – apparently relieved – is ready to remain at arm's length, for a while, at least.

> Despite the United States' decision to recognise the Jewish state there seemed to be no question of extending British recognition until the new country proved its authority and stabilised its frontiers. Britain was deterred partly by the attitude of the Arab states, with which she hopes to restore cordial relations.

Almost 70 years later, Israel is yet to stabilize its frontiers. Daniel, perhaps himself aware of the way differing foreign policy seems to be reflected in differing editorial priorities, has apparently taken the trouble to discover the line his newspaper's London counterpart intends to take. 'The Times of London,' he reports, 'will say tomorrow that the British "share deeply in the sorrow and regret at this failure of a great mission."' Yet still Daniel manages to keep this in context – at least, in the context of what the people around him seem to care about. With a note of the weariness which journalists sometimes experience when they suspect their audience is less interested than they in the story which they are writing, Daniel apparently feels obliged to inject the following note of reality:

> Today ordinary Britons, who were enjoying the first holiday of the spring, the long Whitsun weekend, scarcely seemed to notice that the British sphere of dominion had been contracted by about 10,429 more square miles.[107]

'Newspaper headlines,' he concludes with a hint of weariness, 'were devoted to matters of more general public interest.' There is no such indifference elsewhere in the *New York Times*'s coverage. Sam Pope Brewer, filing from Amman in 'Trans-Jordan' a couple of days later, reports on preparations for the Arab Legion to join the military offensive to prevent the Jewish State getting becoming more than a declaration. He also gives an interesting insight into an early form of embedding.

> Correspondents accompanying the forces are required to wear Arab Legion uniform without insignia of rank – khaki blouse and trousers and red and white checked Arab headdress. This is declared necessary as an identifying mark for the correspondent's safety.[108]

These well-intentioned regulations ostensibly made for the journalists' safety are not necessarily appreciated. Brewer's paragraph ends with the explanation, 'but most Western reporters find it difficult to wear properly.'[109] These sartorial challenges are hardly the most serious difficulty faced by journalists covering the war. Being part of any military operation brings its hazards – as any reporter who has contemplated putting on uniform (less common in the 21st century) knows, such 'identifying marks' as an 'Arab headdress' might lessen the likelihood of a journalist's being shot by the side which they are accompanying. It affords no such prospect of protection from enemy fire. Aside from these dangers, there were also the eternal difficulties of access to reliable technology to send material, and, as already noted, censorship with which to contend. Brewer's report explains, 'Special radio facilities were established here yesterday for correspondents but they are not yet functioning full time. The problems of organisation are causing delays in censorship.'[110] As a modern military might strive to ensure that it provided, or assisted in the provision of, internet access – so the armies of 1948 knew that state-of-the-art technology – radio, in this case – would help them to get their side of the story across. The censorship was there in case they needed to make a more explicit intervention. Brewer himself had reported, in a story datelined Beirut a few days earlier, 'Censorship is now complicating the work of reporting developments in all parts of the Middle East';[111] an Associated Press report, printed in the *New York Times* on 15 May, is headlined, 'NEWS FROM TEL AVIV CENSORED FOR A DAY'.[112] This despatch also has the distinction in journalism history of being datelined, 'Tel-Aviv, Palestine' – normal enough then, of course; a factual error now. The AP report is interesting for another reason, too. 'Correspondents were not notified in advance that officials of the Jewish state, which then was not officially in existence, had imposed security restrictions' it says.[113]

From the point of view of trying to understand the significance of these early days as a starting point for the way the conflict would later be reported, a later paragraph is the most interesting.

At midnight last night, when censorship had been in effect for several hours, public relations officials told newsmen that they had no knowledge of it.

Public relations officers and the chief Jewish censor said today that their failure to notify correspondents was an unintentional error and that they had no intention of censoring dispatches in the future.[114]

Censorship, of course, has endured in Israel – specifically where the reporting of military or security matters is concerned. 'All written material, photographs and recordings dealing with security and defense matters intended for transmission abroad, must be presented to the Censor's Office,'[115] is the beginning of one of the forms which any journalist seeking accreditation from the Israeli government must sign. What has also endured is a practised skill in news management and public relations techniques. Arriving in Jerusalem in 2002 for my own posting to the region, I was told – perhaps half-jokingly – by an Israeli official, 'We will lie to the world, but not to the President of the United States.'[116] The 'public relations officials' declaring that they 'had no knowledge' of the censorship, and that 'their failure to notify correspondents was an unintentional error' reads to me like a fairly clumsy version of the technique which Israeli officials of later years have employed to assist themselves in getting their side of the story across. It seems to have matured and become more sophisticated in parallel with the State of Israel itself.

As will be discussed in Chapter 5, one of the main challenges of covering the Israeli-Palestinian conflict is that of the inclusion or otherwise of context. Israelis, Palestinians, and supporters of both are quickly willing to cry bias if detail which they consider important is omitted. Coverage of the first few days of Israel's existence seems to suggest this was a problem of which correspondents and editors then were only too aware. On 16 May, the *New York Times* gave a whole page over to what would now be called, on a news website, a 'timeline'. It begins with a summary of the first hours of Israel's existence 'Born and Bombed',[117] as the headline has it – but soon explains to its readers the existence and significance of the Balfour Declaration, as well giving an extensive account of the resources and characteristics of what was then the world's newest nation state. At one point, Israel is described as 'as this little land, wedged in a vast Arab world' before the piece goes on to describe some of the forces lined up against it. The phrase anticipates much of the later coverage which would see Israel as an outpost of democracy surrounded by hostile neighbours. It is phrases like these which underline the importance of 1948 as a starting point – a moment when regional roles and international images will be established to be refined and strengthened as the history of the Middle East unfolds. The bolder correspondents, Clare Hollingworth not surprisingly among them, in her piece about Cable and Wireless, also use the world-changing events of this period as a 'peg' – as journalistic slang describes something which makes a story newsworthy – for longer pieces which try to explain to their audience what may lie ahead. Dana Adams Schmidt's work for the *New York Times* is a shining example of such reporting. For the paper's edition of 16 May, he sends a piece of over 2,000 words in which he looks extensively at the nature of the new state, and those who will live in, and alongside, it. His opening paragraph highlights one of the factors familiar to any journalist who has reported from the region: the fact that it is so small that one can travel from the Mediterranean to the Dead Sea, 'In less than a day's drive, war permitting'.[118] The proximity of the important sites and flashpoints is something which journalists more used to covering conflicts spread over greater areas often comment upon – so too is the fact that these relatively short distances can only be covered 'war permitting' even today. That may not necessarily mean armed conflict, but perhaps only physical barriers – such as that built between Israel and the West Bank, or Gaza – which bear witness to its having taken place in the past, and potentially in the future. Schmidt's conclusion – written, let us remember, in 1948 – is gloomily familiar to those of us who would report on the conflict decades later.

> Either the two peoples must be separated by partition, as proposed by the United Nations last Nov. 29, or one of the two must succumb. A combination of the two circumstances, to the disadvantage of the Arabs, has now become reality.

Hollingworth's piece, quoted above, which suggested that Israel would 'provide the United States with a firm foothold in the Middle East' is another such example. Although perhaps only Israel's critics would agree with the description of the Jewish state as a 'foothold' for the United States, few would argue with the suggestion that today, almost 70 years later, the United States and Israel are staunch allies. Reporting such as this shows the value of journalism in understanding the Israeli-Palestinian conflict. Diplomats may reach the same conclusions, but, if so, they may be made public only years later – unless they are leaked, or hacked. The reporting is in the public domain as soon as possible. That is not to say that all the journalism from this time proved to be prescient. In a story for the *Observer* sent from Amman two weeks later – perhaps from the Cable and Wireless office the relocation of which so dismayed her – Hollingworth describes conditions in the Old City of Jerusalem as the warring sides fought for it in the aftermath of the declaration of Israeli statehood. The *Observer* is evidently proud of its correspondent. It promotes the story with the words, 'This is the first uncensored report from inside Jewish Jerusalem. Our correspondent, virtually a prisoner there for a fortnight, was allowed to leave yesterday for Amman.'[119] Still there are some predictions here which do not ring true: the possibility, for example, that the fight for the Jewish Quarter could develop into a 'second Stalingrad'[120] (this to a readership who would not have had to seek out Wikipedia, or Hollywood, to understand the comparison). There is also what seems the unsubstantiated, and astonishingly insensitive, suggestion that, 'Administration of the new State is modelled on Nazi lines.' One wonders again if Hollingworth's near-death experience at the King David Hotel had led her to be implacably antagonistic to the cause which the bombing was designed to advance. Certainly, it seems impossible that such a comparison would pass editorial oversight today, and surprising that it did then. Perhaps in an indication of how closely media coverage of the conflict was monitored then, as now the same edition of the *Observer* carries a letter from a Cable and Wireless Public Relations Officer, Harold J. Wilson. In response to Hollingworth's earlier report, Wilson insists, Cable and Wireless, 'hopes to return to Jerusalem in due course.'[121]

While Hollingworth was 'virtually a prisoner' in Jerusalem, the special correspondent for The *Times* was with Arab Legion forces seeking to capture the city. He or she does not say whether being with the Legion meant wearing the khakis and Arab headdress mentioned by Brewer. Echoing Hollingworth's speculation about a siege implicit in her 'second Stalingrad' line, the *Times* correspondent draws on knowledge of the Old City to build a picture of the military difficulties it presents to both attacker and defender, 'Windows are small, doorways narrow and deep, and the whole quarter is a labyrinth. Hunger and thirst and a shortage of supplies are the weapons most to be feared by the garrison.'[122]

The report, though, is memorable for its extensive use of religious reference. As the correspondent watches the reaction of the 'scores of excited Arabs [who] watched the feud between the Jews and their countrymen, shouting with joy at each explosion and screaming advice and encouragement at the gunners,'[123] there are references to the Garden of Gethsemane, 'the dome of rock covering the place whence Mohamed had ascended to his seventh heaven'; 'the spot where Peter thrice denied his Lord, and the terraced hill of Mount Sion [*sic*], where lie the hidden tombs of Solomon and David.' These references may be a journalistic device to create a sense of place, a sense of recognition, for a readership which would presumably have been far more familiar with the scriptures, especially the King James Bible, than would an audience today. They may also offer an insight into the conflict – an insight which might otherwise be obscured in the fog of war, and journalistic competition to explain sieges and the likelihood or otherwise of a second Stalingrad – and its enduring nature. Perhaps extending the idea of the journalist both as observer, and as representative of the wider, in this case western, world, the paragraph concludes, 'For this, Muslim and Jew are fighting while the Christian world looks on.'

2
Six Days and Seventy-Three

The name 'dog days', for the warmest part of the summer, comes from the rising in the Mediterranean of Sirius, the Dog Star. The coast marking the western limit of the land over which Israelis and Palestinians have fought and argued for so long can be stiflingly hot in the middle of the year. In Gaza, the working day may finish early, around 2 pm, so that people can sleep indoors in the heat of the afternoon. Journalists working in the region may, if their deadlines permit, be tempted to do the same on a slow news day. At times of heightened tension, they may reason that they never know when they are going to get a good night's sleep anyway – so they might as well grab a siesta if there is the chance. During the second Palestinian intifada, or uprising, against Israel, from the year 2000 onwards, Israeli military operations in Gaza usually began, and often concluded, in the hours of darkness. As the BBC's correspondent there from 2002 to 2004, I would go to bed between midnight and 1 am never knowing whether I would sleep for six or seven hours, or six or seven minutes. If attacks came during the day, they were often from the air: missiles from helicopter gunships or warplanes. The helicopters would strike at cars carrying 'senior Hamas operatives' or other 'terrorists', as the Israeli Army Press Office referred to those who swelled the ranks of their enemies. Day or night, surprise was all.

So it was when Israel seized control of the Gaza Strip as the dog days of 1967 approached. By the time the hottest part of the summer was upon the land between the River Jordan and the Mediterranean, Israel had humiliated the armed forces of its neighbours. In doing so, Israel had taken land which it holds to this day – an occupation which, almost half a century later, still lies at the centre of its conflict with the Palestinians. The speed and scale of Israel's military success largely shaped the region as it remains today – a 'crushing victory' which 'suddenly expanded territory under Israel's control almost fourfold'.[1] Most of the journalists waiting for the war to start seem to have been caught off their guard, too – perhaps made dozy by the early summer heat; perhaps fooled by Israel's increasingly sophisticated news management techniques. The 'public relations officials' who dissembled before 'newsmen' almost two decades earlier had evidently sharpened their spinning skills. James Cameron, writing for the *Evening Standard*, on what was actually the eve of war, reported that Moshe Dayan – who had recently been brought into the government as Defence Minister[2] – 'surprised a crowd of fire-eating correspondents by his unexpected restraint'.[3] Dayan, of course, must have known what was about to happen, yet Israel's masterful news management succeeded in throwing journalists even as astute as Cameron off the scent. Only a few days earlier, in his despatch for the *Evening Standard* datelined 28 May, he warned, writing of a war he saw then as inevitable, 'We stand on the edge of a truly tragic absurdity.'[4] Yet with war less than 24 hours away, Dayan told those fire-eaters it was 'too late for the hammer blow'.[5] In reality, the hammer was even then being raised to deliver that blow, but Israel did not want anyone to know, and so the press were hoodwinked. David Rubinger, a photojournalist who was to become famous for the picture he took that week of Israeli paratroopers in front of the Western Wall in the Old City shortly after it was captured, remembers journalists departing – apparently thinking war was not going to break out. 'A lot of them had left already,' he recalls, apparently convinced by a media campaign designed to deceive. 'They had tried a trick,' he says of the Israeli government:

> They sent a lot of people on leave. Units were sent on leave on Friday, and Saturday for shabat [the Jewish Sabbath] which was obviously a Dayan trick. And I know that we had, one correspondent I know from *Life* left for the weekend because they'd been here for three weeks, on and on: 'yes – no' 'yes–no'.[6]

In their account of the Six-Day War – rapidly published the same year – Randolph S. Churchill and Winston S. Churchill (son and grandson respectively of Britain's wartime leader) describe how on the eve of Israel launching its offensive, 'newspaper offices not only in Israel, but throughout the world, received pictures of Israeli troops on leave relaxing on the beaches'.[7] This had been going on for a while, although, as Alan Hart reported for Britain's Independent Television News (ITN) on 24 May, some 50,000 reservists had been called up 'after dark so as not to cause panic'.[8] Hart reported too that hospitals had been emptied to make way for a possible influx of military casualties – but his report also showed pictures of summer crowds on the beach at Tel Aviv. A *News of the World* interview with Dayan was another part of the media campaign to mask Israel's intentions. Persuaded on the basis of the interview that Israel had no immediate plans to launch an offensive, the Churchills tell us, 'the correspondent took plane for London on Sunday morning – the day before the outbreak of war. He was followed at 8 am the following morning by a Sunday Times news team.'[9] Presumably there were red faces – and rapidly booked return tickets – all round. No journalist likes the realization that they have been fooled. They like it even less when they learn that not only have they been duped themselves, they have unwittingly been used as part of a media campaign designed to mislead. In the introduction to their book, the Churchills explain that Winston Churchill 'was in Israel (briefly also in Jordan and Lebanon) for three weeks before the war'.[10] They do not disclose that the departing correspondent who 'took plane', and was thus absent for the actual start of the war, must have been Churchill himself! It is his story in that week's *News of the World* – 'Winston S. Churchill reports from the foxholes of Beersheba'[11] – which includes the interview. Churchill seems to have been given extensive access, and seems to have been impressed both with Dayan, and the troops he commanded. Dayan's recent appointment as Minister of Defence had been made as Israel weighed its options in the face of expected war. This leads Churchill to compare Dayan with his grandfather and namesake, Britain's prime minister during the Second World War. 'When I remarked that it took Hitler to make [my] grandfather Prime Minister he laughed and added: "Yes, and it took 80,000 Egyptian soldiers to get me into the Government." '[12] With the benefit of half a century's hindsight, and the knowledge of what was to come, Dayan's message in his interview with Churchill seems very carefully crafted to do at least two things: firstly, to tell an international audience, especially in Britain and the United States, what they want to hear; secondly, to suggest Israel's willingness to pursue a diplomatic solution to the conflict with its neighbours. Churchill wrote:

> General Dayan declared: 'We don't want anyone else to fight for us. Whatever can be done in a diplomatic way I would welcome and encourage but if fighting does come to Israel I would not like American or British boys to get killed here and I do not think we need them.'[13]

The talk of 'whatever can be done in a diplomatic way' serves its purpose. Churchill says he meets Dayan 'on the evening of Friday 2

June'[14] – a point at which, one assumes, the General must have known that Israel was due to launch its attacks on the Monday morning. Churchill's analysis shows his conviction that war was not about to start: presumably exactly the message which Israel wished to send through the interview. He tells his readers, 'Contrary to what some people supposed (and many of his supporters believe) Dayan's appointment will not necessarily mean that Israel will respond immediately with military force to the closure of the Straits of Tiran by the Egyptians.'[15]

It is not just Churchill who writes a later account of his encounter with Dayan. The General himself, in his 1970s autobiography, *Story of My Life*, also mentions his meetings with the press. 'I was hoping,' he writes, 'that the impression might be gained that we were not about to go to war but were intent on exhausting all the diplomatic possibilities.'[16] Dayan is keen to gauge whether or not his tactic has worked. Checking later with his advisor, Moshe Pearlman, he seems pleased to learn that 'this was indeed the impression of the correspondents, judging from what they were saying, and from the reports they had filed.'[17] Pearlman was the man to judge, having been the first spokesman for the Israeli Army, and the founder of the Israeli Government Press Office.[18] Of the interview with Churchill, Dayan is content to mention his remark about the massing of Egyptian troops assisting his return to government.[19]

Much of the rest of Churchill's piece reports on his visit to the 'foxholes of Beersheba'. Here again, as with Dayan himself, Churchill writes favourably of what he sees, 'The cool self-assurance of these men – factory workers, farmers, students, actors – I spoke to in their slit trenches impressed me deeply.' Churchill tells us that the unit he visits is 'close to the Gaza Strip', and so may later have been involved in occupying that territory for Israel. What is interesting too is the space which the *News of the World* gives to weighty news of foreign wars and diplomacy. For much of that newspaper's history, until its closure in 2011, its principle stock-in-trade was crime and scandal. George Orwell's 1946 essay, 'The Decline of the English Murder', for example, mentions the *News of the World* by name as a part of the quintessential English Sunday afternoon. In later years, while it continued to deliver impressive scoops – the exposure of a match-fixing ring in international cricket being one example[20] – many of these focused on celebrities rather than affairs of state. Indeed, it was the use of illegally obtained voicemail messages as sources for some of these exclusives which, once these methods were exposed, led the newspaper's owner, Rupert Murdoch, to decide to close it as a means of mitigating the scandal. A *News of the World* which discussed in some detail sessions at the United Nations, rather than the sex secrets of soap opera stars, seems to belong to a different journalistic era. The admiration expressed for Israel's Army marks a new departure, too. In 1946 and 1948 men taking up arms to fight for the Jewish state were terrorists battling British interests. Now they are 'cool', self-assured, soldiers.

Leaving their readers to guess who might have been the correspondent who 'took plane' notwithstanding, the Churchills' book as a whole is impressive considering the speed with which it must have been written. In an echo of the *Times* story quoted at the end of Chapter 1, perhaps the most interesting aspect of the Churchills' book from the perspective of journalism history is its opening chapter. In a commendable attempt to provide context for readers – many of whom would have been familiar with the basic facts of the war from recent news coverage, including the stories sent by Winston Churchill himself – the book's first chapter is entitled simply 'The Past'. From a journalistic point of view, it is curious because it relates stories from scripture as if they carry exactly the same weight as verifiable, relatively recent (i.e. 20th century) historical events. For example, the second paragraph begins with the assertion that 'Three thousand five hundred years ago, Moses led the Jewish people back from captivity in Egypt,'[21] and ends with the victorious British military campaign in Palestine in the First World War, and 'the establishment of the British Mandate in 1920'.[22] Like the *Times* correspondent almost 20 years earlier, the Churchills, writing almost 50 years ago, have readers who would be much more familiar with the Bible than might be many people in Britain today (though that might be different in the United States, with its higher proportion of churchgoers). Of course, the Bible might still be used today, too. But it would be much more likely to be referred to as one might a legend: that is, to illustrate a story, or explain the spiritual significance it has for one or more of the protagonists. It would be presented in those terms, too – not alongside, and apparently treated as equally reliable as, events which had taken place within what was then living memory. One is left to conclude that religion's more prominent role in the lives of the readers ensured it a wider role in journalism than it would be likely to have today.

While Winston Churchill was interviewing Dayan, and reporting that Israel was getting ready for war, yet hoping for peace, the picture on the side of one of the young Jewish state's enemies, Jordan, was different. Dana Adams Schmidt, who had reported on the war of 1948 for the *New York Times*, was witnessing the preparations for this one, too. 'The people of Jordan have been contemplating the prospect of war for more than two weeks and smiling about it,'[23] he wrote from

'Jerusalem (Jordan)' on 4 June, one of the last days in history when that dateline – like the 'Tel Aviv, Palestine' one cited in the previous chapter – would have been correct. Jerusalem was very shortly to fall under Israeli control. Schmidt's great advantage as a correspondent of this war is his experience of covering the earlier one. He describes, 'the national humiliation of mass flight in 1948 for nearly a million Palestinians, three-quarters of them now in this country'[24] as a powerful motivating factor. The war, he writes, is 'an opportunity for revenge and redemption: a chance to go back to the land and homes many remember abandoning 19 years ago'.[25] Schmidt does his best in his piece to try to report on what is happening on the other side, too – although from where he is, his perspective is distant. 'You sit on a roof in the old city and look out over the shadows of no man's land to the lights go the new Israeli city and watch the people and cars moving,' he tells his readers. He makes up for the restrictions on his own first-hand reporting by cultivating sources who are able to see a broader picture. 'The diplomats who slip back and forth across the border at the Mandelbaum Gate say that there is more excitement and tension here than on the Israeli side.' The Mandelbaum Gate was a checkpoint, 'the only border crossing with the Kingdom of Jordan, connecting between the two parts of Jerusalem,'[26] between 1948 and Israel's taking of the rest of the city in 1967. The greater access afforded to diplomats then seems remarkable to later generations of correspondents, free, unlike today's diplomats, to talk to representatives of groups designated 'terrorists' by the United States and the European Union: Hamas being the most prominent example. Once the war started, on the morning of 5 June 1967, the reporters found themselves in the thick of it – as did, once again, the King David Hotel. As in 1948, Jordanian forces were firing from the Old City across towards West Jerusalem. So perilous could this area be – even in peacetime – that after 1948 the Israelis had built a trench in order to enable them to supply the positions which they held. Parts of the 'Mount Zion trench' are still visible today, on the road leading away from the Jaffa Gate of the Old City. A plaque describing what the onlooker sees explains that, 'The trench remained in use up until the Six Day War.' After that was over, Jordanian troops no longer represented a threat. At the beginning of the conflict, though, these slopes below the city walls were in the thick of the fighting. Despite that, and perhaps also because of it, the King David seems to have become the international journalists' residence of choice. With Jerusalem being fiercely fought over as the Israelis strove to capture it, Robin Stafford reported in the *Daily Express* on 7 June, 'Most Israelis are sleeping in their basements. Last night a few women and two American tourists slept on mattresses on the floor of my hotel, the King David, by candlelight.'[27] In conditions of hardship and danger, reporters are reduced, as is common even today, to pooling their resources. Christopher Dobson, in the *Daily Mail*, credits Stafford of the *Express* with helping him to send his article, 'from the blacked-out King David Hotel, where a shell landed earlier today and wounded four people'.[28] The blackout means that the catering facilities have been reduced from their normal luxury standards – something which Dobson concludes is newsworthy. 'We dined by candlelight with the waiter apologising for the restricted menu – paté and filet mignon!'[29] In January 2014, the King David menu included 'Filet of Beef Financier'. The name of the newer dish reflected perhaps how the hotel's clientele had changed from when it was on the front line of a war to control Jerusalem. Dobson does not say how much he had to pay in 1967, but in 2014 the filet would have cost him 180 shekels, then a little over £30 or $50 – in the 21st century, more readily in the price range of a financier than a reporter.

Dobson goes on to talk of more weighty matters than the menu. He tells his readers that he has arrived in Jerusalem 'with a convoy of bearded brigands on half-track vehicles'.[30] Others too are keen to get out as close to the fronts as they can. Harold Jackson for the *Guardian* reports 'seeing line after line of Egyptian bodies in the Gaza Strip';[31] Hans Benedict described for the Associated Press, 'A group of dead Palestinian Liberation Army commandos in tennis shoes sprawled grotesquely behind the barbed wire of a strong point.'[32] On 6 June, the second day of the war, Jackson had been to Sinai with Israeli tank forces. He describes:

> the steady banging of the heavy artillery in the distance. We are unable to go farther forward because the road, which is not exactly the M1, peters out altogether in the sand. Two convoys waiting to go through stretch as far as the eye can see, and reporters take second place.[33]

Here Jackson encourages his readers to imagine a desert battlefield by comparing in to a major motorway leading north out of London. As he makes his way around the war-torn streets of Jerusalem – 'The whole city was blacked out and explosions rumbled as I tried to find my way about the streets'[34] – Donald Wise of the *Daily Mirror* recalls the classroom to draw his audience in. 'All the places you read of at school lay spread out before me. The Mount of Olives, the Holy Sepulchre, and the olive grove where Samson wooed Delilah. All overhung by the smoke of war.'[35] From their later, longer, more analytical despatches, it is clear that the reporters understand the strategic significance of what they have witnessed. Sydney Gruson writes in the *New York Times*:

> On one thing all Western diplomats and Israelis seem to agree: too much blood has been spilled – more perhaps than is yet realised in the great flush of victory – to expect that Israel would willingly return the frontiers to what they were before the war began on Monday.[36]

Almost half a century later, of course, they are yet to do so – and the 1967 borders have remained the focus of every unsuccessful round of peace talks since. So the correspondents of 1967 face the eternal challenges of reporting on armed conflict: telling the story of the day; trying to explain to their audiences what the longer-term consequences of the day might be; and danger. In his AP despatch carried in the *Express*, and referred to above, Hans Benedict describes on entering Gaza, 'a blinding flash and a car ahead of us carrying three journalists and cameramen and an Israeli officer was blown up by a booby trapped mine hidden in a roadblock.' The cameraman was named as Ben Oyserman, who was working for the Canadian Broadcasting Corporation – one of three journalists[37] killed covering the Six-Day War. The 'booby trapped mine hidden in a roadblock' which claimed Oyserman's life became a common feature of Gaza in time of conflict. As the second intifada, or Palestinian uprising against Israel, raged from 2000 onwards, piles of sand appeared in the bumpy, badly-surfaced, roads of Gaza's refugee camps. They were placed at short intervals on opposite sides of the road, making a chicane that forced any vehicle to slow down. Given that the streets of the seaside territory's shanty towns double as playgrounds for thousands of children, you might assume these were traffic-calming measures. If so, they doubled as part of Gaza's defences against Israeli military incursions. As night fell at times of heightened military activity, Palestinian fighters would conceal explosives in the piles of sand – hoping to damage or destroy any Israeli armour that advanced that way during the hours of darkness.

Faced then with their own pressing dangers – Stafford writes that 'mortar bombs, machine gun fire, and sniper shots are exploding all around us'[38] – some reporters, as noted above, decided to assist their competitors. Others recorded the challenges they faced in getting their stories out to the world. James Reston tells *New York Times* readers 'running copy to the telegraph office was an obstacle race, with perky instant commanders at every corner.'[39] Correspondents today would be fretting over the reliability or otherwise of the hotel's wi-fi connection, and would not have to worry about physically getting to the telegraph office. Perhaps Reston's enforced nocturnal outings gave him time to think on what he had done during the day – at least once he had the satisfaction of knowing that he had been able to send his story. For his story 'A War's First Hours', published in the *New York Times* on 6 June 1967, and from which the line above is taken, is a fascinating reflection on the challenges and pressures of reporting this war in particular, and indeed war in general. Perhaps stunned by the suddenness with which the war, even if expected, finally came, Reston admits to being unsure of what is happening around him. He writes of a Jerusalem, 'blacked out physically and factually tonight' one which is 'jumping with propaganda about who fired the first shot'. Of the radio stations' competing versions of events, he writes of the BBC's 'cool accounts', and the 'angry voices' of the broadcasts from Moscow, Damascus, and Cairo. He encapsulates the bewilderment a reporter can feel faced with the task of putting together a story when the sources at hand are 'the wildly contradictory and uncheckable reports from the different warring capitals'. Even after these have been reconciled, or at least dealt with as well as possible, there remains the obstacle of 'censors eliminating things the enemy obviously knows'. Perhaps, given that his deadline fell in a time zone far behind the one from which he was filing, Reston did have time to reflect not just on the story, but on the journalistic process. His account is highly informative for us know, as one imagines it was for his readers then. In the *Guardian* of the same day, 6 June, David Hirst turns the confusion, claim, and counter-claim which surround him into the opening line of his story, declaring, 'There are two wars – the real war and propaganda war.'[40] He is writing from Beirut. His story reflects the fact that everyone in the region has much at stake in the war as it unfolds, and the media are being used as part of that 'propaganda war' much as the armies are fighting the 'real one'. Hirst echoes Reston's impressions from Jerusalem when he talks of 'fierce rhetoric pouring in' from Arab radio stations, and 'Arabic counterblast from Israel'.[41] In an era long before 24-hour television news, let alone social media, Hirst writes that radio speakers have been set up on the campus of the American University so that no one misses anything. It seemed to do the trick. Looking back, Hirst recalls an atmosphere in which, 'In the early days of the war – we're talking not more than one or two days – the Arabs believed what the Egyptian media was saying. And they thought that victory was on the way.'[42] In Israel, as presumably across the region, this craving for information had begun before the first shot was fired. The propaganda war began in advance of the real one. For the *New York Times*, Terence Smith described Jerusalem on the eve of war, a city where the cafés were lively after the evening cinema screenings had concluded. But, he writes, the 'conversation halts each hour on the hour while the news reports are being broadcast.'[43] By the time Smith's report was being read on the breakfast tables of the East Coast of the United States, the propaganda war of which he described a part had taken second place; the real war had been under way for several hours. At the same time as they tried to describe and to understand the media war, correspondents, like Churchill, were being used in it, too. The same day that Churchill's interview with Moshe Dayan appeared in the *News of the World*, Dayan was giving a news conference – presumably this was the meeting at which, James Cameron wrote, the correspondents were 'surprised' – repeating the line about Israel's not wanting 'American or British boys to get killed here'.[44] The *Guardian*, which carried Harold Jackson's report from which that line was taken, seems, though, to have suspected that something may have been up. Whatever weight they give to Dayan's words, the headline chosen for Jackson's story is 'Israelis Cloak Their Aims'.

Those aims were soon clear, and accomplished with devastating effect. Perhaps consciously echoing Dayan's 'military hammer blow' phrase of a few days earlier, Cameron talks of the 'first sledgehammer day of the new Middle Eastern war.'[45] Two days later, he says that as the day dawned in Jerusalem, 'the first stage of this Middle Eastern blitzkrieg was already over.'[46] Israel had started by attacking Egypt, destroying over 300 aircraft, before striking at the Jordanian and Syrian air forces.[47] The Jewish state's enemies had been crippled before they could begin to fight in earnest. The extent of Israel's military success was not immediately obvious – and one correspondent in particular suffered the miserable fate of not being believed by his editors. Michael Elkins was a BBC correspondent, and an Israeli. Elkins's nationality, as Jeremy Bowen wrote in his book on the Six-Day War, led editors in London to suspect that he had 'spoken with the tongue of the prophets'[48] – in other words, overstated Israel's feat of arms. As a result, his story was not broadcast until the evening – one of those infuriating cases for a journalist when an exclusive is so good and so complete that not even the newsroom is willing to credit it. Hirst remembers with 'shock and disbelief' such a moment, when Michael Elkins 'said the war was over before anybody else – with details'.

Once Israel's victory became clear, some of the foreign correspondents were ready to share their sense of triumph. On 7 June, the *Guardian* described the capture of the Old City of Jerusalem as the realization of a dream 'which had sustained Jews for 2,000 years'.[49] David Rubinger was there, about to take the picture which ensured his enduring reputation. Getting into position for the shot, though, was a matter of an overnight journey. As Rubinger remembers, the evening before, he had been in the Sinai with advancing Israeli troops:

> And I was – you know journalists, keep your eyes and ears open – I heard something on the intercom. A General speaking, Jerusalem was mentioned. A helicopter came in to pick up wounded. I hopped on. You don't need any papers, I hopped on the helicopter, flew back – and raced to Jerusalem. Arrived in Jerusalem about six in the morning. Went to see if my family was alive. I hadn't seen them for three weeks – you know, because I was out with the troops, and made my way to the Old City and arrived there about ten, fifteen minutes after the place was taken. Lying down on the ground because there was a lot of hovels still standing. The width between them and the wall was about ten feet. So I wanted to get a little bit of the height of the walls. That's why I was lying down.[50]

The 'hovels' which Rubinger remembers being so close to the wall were among the buildings which Israel demolished following the conflict in order to make room for worshippers to pray at the site, which is revered as the last remaining part of Jerusalem's ancient Jewish temple. The houses destroyed included one in which the Palestinian leader, Yasser Arafat, is thought to have spent part of his boyhood.[51] While the Old City has changed since Israel captured it in 1967, Rubinger's picture stands as an unchanging record of a particular moment in Middle Eastern history. Three Israeli paratroopers stand at the front of a crowd of their comrades, taking in the realization that they have seized a site which the Jewish people have dreamed for centuries of holding. The central figure, handsome, has removed his helmet – perhaps a reflection of relief that he is no longer in danger, perhaps better to look up at the wall reaching above him (which Rubinger achieved by lying on the ground). The soldiers' emotions are hard to guess – fatigue, wonder, lingering fear, relief – all seem to combine.[52] Rubinger remembers chaotic scenes as those present tried to understand the significance of what had happened – and he remembers one colleague whose scoop had now been recognized for what it was. 'Mike Elkins was there with me. And I don't remember photographers. I can't recall any photographers. It was pandemonium. I was lying on the ground and lots of moving around.'[53] Rubinger still lives in the house in Jerusalem to which he returned to develop the picture – although his dark room has now become, in his words 'where you throw everything that you don't need'. He laid out the contact sheets on the desk at which he still works today. By the evening, the Israeli Government Press Office was distributing the picture for a small sum to all comers. While this was later to become the subject of a court battle for Rubinger over copyright – he suggests that some of those who picked the picture up later tried to pass it off as their own work – he now says 'thank you all the thieves' without whom, he believes, the picture would not have become so widely known.

In a few days, Israel's stunning feat of arms had transformed the region, and Israel's position within it. For Hirst, full comprehension of the scale of what had happened was only to come later:

> when I realised that the Israelis were not actually going to withdraw from the territories they'd occupied – in my naiveté I'd assumed that they would – when that became clear, and the sheer scale of it, the amount of territory which they'd actually taken: four or five times their own size.

For the Arabs, who had 'believed what the Egyptian media was saying, and they thought that victory was on the way,' Hirst remembers defeat as 'a colossal shock'. The newest state in the Middle East, less than 20 years old, had fought and defeated enemies on three fronts. It had taken control of Jerusalem, and those parts of Mandate-era Palestine which it did not already control. The war had also created other problems, including 'Some 200,000 more Arab refugees [who] crossed the Jordan to the East Bank.'[54] With the 'Middle Eastern blitzkrieg' over, reporters were able to travel to try to make sense for their audiences of what had happened. In an unforgettable despatch for the *Evening Standard* Cameron describes a flight over Sinai, during which he is able to appreciate the scale of damage and death which Israel's campaign has inflicted. 'The tanks and vehicles litter the desert like the nursery floor of an angry child,'[55] he writes. His simile is perfect, describing both disorder and uncontrolled rage. As they tried to summarize what the far-reaching consequences of the war would be, correspondents were in a more pensive mood – in at least one case, bordering on self-criticism. In the *Guardian*, Harold Jackson reflected, 'Intellectually it is easy to deplore "aggressive nationalism". Politically it is a bad mistake to ignore it and one which I and a number of reporters fell into last week.'[56] The fault, he believes, is that, 'we assumed that the tortuous ennuis of diplomacy and compromise would hold sway as usual'.[57] Working for a weekly, Churchill had seven days to come up with what the *News of the World* trumpeted as 'another brilliant dispatch'.[58] Churchill called Israel's military success, 'a victory unprecedented in the history of the world.' He correctly assessed that the balance of power in the Middle East had been altered, 'for a generation or more'. Cameron is even clearer, and, as one might expect of a correspondent of his limitless talent, completely correct. 'For good or ill, from today nothing can ever be the same again in the Middle East,' he writes on 12 June. 'The new book must start today.'[59] And so it did. The conflict which I arrived to cover 35 years later was defined by what had happened in those six days, as is the region today. Israel continues to control the Golan Heights, the Gaza Strip, the West Bank – where the continuing building of settlements has called into question the very possibility of there ever being a Palestinian State, even assuming that the political accord necessary for one to come into being can be reached.

The general tone of the coverage of the Six-Day War is one of surprise, shock, and then recognition: recognition that the reporters covering that conflict had witnessed a seminal moment in Middle Eastern history. In the week after the war had been won, Richard Lindley reported for ITN from the Old City, speaking over pictures of long queues of Jewish worshippers going to visit the Western Wall. 'In their minds,' Lindley suggests in his script, 'are the words of the prophet Jeremiah. "Thus said the Lord, refrain thy voice from weeping, and thine eyes from tears. For thy work shall be rewarded, and thy children shall come again to their own border." '[60] Lindley's drawing on the Old Testament touched on an important trend in the way in which the conflict was portrayed. Hirst, in his book *The Gun and the Olive Branch*, writes of 1967 as a moment when 'modern Israelis rediscovered overnight something of the zeal and vision which had moved the early pioneers. It all gushed forth, this Zionist renewal, in a torrent of biblico-strategic, cleric-military antics and imagery.'[61] The Western Wall lies at the heart of this, its religious significance reinforcing its importance as a military objective. Among the soldiers taken to see it in the days which followed was the Israeli historian Shlomo Sand. Sand, who disputes the widely held belief that the wall is part of the ancient temple, remembers from those days 'secular agents of culture who sought to re-create and reinforce tradition through propaganda'.[62] While this new imagery and propaganda was emerging on the Israeli side, Hirst argues that the seeds of another force had been sown, too. 'The 67 war was clearly a landmark in the rise of

Islamism in the region,' he says now. 'You couldn't see it at the time, but it clearly was.'

Israel had consolidated its existence, which must have seemed in doubt during its first two decades. The map of the land between the river and the sea – whether or not the de facto borders thereon are accepted – had been redrawn, and remains largely the same today. That is not to say that there were not attempts to alter that. Six years after 1967, Syria and Egypt sought to reclaim what they had lost in 1967. Jordan, which had lost so much territory, including the Old City of Jerusalem, to Israel during the Six-Day War, was deliberately excluded. Cairo and Damascus feared that the Jordanians' lack of the Soviet-made air defences which they themselves possessed made them a chink in Arab armour.[63] They were not therefore involved in the attack on Israel launched on the night of 6 October 1973, the Jewish Holy Day of Yom Kippur.

This time it was Israel's turn to be taken by surprise. Some of the British newspaper coverage seems to have been influenced by the brash confidence which reporters encountered among Israelis. Israel was to come out of this war with no loss of territory, but with much heavier casualties than they had suffered six years earlier. The sledgehammer of 1967 seems to have engendered a continuing sense of self-belief among Israelis and their supporters. In the *Daily Express*, Michael Brown describes arriving on 'the first plane into Tel Aviv since the war broke out', amid something of a party atmosphere, 'like a jamboree, singing, clapping, and drinking all the way'.[64] Having arrived in Tel Aviv, Brown encounters 'a definite optimistic cockiness'. Two days later, Brown has been to the front near the Suez Canal, travelling more than 200 miles by taxi. 'Some men wear their religious skull caps under their battle helmets,'[65] he tells his readers of the Israeli soldiers he encounters, a reminder that they had come from their Yom Kippur fast and prayers to fight. The *Daily Mirror*'s Peter Stephens had also taken a cab to the war, although he perhaps managed to make more of the fact than Brown. 'Israeli troops turned and stared in amazement and then began waving and cheering as I rolled up to the northern end of the Suez battle-front – in a taxi.'[66] Once there, Brown and Stephens's admiration for the Israelis is not unqualified (Stephens judges the 'show' 'slightly scruffy' 'by European military standards'[67]), but both seem convinced that Israel will prevail. There are notes of caution, though: for the *Daily Mail*, William Lowther speaks of an 'indefinable buoyancy in the air' in Tel Aviv, yet adds 'despite all the official statements that Golan Heights is where the major action is, one senses that the greatest carnage in the history of Israel is in fact going on right now at Suez.'[68] The next day,

Lowther travelled 300 miles (was there a distance competition going on between the rival correspondents?) to get to the front. He saw wounded and dying members of tank crews, 'swathed in bandages' from burns, being comforted by rabbis.[69] Of his return journey, he reported, 'The Israelis are also encountering a nasty battle nuisance from some of the Arabs who are resident in Israel, particularly at the Gaza Strip.'[70] Gaza had by then been under occupation for more than six years. The territory's residents perhaps sensed a chance to strike at the occupier, or create 'battle nuisance', as Lowther saw it. It is interesting now that he seems to suggest Gaza is part of Israel. A slip, perhaps, or a reflection of Israel's ability to hold territory it had taken in the earlier war, an understanding on the part of western correspondents that the Middle East really would never be the same again after 1967.

Not all reporters saw the Israeli side of the front as the main destination. For the *Daily Mirror*, John Pilger reported from an Egyptian village in the Nile Delta. Israeli warplanes had bombed the main street. Pilger's focus is the civilian victims. He warns his reader from the outset, 'I shall not spare the descriptions.' He goes on to write of a five-year-old girl whose 'arms are gutted and her hands are charred and petrified in front of her, one turned out, one turned in.'[71] She is one of many victims of the air raid, and her fate is a consequence of the Israeli military response which Brown's fellow air passengers had rushed so enthusiastically to join. Pilger explains his approach with reference to one of the great journalists of the Second World War, and to more recent conflicts:

> In any war, you will find truth among its victims – 'truth from the ground up', as Martha Gellhorn would say, 'seldom from the top down'. Most so-called mainstream reporting is from the top down, and military or government public relations is the source of most news. What this suppresses is that most wars are not between armies but are waged against societies and civilians and are atrocious. Iraq is a vivid example.[72]

Situations such as the civilian deaths Pilger described will become an eternal feature of reporting the Israeli-Palestinian conflict. In Gaza in the summer of 2014, much of the reporting was focused on the civilians killed as Israel pursued its military aims. Here, for all the 'battle nuisance' in that territory in 1973, Israel's enemy was Egypt – but the journalistic principle is the same: how accurately to reflect on Israel's military operations without including their civilian casualties? How does the reader's response to the 'jamboree' which Brown describes shift once we imagine the child's 'charred and petrified' hands?

The coverage of the 1973 war is also notable for another emerging trend: the Israeli military's control over reporters. While censorship, as we have seen from accounts of 1948, is as old as the state itself, accounts of the military sending reporters packing are absent from the 1967 coverage – so one is left to assume that if it happened, it was relatively rare. Instead, we saw Winston S. Churchill in the foxholes of Beersheba; James Cameron's flight over the carnage in the Sinai must also surely have been an Israeli military facility for reporters. Now, perhaps because Israel had not expected war to break out exactly when it did, there is a firmness with foreign journalists. Those who encounter the Israeli Army seem to get the chance to chat with soldiers, but Lowther, the fact that he had travelled 300 miles notwithstanding, is sent on his way. The soldiers he has met, 'radioed back to Tel Aviv and were told that we had to be moved out of the firing area. No photographs were allowed and after the coffee the friendly brigadier made us move back.'[73] There are frequent references to censorship and restrictions in the newspaper coverage of this time, with Brown shrewdly observing in one of his stories, 'History revealed that in the Battle of Britain losses were much greater than admitted in the 1940s. The same could apply to the Israelis today.'[74] Impressions from the front had obviously betrayed the fact that this war did not start well for Israel – even if, at the end it, they 'snatched a stunning military victory from initial defeat'.[75] The cost, though, was high – with more than 2,000 Israeli deaths in the first week of the war.[76]

Some of those deaths were movingly reflected upon by Sandy Fawkes, a woman whose own life seems to have been more remarkable than many she might have written about. Her obituary, published on her death in 2005, tells an astonishing story of a life which began as an abandoned baby, continued as an abused foster child, artist, writer, lover of a serial killer, prodigious consumer of whisky.[77] Here though, writing for the *Express*, she paused to consider the contrast she found between her own reaction to war, and that of her male journalist colleagues:

I guess most people know the difference between men and women, but war, I can assure you, brings them out in a way that is usually reserved for adolescents.

While the men behave like boys in a playground showing their knowledge of names of guns, discussing the angles and number of shots needed to destroy an armoured lorry or a tank, I noticed that each of the hundreds of destroyed and discarded vehicles were tombs to at least four of some mothers' sons.[78]

For the *New York Times*, Terence Smith in Jerusalem is more matter-of-fact. His report, datelined the day after fighting broke out, has none of the correspondent as happy-go-lucky taxi passenger; none of the reflection upon the boys in a playground. This is old-school, well-sourced, American journalism – to the extent that even his opening line, 'Heavy fighting erupted yesterday', is attributed to 'a military spokesman'.[79] The reporting is already beginning to identify patterns of conflict and anticipated ceasefire in the Israeli-Palestinian conflict. Smith quotes Chaim Herzog, former head of Israeli military intelligence, and future president of Israel, as saying that Egypt and Syria have launched the offensive to 'make a point before the United Nations General Assembly debates the Middle East again'.[80] The phrase seems to echo 'facts on the ground', used so often to describe military gains, or the building of settlements – moves made with the longer-term purpose of entering negotiations from a position of strength. Smith's coverage of Moshe Dayan's assessment of the situation when talking to the press is worth considering at length:

> In his press conference and during an earlier address to the nation over television, Mr Dayan sought to allay the initial Arab successes. He said that Israel had known about the planned attack before it had begun but it had deliberately decided against a pre-emptive strike in order 'to have the political advantage – or whatever you want to call it – of being the side that is attacked.'

Brown's suspicions, quoted above, about the real scale of Israeli casualties, and the later revelation that Israel had lost 2,000 killed in the first week of the war, make Dayan's claim harder to take at face value. While there may have been 'political advantage' in being attacked, it cannot have been great enough to be worth sustaining the losses which Israel suffered. Nevertheless, presenting Israel's setbacks as part of a deliberate decision could only deliver political advantage if carefully presented to the news media. While Moshe Dayan was brought back into the cabinet on the eve of the 1967 war because of his military abilities, then, as here six years later, he is also playing the role of a commander in the information war. Smith tells us that Dayan speaks both 'in a press conference' and 'over television', aiming 'to allay the initial Arab successes'. As in 1967, when he sought to suggest that there was little prospect of immediate war, hours before Israel launched its attacks, Dayan is seeking to manage the news as he might command troops. The military and the media wars are being prosecuted in parallel, and the Minister of Defence is at the centre of them both, devising and delivering Israel's strategy. It seems to be becoming increasingly sophisticated. From the disingenuousness of the 'public relations men' denying all knowledge of censorship imposed as the State of Israel came into being, to the impression in 1967 that there would be no 'hammer blow', to this, presenting the most serious setback of Israel's short history as having 'political advantage', the young nation is a pioneer not just of agriculture in desert regions, but also of spin in wartime. The public relations tactics which are devised to present Israel favourably to the world are coupled with stricter controls on the international press when things are not going well: compare Winston Churchill's tour of the foxholes, or James Cameron's flight over the murderous playroom of the Sinai, with the reporters of 1973 being given a cup of coffee and sent on their way.

From writing about solitary pipers and sun-drenched Union Jacks at the end of a chapter of British imperial history, from watching as Israel came into being, the tone of British and American newspaper coverage has changed as reporters look on at the state, now quarter of a century old – and hardened like a 25-year-old army officer who has seen and survived combat. Talk of 'Jewish terrorists' committing outrages against 'our troops' has gone from the British news coverage – although in 1973 the Israeli Army would still have included those who fought the Mandate forces. Instead, some reporters seem to look at the Israeli Army with a mixture of fascination and admiration. They are thrilled to be jumping onto the last planes into the war zone as Israelis return to fight for their country. Distance and suspicion still linger in places though, as when Israeli soldiers are seen by Stephens as 'scruffy' by European standards. Then there is reporting which refuses to join the cheering, the 'jamboree', but which, like Pilger's or Fawkes's, does not flinch from showing its readers the dead and maimed children, or the tank tombs containing the burned bodies of young soldiers. The purpose of these first two chapters has been to try to identify some of the characteristics of the journalism of the Israeli-Palestinian conflict in its early stages in order better to judge how they develop later on. For while there is endless debate about the real influence of war reporting on public opinion or policy making – consider the fact that television is, especially in some military and political circles still widely believed to have 'lost' the Vietnam war – journalism is the primary source of information for members of the general public, and an important source for diplomats. In this respect, the reporting of the Israeli-Palestinian conflict occupies a place of special significance in international journalism. Unlike a military campaign which comes and goes, this has continued – with pauses for periods of peace talks, of course – for decades. It has found itself at the heart of Cold War confrontation; it has been portrayed as a front in the 'war on terror'. It has dismayed, distressed, and angered advocates, adversaries, and governments the world over – and fascinated journalists.

3
Any Journalist Worth Their Salt

However you approach Jerusalem, you ascend. The commonest way for new arrivals is from Ben Gurion airport near Tel Aviv. Even in winter, the coastal plain is warm in the middle of the day – pleasantly so if you have come off a flight from Europe. The journey to Jerusalem begins through flat agricultural land, then takes the traveller through rising, rockier, ground until you arrive on the outskirts of the city. The landscape here has been transformed over the last half-century. Modern blocks of flats stand on hillsides which look as if for hundreds of years they have been home to villages and fields for subsistence farmers. The Old City, which contains almost all that makes Jerusalem sacred to so many people around the world, is seen only at last: still walled like a medieval citadel, and even higher than the surrounding hills upon which the modern town stands. Coming from the east, the ascent is even more dramatic, passing as it does areas of the desert which are below sea level, crossing landscapes which are even rockier and more barren. Here you might still see camels tethered at the edge of Bedouin camps – a scene which for Europeans like me might more readily come from a children's Bible than real life. Jericho, Bethlehem, Hebron: the names of West Bank towns and cities fire the imaginations of those travelling towards Jerusalem, a place which in recent decades has drawn journalists in large numbers, 'It's one of those places that any journalist worth their salt wanted to come and try their time in,'[1] says Crispian Balmer, Bureau Chief for Reuters from 2010 to 2014. Balmer believes this is a place which fascinates the wider world, too:

A lot of countries, a lot of peoples, feel that they have got a stake in this story and it's a story that they engage in, and are committed to over and above any other conflict for religious reasons, for historical reasons – you know, so many European, American countries deeply involved here over a long period of time.

For some who come to report from Jerusalem, those national ties are combined with religious ones. Jodi Rudoren, Bureau Chief of the *New York Times*, describes her first visit to the region as 'one of these Jewish-American teen tour type things'.[2] Even as a 17-year-old, she remembers, 'a place that everybody thought was particularly special and important and that people were fighting over struck me as a perfect kind of Petrie dish for journalism. And I think I held that with me throughout my career.' Finally coming to Jerusalem in 2012, after 15 years with the *New York Times*, she says that she 'felt it would be a challenge that would really push me journalistically,' before adding, 'I underestimated how hard it would be.' That does not seem to put journalists off coming to cover the Israeli-Palestinian conflict. Their personal reasons for being drawn to Jerusalem, along with some of the challenges which led Rudoren to conclude that she had underestimated the difficulties she would face, will be considered later. First, though, this chapter will consider their views on why the conflict has received such a huge concentration of media attention.

'If it bleeds, it leads,' goes an old saying in British journalism. In other words, violence can be sure to find its way into the headlines. On that basis, the Israeli-Palestinian conflict has frequently been able to grab the attention of editors. Violence will often succeed in securing airtime where drier, but still important, events cannot. In the spring of 2014, the United States' latest attempt at seeking a diplomatic solution to the conflict – a series of negotiations sponsored by the Secretary of State, John Kerry, collapsed. There was simply not enough common ground for the talks to proceed. Conflicting demands became impossible obstacles. Despite the scepticism which surrounded the talks from the outset, and the lack, at least until the talks fell apart, of any major development, this was an important story. At a time when the Middle East was altering in an unprecedented and unpredictable way, the Israelis and Palestinians remained stuck in their long and firmly held views – while the neighbouring region changed around them. By the summer, the deaths first of three Israeli teenagers – Naftali Frenkel, Gilad Shaer, and Eyal Yifrach – and then of a Palestinian teenager, Mohammad Abu Khdair – apparently to avenge that of the three Israelis – took the conflict back to the front pages. Abduction and killing had crossed editorial thresholds which diplomacy could not reach, especially as the three Israelis had disappeared while hitch-hiking back from their place of study on the occupied West Bank. The violence spread. There were stone-throwing protests in East Jerusalem; Palestinian fighters in Gaza fired rockets at targets in Israel; the Israeli Air Force bombed targets in Gaza; eventually, Israel launched a ground operation in Gaza for the first time in five years. The Israel-Palestine story bled again, so it led again – albeit sharing the top of the international news agenda then with the ISIS uprising in Iraq, and the Ukrainian government's attempts to re-establish by force its control over its separatist Eastern regions.

Yet bloodshed alone cannot explain the international focus on the Israeli-Palestinian conflict. If deaths were the only criterion, then Rwanda, Congo, and Darfur would have commanded far more airtime than they did. So too would the wars in Chechnya late in the last century, and at the beginning of this one, as Russia struggled to control the separatist tendencies which had come with the collapse of the Soviet Union, and, in the case of the North Caucasus, been further fuelled by that region's own version of militant Islam. The journalists who were interviewed for this book agreed that the Israeli-Palestinian conflict commanded a huge degree of editorial attention. 'It's not just about the body count,'[3] says the BBC's Middle East Editor, Jeremy Bowen. 'Because actually in recent years the number of dead have been nothing. Nothing compared to Syria. And nothing compared to almost any conflict you can think of.' Chris McGreal, who covered the conflict for the *Guardian* for more than a decade, echoed Balmer's view that reasons of history were key – although he argued that the interest was most keenly focused in certain parts of the world. 'I think for Europe and for America – which are the ones that take interest, I'm not sure the rest of the world does take that much interest – I think it's historic.'[4] He explains further:

> If you're my generation – I'm in my 50s – you very much grew up aware of Israel and Palestine's struggle for survival, 1967 war, 1973 war, context of the holocaust, and so the idea of Israel and the creation of a Jewish state is imprinted on our history, it's not something abstract.

More recently, though, McGreal senses a shift. He goes on:

> I think I am on the cusp of a generation. I think people older than me on the whole have tended to be very sympathetic to Israel's situation, because of the whole Holocaust, the history of the war and survival. And the generation which comes after sees Israel in a different context: as an oppressor and as an occupier.

'In that part of the world there's a confluence of various factors and issues,' says Bowen. 'Various international fault lines, of religion, politics, issues of colonialism come up, which has always been a big thing for Europe especially. We were leaving colonialism behind when Israel was starting its own colonies in the West Bank.' Harvey Morris, who has reported from the Middle East for Reuters, the *Independent,* and the *Financial Times,* identifies certain moments in history which secured the Israeli-Palestinian conflict its prominent place in the global news agenda: chiefly the 1967 war and 'after Arafat took over the PLO.'[5] While noting these two seminal events, Morris also argues that it was only in the post-Cold War era that the news coverage became so concentrated. 'It only became truly obsessional – I won't say since Oslo – but since the first *intifada.*'[6]

Intifada was the name given to the Palestinian uprising against Israeli occupation which began in Gaza in December 1987. The intifada broke out after a fatal traffic accident in the Jabaliya refugee camp in Gaza in December 1987.[7] From the point of view of journalism history, it was significant because – especially from a broadcast perspective – it provided pictures which were eye-catching: the lifeblood of television news reporting. Perhaps realizing that they had few strengths to play to, the Palestinians might almost be said to have tried to play to their weaknesses. This is the era when teenage boys throwing rocks at armoured jeeps or tanks became a standard image of the conflict – contributing to the transition in the minds of some audiences which McGreal describes above: from survivor to oppressor. The gesture of stone-throwing itself, of course, contains a reference, in the eye of many beholders, to the Biblical story of David and Goliath – except that the stone-slinger then was a Jewish underdog, not a Palestinian one. Yet this transition is part of what makes covering this conflict so challenging, and so interesting. In the case of the first intifada, there was another transition underway: the emergence of Islamist groups, Islamic Jihad and Hamas, as forces in the Palestinian fight against Israel. There are hints of it in the reporting of the time. Writing in the days after the outbreak of the uprising, Ian Black explained in the *Guardian,* 'Disturbances have occurred with increasing regularity in recent weeks with rising support for Muslim fundamentalists.'[8] In the *Los Angeles Times* the same day, a story written by a staff writer on the foreign desk stated that, 'Gaza is the stronghold within Israel [*sic*] for a militant form of fundamentalism symbolized by the Islamic Jihad, a movement that has emerged over the past two years.'[9] In the following day's *Daily Telegraph,* Con Coughlin reported that, 'Palestinian activists have become increasingly militant in recent months, moving away from their traditional support for the Palestinian Liberation Organisation towards the radical appeal of Iranian inspired Islamic fundamentalism.'[10] Looking back now, at a time when Hamas is the focus of armed opposition to Israel, this seems a significant shift. It is important to remember, though, that it would be a gradual process. Four years later, analysing clashes which had taken place in Gaza between Fatah and Hamas, the late Graham Usher, the respected writer on Palestinian affairs, noted that, 'political wisdom had it that with the "July clashes" Hamas lost the street; when it came to the crunch, Palestinians were nationalist first and Islamist second.'[11]

Many journalists, perhaps, in part, at least, because they have been schooled in a British or American school of objectivity, point to a complexity in the conflict: the many factors which it involves. These can principally be divided into the following categories, what I will call 'global connections' because they link the conflict to audiences outside the region. They are principally: history, foreign policy, religion, and journalistic tradition and media ownership.

The United States and Britain, whose news media are the principal focus of this book, have strong historical ties to the region: the former having succeeded the latter, in the second half of the 20th century, as the dominant outside power. Clare Hollingworth's concern over the United States' taking over the wireless station used to send reporters' copy seemed to stand for something more. A few days later, the 'sun dried' union flag, which had flown as a symbol of imperial Britain's presence in Palestine, was back in Victoria station in London – a short distance from Buckingham Palace. It may not have been until later in Israel's history that the United States became the almost uncritical supporter it is today, but Washington was also the first global power to recognize the fledgling Jewish state, only hours after it had declared independence. William Booth, who has been the *Washington Post*'s Jerusalem Bureau Chief since 2013, senses these long-term influences. He points to international involvement in Israel's creation, and subsequent development, recalling the fact that 'Truman acknowledged the State of Israel', and that today, in terms of its support for that state, 'the U.S. is all in'.[12] The Jerusalem Bureau Chief for the Associated Press, Dan Perry, who has covered Israel-Palestine on and off since the 1990s, suggests strong reasons of Jewish history in particular explain the United States' news media's focus on the story:

The history of the Jews is important in the U.S. for obvious reasons: Jewish people are a big factor in the country. There is also the narrative of the close ally, the sole democracy, which touches people in the U.S. And you have what is perceived to be a Western society in conflict, and until recently that was unusual in recent decades. Also, it's a factor that in some ways Israel sprang out of the Holocaust and the Holocaust is one of the most incredible things to ever occur.[13]

Harriet Sherwood was Jerusalem correspondent for the *Guardian* from 2010 to 2014. She too identifies a combination of historical factors. She includes, like the speaker above, Europe's role in the Holocaust as one of them:

> I think it has historically been covered a lot because it is seen as an absolutely kind of crucial element in the whole wider Middle East region, and the conflicts between East and West, and the rise of Islam. And in terms of the Jewish homeland angle, most European countries feel this is an important story to cover because of Europe's particular history in this area and its role in creating such an obvious need for a Jewish homeland.[14]

For Sherwood, who still works for the *Guardian*, there is a particular factor relating to her own newspaper's history. In the early 20th century, the *Manchester Guardian*, as the paper was then called, campaigned strongly in favour of the Zionist cause. A friendship between C.P. Scott, the then editor, and the leading Zionist, Chaim Weizmann, was Weizmann's introduction to the British political elite – facilitating Weizmann's role in the British government's decision to make the Balfour Declaration.[15] As Sherwood notes, 'The Guardian itself has kind of had a very, very, long history in this area and was actually kind of pretty instrumental in the Balfour Declaration and I think we've always felt a very strong attachment.'

The *Guardian* actively supported the creation of a Jewish Homeland in Palestine at a time when Britain was playing a decisive role in the region. This was not just an example of a newspaper having a view on international affairs. As Scott's ability to take Weizmann to breakfast with Lloyd George demonstrates,[16] this was an example of a leading newspaper in the world's pre-eminent diplomatic and military power seeking to shape policy. It was a policy which would come to affect thousands of British troops and other service personnel, including Peter Tooley and Donald Christie, mentioned in Chapter 1. The extent of British ties to the Holy Land has perhaps been forgotten in the public imagination after a decade when wars have been fought further east, but there are reminders everywhere of how strong those historical connections are. To give just one example: walking into my local church, St Nicholas' in Chiswick, West London, on a wet winter afternoon early in 2014, I wandered over to the war memorial which is a common feature of so many English parish churches. A small cross hanging above the book of remembrance caught my eye. Looking at it closely, I learnt that it had been carved from wood from the Mount of Olives, where men from my local area had been part of the force which captured Jerusalem in December 1917. Not all of them had survived the victory. Looking at the names before me, I discovered that they had died later that month, fighting the Ottoman forces who still sought to hold onto positions on the hills overlooking the Old City. In Jerusalem a week or so later to gather material for this book, I found the graves of some of those who were remembered around the corner from my home in London. The conflict in which they died, a century old now, helped to shape the Middle East as it is today – even if more recent events in Iraq and Syria suggest the borders defined then, by Imperial Britain and France dividing up the spoils of the Ottoman Empire, have now been altered, perhaps for good. Still, this shared history has been a factor in placing Israel-Palestine at the heart of British international news agendas. A similar process, that of being the dominant power in the region, has done the same in later years for the editorial priorities of United States-based news media. Donald Macintyre, who covered the conflict for the *Independent* for nine years from 2004, echoes the conclusions of other long-serving correspondents as to the importance of historical connections:

> I think it's true that Israel, certainly in terms of the United States, and to some extent in terms of European countries, exercises a fascination partly because of its shortish history and the importance of both Europe and the US in the creation of that history.[17]

He adds:

> But partly I guess because there's a sort of – and I'm much less comfortable with this point – there's a sort of fascination with what is conceived to be, rightly or wrongly, Western-style democracy, in the middle of this not entirely friendly Middle Eastern world.

Macintyre's second point leads onto the second of the global connections: foreign policy. One of the other reasons which William Booth offered to explain why he felt the conflict was covered so much was, 'it's just like a constant running story with an ally, right? Because the U.S. supports Israel to such an extent.' This is a point echoed by Perry, cited above, 'the narrative of the close ally, the sole democracy'. These diplomatic priorities seem inevitably to influence editorial ones, a phenomenon which, as Morris points out, pre-dates the 9/11 era. 'There was a perception during the Cold War that it was a major clash point in a possible future war,' he says of Israel-Palestine during the time when the Soviet Union supported Israel's enemies – not only the Palestinians, but also Syria – and the United States' support for Israel continued to grow stronger. It is hard to imagine now that the United States once had a policy of not selling arms to Israel,[18] but, from the 1960s, when, as Avi Shlaim writes, 'Kennedy continued to tilt America's Middle Eastern policy in Israel's favour'[19] onwards, the 'narrative of the big ally, sole democracy' has become more powerful not only in public opinion, but also in Washington's foreign policy. Journalism has followed this deployment of diplomatic resources. As Rudoren of the *New York Times* puts it, 'It's very clear that Israel for sure and that this conflict in general gets vastly more coverage than anything else.'

In the immediate post-9/11 era, Israel, by then facing the fury of a second intifada, was more than ready to make common cause with the United States' so-called 'war on terror'. The second Palestinian uprising against Israel had been ostensibly provoked by the visit in September 2000 of the then leader of the Israeli opposition, Ariel Sharon, to the Temple Mount, known to Muslims as the Haram-as-Sharif, or Noble Sanctuary. Sharon's visit was the spark for an uprising for which the time was already ripe. A year later, after the United States had been shocked by the airborne attacks on Washington and New York, the Israelis were ready to place in a wider context the renewed conflict in which they had already been engaged for twelve months. As McGreal recalls, 'There was the added twist of 9/11. You have the "war on terror". Sharon and the Israelis very cleverly cast the context of the struggle with the Palestinians in the context of the war on terror.' They were not alone. Russia was another country fighting a regional insurgency, in the North Caucasus, which, following international concern over civilian casualties and human rights abuses, it sought to reposition as another front in the global war which Washington had decided to prosecute. Israel, though, had greater success – at least in the short term. The word terrorist was so widely used at the time by both Sharon (who had been elected prime minister months after his controversial visit to one of Jerusalem's holiest sites) and by the then president of the United States, George

W. Bush, that the two 'wars on terror' Israel's against armed Palestinian groups, and the United States' against Al-Qaeda, must frequently have seemed, in the minds of audiences, to be part of the same battle. This, after all, was a time when the United States administration's claims that Saddam Hussein was connected to the 9/11 hijackers, and that his regime possessed weapons of mass destruction, were widely accepted, not least by the British government of Tony Blair. It may be, too, that presenting the intifada as part of a 'war on terror' enabled Israel to draw on earlier stages of the conflict with the Palestinians to portray their enemy, and their enemy's cause, as illegitimate. Although he identifies the first intifada as the moment when the Israeli-Palestinian conflict first began to be covered in great detail, Morris continues, 'I think there are a variety of factors some of which pre-dated that.' These include, he argues, the fact that, 'the Palestinians invented modern terrorism in the form of hijacking and shooting and everything else in the 70s – and that's a big story. As I say, unfortunately, it drew attention to the topic.'

While Israel may then have been drawing on memories of earlier stages of its conflict with the Palestinians, it understood also that there was a risk it would be drawn into the United States' expected attack on Iraq. Early in 1991, when the administration of President Bush senior had attacked Iraq, part of Saddam Hussein's response had been to launch missiles at Tel Aviv. All but one of the casualties which resulted from these inaccurate strikes were from indirect causes, such as heart attacks.[20] When I was reporting from Gaza a decade later, during the second intifada, and as a new invasion of Iraq seemed increasingly inevitable, Palestinians remembered dancing on their roofs, and chanting support for Saddam Hussein, even as they lived under the restrictions of an Israeli-imposed curfew. In 2003, Israel was worried it might be attacked again as it had been in 1991. The United States was keen for Israel not to get involved if that were to happen.[21] Persuading Arabs – the vast majority of them Muslims – that the 'war on terror' was not a war on them and on Islam would be all the harder were Israel actually to join the United States in a military operation against an Arab country. Nevertheless, the fact that Saddam Hussein was then Israel's most prominent, and possibly most powerful, enemy, as well as America's favourite villain, probably made it easier for Sharon's administration to make their fight seem part of a global cause. Another factor was that British and American correspondents living in Jerusalem (the majority of them in Jewish West Jerusalem) understood all too well the threats which Israelis faced on a daily basis. As McGreal recalls of the time when Palestinian suicide bombers frequently attacked Israeli shopping centres, restaurants, and public transport:

> one of the things about being a correspondent in Jerusalem is that you're not just writing about it, you're living it. And I was living it with two small children who I had to walk to school every day past buses which could potentially blow up, I think as a correspondent you're very conscious of it.

Living in such circumstances probably made it harder for reporters to separate the personal from the professional. Moreover, in addition to the historical and policy reasons why the Israeli-Palestinian conflict receives so much news coverage, there is another dimension which overlaps with those two aspects. As Rudoren summarizes it:

> The core is that there's a religious component to the struggle, and in particular that all three religions find this place…you know, attach special importance to this place. So it's a struggle that resonates worldwide for that reason.

These three religions: Judaism, Islam, and Christianity, and the fact that they have adherents worldwide, are clearly factors. Rudoren herself mentions having come to Israel the first time on a 'Jewish-American teen tour', but stresses too 'the idea that Christianity also holds this place dear'. McGreal, who now lives in the United States, observes, 'I think in America you have a very large Jewish community, an influential Jewish community, a large portion of it based in New York and that has obviously always helped to define the interest in Israel and its fate.' Aside from those ties of faith, there is, as Macintyre points out, a more politicized form of religion which keeps the conflict in the headlines.

> In the United States, I think this is much less true in Britain, there is the added point that there is a very and, in my view, not entirely healthy, interest in Israel particularly by some very vociferous members of the Jewish population, and to some extent politically for Christian Zionists and others.

The role in particular of the American Israel Public Affairs Committee (AIPAC), which describes itself on its website[22] as America's Pro-Israel Lobby, has been considered in some detail, especially by John

J. Mearsheimer and Stephen M. Walt in their book *The Israel Lobby and Foreign Policy*. Lobby groups seeking to influence not only policy, but public opinion, will often try to affect the reporting of the conflict by harassing reporters. Anyone who has written in public about the issues relating to Israel-Palestine will recognize this. After I had had an article published on a news and discussion website last year, I received an email from the editor of a Jewish newsletter in the United States. 'So I have two words for you, and they are not happy birthday,' was one of the more reasonable lines in my unsolicited correspondence which also, incidentally, drew on the kind of history mentioned above to make some of its other points. 'We know England caused this whole mess in the first place,' ran an apparent reference to the British Mandate.

Morris sees not only Jewish interest, but massive support for Palestinians too, as factors.

> The Palestinian side is one that attracts an almost mindless level of support from people in the West, particularly in the West: very unquestioning support. Obviously Israel has a lobby of supporters because of the Jewish communities all around the world and that's another reason why there's international interest.

This kind of international interest – lobbying, or protesting – seems almost to exploit religious ties in order to promote political causes. Still, the fact that this combination of politicised faith is so strong is one reason why the Israeli-Palestinian conflict receives the media attention which it does. 'There is something beyond journalism that makes it covered,' says Matt Rees, a former correspondent for the *Scotsman*, *Newsweek*, and from 2000 to 2006, bureau chief for *Time* Magazine. Rees speaks of:

> an almost evangelical perspective on the Middle East, and on this place in particular which most of us might not think we share, but you know, if you in any way have any kind of Christian upbringing, even if it's just a very, very formula you know, you celebrate Christmas, you have some kind of element of that in your thoughts, you know in your DNA. So it's just something that you can relate to. It's a relatable story.[23]

Bowen agrees. 'It's the Holy Land, we grow up with this stuff in traditional Judeo-Christian, Christian societies. You grow up with Bethlehem, Hebron, you read about it at school, you hear about it at

Church if you're religious.' Rees also writes fiction, in which the main character is a Palestinian detective. To support his point about the 'relatable story', he describes his New York-based literary agent's concern when he planned to set a novel in Nablus, on the West Bank. An earlier book, in which the action took place in Bethlehem, had benefited from an instantly recognizable location. Rees's agent was worried that no one would know where Nablus was. He insisted that surely they would. To test the idea, she emailed 40 of her friends – all newspaper readers. Despite the fact that they had all read coverage from Nablus, none of them recognized the name. The story of the nativity had a power which extended far beyond its religious significance in that it can hold the interest of a non-religious audience – including anyone with 'a kind of Christian upbringing' – while presumably also attracting the attention of believers too. Nor, of course, is this a phenomenon confined to journalism, as Rees notes of his own fiction. In the title track of the American country singer Steve Earle's album *Jerusalem*,[24] the narrator's reflection on the bloodshed in the Middle East is sparked by his hearing from news coverage of more violence.

The sense of identification goes beyond the religious, politically religious, and culturally religious. For McGreal and Rudoren, although coming from different countries and working for different news organizations, also identify a dimension of ethnicity. Rudoren, for example, argues that, 'there are not so many conflicts that involve white people. So that's something.' McGreal, who reported for many years from South Africa, says:

> for the same reason that the Apartheid struggle in South Africa attracted much more attention in Europe, the idea of the Apartheid struggle, rather than other things in Africa which were creating dreadful human rights abuses and great numbers of people being killed. Why? White people.

He elaborates:

> in that sense, a very loose sense, Israelis or many Israelis, are of European origin to the extent that they immigrated from Europe and they fall into a kind of loose definition of European or white people, or whatever, in the minds of a lot of people on the outside. There's an element of they share our values, they share our history, there's something of them about us, or something of us about them, and therefore a connection.

In other words, these ethnic and cultural characteristics, whether real or perceived, it does not seem to matter, are yet another powerful factor which, journalists suggest, makes the conflict 'relatable'. The narrative of the only democracy in the Middle East is strengthened by a wider idea that 'many Israelis' 'share our values' – although Israel's critics would disagree, and even its critical friends might fret that such values are often not upheld in Israel's conduct in the Palestinian territories. The whole combined effect of these connections is to make the Israeli-Palestinian conflict unique in terms of its importance to British and American news organizations. No other international story, with the exception of foreign wars in which one or both of the countries have deployed troops, can be counted on to hold such a prominent place on front pages and in running orders. In addition, as a senior member of the international press corps working on the story since the 1990s points out, 'You have what is perceived to be a western society in conflict, and that until recently was extremely rare,' adding, 'when wars first started happening again that involved the west in the 90s, the idea seemed preposterous. Now of course we're in an era of warfare. But until recently it was rare for a first world country to be in that situation.'

In an international media world, in which, despite changes of recent years, the west still holds sway through the dominance of news agencies and international broadcasters such as BBC World News and CNN, these are factors which lead the Israeli-Palestinian conflict to have a huge presence in global news too. 'For much of the 60 some years of this conflict, the dominant media power was the U.S.,' says the journalist cited above. Rudoren also highlights media power, in the sense that those countries linked to the Holy Land by the historical, policy, and religious ties discussed above are also those which dominate international news. 'There's much more connection through dual citizenship, through academic exchange, whatever, between America and the other great western powers that kind of set the international media debate and this place than probably any other.' It might be observed that the expansion of satellite news stations, especially in the developing world, and the rise of social media for newsgathering and distribution might undermine this. If so, it is worth remembering that in an era when budget cuts are leading to the cutting back of international coverage, the big western news agencies: Reuters, Associated Press, and Agence France-Presse, are increasingly relied upon to make up the shortfall. The rise of digital media has also permitted previously national western media, such as the *New York Times* and the *Guardian*, to become international news organizations in a way unforeseen and unimagined until this century.

Rudoren sees a further factor which combines many of the connecting factors considered in this chapter with that of ownership, especially in the United States, 'maybe there's also something to do with the Jewish hegemony in the media,' she suggests. As will be discussed in more detail in Chapter 5, this is a factor, together with the points made by both McGreal and Rudoren about 'white people' which often leads to the western media being accused of pro-Israeli bias – even if that is not the way some critics, like the American email correspondent who had 'two words' for me, see it.

In addition to the global connections identified and discussed above, there is another set of strong reasons why journalists seem to have been drawn to cover the Israeli-Palestinian conflict. As Crispian Balmer of Reuters noted at the beginning of this chapter, 'any journalist worth their salt wanted to try their time in' covering the Israeli-Palestinian conflict. Balmer describes the professional attraction of working in the region in terms of taking up membership of an elite.

> It's a place that has traditionally attracted some very, very, high quality journalists and produced some high quality journalism. When I look back at previous bureau chiefs of Reuters, I just wanted to have my name on the honour board, next to them.

Added to this sense of being part of one of the biggest international stories (a sense shared by diplomats who work in the region) there is, for some correspondents, a personal fascination with the region. Just as Rudoren spoke of one of her first impressions of the Holy Land being that it was a 'Petrie dish' for journalism, Yolande Knell, who has been the BBC's correspondent for the West Bank and Gaza since 2013, and who has also spent three years in Cairo, speaks of being struck by the potential for working in the region as a journalist. Of her first visit, in 2005 as a BBC News producer on a short-term assignment, she recalls, 'I was fascinated by the situation on the ground and how different it was from what I had had to report as a reporter in London,'[25] noting in particular, 'the interactions of Israelis and Palestinians in everyday life'. Knell's initial experience, left her 'hooked on the Middle East and its possibilities'. Her next career steps were dictated by a desire to satisfy that curiosity. 'So not long after that,' she explains, 'I took a sabbatical, I went to do another Master's in the U.S., I did a focus on Middle East studies and U.S. foreign policy, and started learning Arabic.' Knell's plans may have been prompted by a desire to increase her own understanding, but they also reflect how sought after postings in the region can be, and the efforts to which some reporters decide to go in order to strengthen their chances of landing one. Simon McGregor-Wood, a British journalist who spent nine years covering the conflict for ABC News, as bureau chief, correspondent, and finally in a combination of the two roles, also saw this as a story with special characteristics. Like Knell, he had travelled to the region on holiday while working in London:

> I made several trips to places like Syria, and Lebanon, and Jordan – although strangely enough, not Israel and the Palestinian territories – and those visits just cemented my interest. And as a young journalist, it was clear that there was a special kind of allure for a journalist in the Middle East.

Sherwood experienced a similar fascination: even using, like Knell, a word, 'hooked' derived from drug addiction. Sherwood's experience differed, though, in that she was already a senior journalist when she came to the story. 'When I was appointed the Guardian's foreign editor, I had no background in foreign news at all,' she remembers. 'And I was a bit surprised to be appointed, and a bit frightened of the job.' One area of coverage in particular sparked that alarm:

> the story that I was most frightened of was the Israeli-Palestinian story because it's one that the Guardian has a huge amount of exposure on and we're very closely scrutinized in terms of what we write and accused by both sides of favouring the other side and as you know it's a very kind of toxic area.

In order to confront this fear of dealing with this 'toxic' story, Sherwood decided to take a trip to Jerusalem. Her impressions were what led her later to seek the post of correspondent there. 'I thought it was just the most interesting place I had ever been; the most complicated place I have ever been to; in every respect it was just fascinating.' This sense of uniqueness, of being hooked, of wanting to join a top team may be widespread, but it is not shared by everyone – at least not to begin with. McGreal, for example, got a call from an editor at the *Guardian*, one of the titles for which he had been working in South Africa, asking him if he wanted to go to cover Israel. 'To be frank, at that point, I'd never given it a thought,' he recalls. 'And I thought, "That sounds interesting." But I didn't have deep desire.' He decided to go for a visit, returning a week later to accept the post. But, he says, 'It was a move, it wasn't an enthusiasm.'

Some reporters, though, view their fellow correspondents' motives very cynically. Not surprisingly, this is directed – sometimes with justification – at star names who venture to the region for a short time only, although they are not the sole targets. Matt Rees sees the fact that 'for a long time it was a very easy place to operate'.

> A place where you could go to the kinds of locations that in other parts of the region you'd have to really go through some hardship to get to, and to stay in, you could go there and then you could come home and you could have a steak in an Israeli restaurant. So it was really perhaps a dirty little secret because you could look like a war correspondent whereas actually you were just going there for three hours.

One long-standing member of the foreign press community in Jerusalem shares these suspicions, taking particular issue with visiting reporters who stay in a Jerusalem hotel which is a byword for good living, and where the bar in particular has historically been a favourite meeting place for reporters.

> It's the Five Star war. It's a place where foreign correspondents can come, they can wake up in the luxury of the American Colony hotel in the morning, they can be down a smuggling tunnel with terrorists with guns by lunchtime, and having filed the story they can be back in time for cocktails in the American Colony by dinner time. That's not something you get in Syria, or Iraq, or Afghanistan, or in the conflict zones in Africa.

The same journalist suggests that the attention focused on Israel-Palestine constitutes 'an obsession that goes way beyond the foreign interest in any other conflict in the world' and argues that the 'concentration on this place is completely lopsided'. This, though, may be changing. In some respects, the obsessively covered, easy-access war is an outdated stereotype. While one of the characteristics of the Israeli-Palestinian conflict is that the land being fought over is relatively small, steak dinners and cocktails at the American Colony are beyond the budgets of many reporters today. A quick look at the hotel's website in July 2014 revealed the cheapest nightly room rate to be over $350 (at that time, approximately £205). While big news organizations would probably have corporate discounts, and those discounts might be substantial, it could hardly be considered a budget option. As the BBC's correspondent in Gaza from 2002 to 2004, I would visit the American Colony bar during weekend trips to Jerusalem to meet other reporters over a drink. Then, there would often be a big crowd of journalists, especially on Thursday and Friday nights. Visits in more recent years suggest that is a thing of the past. Talking to some former colleagues in the late summer of 2011, I learnt that they had barely travelled to the West Bank (but a short distance from where we then sat) in the preceding twelve months. Instead, they had found themselves in some of those locations which, in Rees's words, 'you'd have to really go through some hardship to get to': battlefields in the deserts of Libya, riots in revolutionary Egypt. So while the traditional reasons for covering the conflict endure, they are not as dominant as once they were. The Arab uprisings changed that.

'I think it has really gone down in the hit parade of international stories,' Sherwood says of the story which got her 'hooked' before she went to cover it. Asked why he thinks the conflict is covered so much, McGregor-Wood replies, 'I don't think it is any more. If we're talking about the core of the conflict, which is the Israeli-Palestinian conflict, one of the interesting things is that interest in it has diffused.' Knell seems sympathetic to the idea that at times in the past attention has been 'lopsided' but believes that has changed. 'For a long time you could argue that there was perhaps a disproportionate level of coverage of the conflict and the day to day events that took place,' she says 'partly because there was such a concentration of international correspondents here.' This was already changing when she moved to the region full time. 'Very soon after I arrived,' she remembers, 'I was back in Cairo, where I had started, covering the 2011 uprising and all that followed.'

Despite the reasons outlined above why this conflict holds such a fascination for audiences, editors, and reporters, there have been, in recent years especially, other factors which have led to a reduction in coverage. These include cost. Falling readerships and advertising revenues have made this worse. As Richard Sambrook noted in his important 2010 study, *Are Foreign Correspondents Redundant?* even in the good old days – if they existed – 'There is little evidence however, outside of niche publications and services, that foreign news drives profit.'[26] He also, with the benefit of his experience as the BBC's Head of Global News, reminds his reader that, 'Overseas offices are inevitably expensive'.[27] To coverage of the Israeli-Palestinian conflict has been added the additional challenge that the region around has been full of stories – not just during the Arab uprisings, but in the invasion of Iraq before them – which have been unprecedented, exciting, potentially world-changing. McGregor-Wood elaborates on his reasons for arguing that the conflict is not covered as much as it once was:

> Both because of other more interesting things happening in the region, but also I think because of a sense, shared by both editors and consumers, that it's no longer as interesting as it was because you can't keep reporting something that doesn't fundamentally change, and hasn't really changed in ten or twenty years.

The lack of a meaningful peace process which might place Israel-Palestine in such categories means that it has sometimes been possible for editors to pay less attention, if not to ignore. So too does the lack of violence. The expansion of Israeli settlement on the West Bank, or the worsening living conditions in Gaza, can only hope to gain any major editorial attention at a time when there is violence, too. Since the ending of the second intifada, and the evacuation of Israeli settlements from the Gaza Strip in the summer of 2005, the territory has had four main periods among the lead stories in international news: Hamas's struggle with the Palestinian Authority to take control of the territory in 2006–2007; and Israel's major military operations there in 2008–2009, 2012, and 2014. All of those stories, it goes without saying, have been times of armed conflict and major, violent, loss of life. In this chapter I have argued that blood and death are not the only reasons that Israel-Palestine is covered to the extent that it is. They are, though, still important reasons. They are dramatic, attention-grabbing, extreme. In that journalism relies on 'pegs' – journalistic slang for an event or a date which means a story is topical – violence often provides a peg for discussion of deeper issues, but can also, inevitably overshadow them. On a day when dozens of people are being killed, as happened frequently in Gaza in the summer of 2014, it can be hard to justify an in-depth report explaining the longer-term causes of the conflict at the expense of covering the day's events. The huge benefit of the internet, as will be discussed in greater detail in Chapter 7, is that a news website provides the opportunity for those background, contextual stories to be displayed prominently where a traditional broadcast bulletin or newspaper would not have had the space. The idea of change, or, in this case, an absence of it, raised by McGregor-Wood above, is fundamental. The difficulty with the Israeli-Palestinian conflict is that there has been so little change, as he points out, for the last two decades. That is not to discount the changes that have occurred: the removal of Israeli settlements from Gaza; Hamas's rise to power in the territory, and its emergence, at the expense of the PLO, as the main armed opposition to Israel; Hamas's vicissitudes in the light of shifting political power elsewhere in the region. This latter point relates most particularly to Egypt, where Hamas's close ideological allies, the Muslim Brotherhood, went from being banned, to being the democratically elected government, to being banned again all in the space of a couple of years. What has not changed, or really even been addressed, are the issues which make enemies of Israel and the Palestinians in the first place: issues of territory and of political rights. The global connections which make the Israeli-Palestinian conflict of such interest to editors and audiences mean that this change is sought at every turn. New peace initiatives are still covered even if, like the process sponsored by the US Secretary of State, John Kerry, in 2013–2014, it received nothing of the fanfare which had announced the Roadmap a decade earlier. There are two reasons for this. Firstly, as the BBC reported in November 2013, 'the talks were held in secret locations and at undisclosed times as part of a US-requested media blackout.'[28] Secondly, the experience of previous rounds of negotiations, all of which had failed to produce a lasting settlement, gave little grounds to think that it might be different this time. For change, that which is new, is the lifeblood of journalism. With little prospect of change, there is little prospect of news, so there is little to quicken the heartbeat and pump the lifeblood of journalism. So there have, especially in recent years, been reasons – editorial and economic – why this conflict has been covered less than it had been historically. This may, though, just be temporary fatigue. The huge and rapid return of international editorial attention to Gaza in the summer of 2014 demonstrated that the global connections were just as powerful as ever, even if they had been dormant, or at least less prominent, for a while.

In the sense that change is the lifeblood of journalism, the Israeli-Palestinian conflict has one other element which makes it stand out. It is less than 70 years since the founding of the State of Israel, but so very much has happened: creation, fears of annihilation, victory, survival, dominance. Perry highlights this as one of the reasons why the country and its conflict has been covered in such detail.

> Israel started off with a narrative, as seen in the West, of a kind of admirable place scrappily carving out a model country, or so they said they would, also helping Africa, building roads in Ghana, and trying out socialism with the kibbutz movement. Swedish people come here to see and admire and be volunteers. There was positivity, and all of a sudden it turns on a dime, and David becomes Goliath,

and increasingly the narrative, in many circles and in particular in Europe and the developing world, is that of bad guy occupying the Palestinians. That kind of narrative shift has drama and therefore power as a story.

The Israeli-Palestinian conflict combines some characteristics which it shares with wars around the world: violence, death, arguments over just causes, the influence and interest of outside players. All these are elements which fascinate journalists and their audiences. What sets the Israeli-Palestinian conflict apart, though, is that to these characteristics are added others: multiple injustices; the difficulty in deciding where the truth lies, even in an incident, such as an explosion, where it might seem straightforward; the presence of divine inspiration for both belligerents; the fact that the conflict is taking place over the land where the events of the scriptures are set. This is what makes the Israeli-Palestinian conflict unique: the drama and change of worldly events set against the immutability of faith.

4
The Roadmap, Reporting, and Religion

The young man's face changed as if it had suddenly been cast into shadow; as if the air temperature around had unexpectedly fallen sharply. The minibus passing by, already slowed by heavy traffic, had stopped. The window, half open in the afternoon heat, had been wound down further. 'Your country, your country,' began the voice the voice from the seat inside, half speech, half snarl. Yusef, the young student who seemed so shocked, looked anxiously round. His fluent English had come to a halt. Now, lost for words, he smiled nervously, trying to calm the situation, and his own obvious fear. 'Your country is in the grave,' growled the voice.

It was early June 2003. At the roadside, it was hot. There was a breeze from time to time, but mostly the air was as still as the long queue of traffic trying to head uphill towards Jerusalem. It was a time of deadly Israeli military incursions into Gaza and the West Bank. It was a time of suicide bombers in the buses, bars, and cafés of Israel. That was the reason given that afternoon for the extra security measures which had caused the traffic jam. It was a time, too, of diplomacy. Later that week, a summit was due to be held in the Jordanian Red Sea resort of Aqaba to discuss, 'A performance-based Roadmap to a permanent Two-State solution to the Israeli-Palestinian Conflict,' ('The Roadmap'). The 'destination' to which this map showed the way was 'a final and comprehensive settlement of the Israeli-Palestinian conflict by 2005'.[1] That afternoon, there was little prospect of anyone getting to any destination. The traffic moved so slowly that some passengers in the elongated Mercedes cars which served as shared taxis had opted to become pedestrians. Here a woman balancing a bundle on her head with one hand, and holding the hand of a small child with the other, made her way in flimsy sandals along the stones at the side of the road. On the other side, across the lines of traffic, another woman, dressed like the first in a brightly coloured traditional headscarf, and ankle-length dress, made her way up a rocky hillside path. A teenage boy, perhaps her son or grandson, walked a short distance ahead of her. The boy carried two plastic bags, one in each hand, of the kind a market stall holder might have used to pack vegetables. The woman bore a box on her head, steadying it with her hand as she climbed higher. The sky was cloudless blue, and it was just long enough after midday that small shadows spread at people's feet as they walked. Still it was hot, uncomfortably so if you were stuck in a stationary car. That was what had driven some car passengers out on to the roadside. Walking was the only way you could be sure of getting anywhere that day. I was gathering material for a report about how Palestinians and Israelis viewed the forthcoming summit. I had stopped Yusef to seek his views, pleased to find a good English speaker among the hundreds, probably thousands, of people stuck in traffic that afternoon. Before the window of the passing minibus was wound down, Yusef spoke with clarity and passion of the situation in which he, as a student trying to make his way along the main road from the West Bank city of Ramallah to Jerusalem, found himself.

'Everywhere there is a checkpoint,' he said. 'In which time will they remove these checkpoints?' Yusef had already told me he was a student. The steel-rimmed glasses he wore almost made him seem more studious, more thoughtful. As he spoke, he became more animated. 'We are living in the Palestinian country – our country. Why are we not moving in freedom?' As he said these last words, the traffic started to move slowly, bringing the yellow minibus alongside, where it halted. The occupants of the bus, Jewish settlers living on the West Bank, had heard Yusef talking of 'Palestinian country – our country.' This is what had prompted their mocking, menacing, response. Maybe Yusef had had a previous unpleasant encounter with settlers. Maybe he feared a beating. Whatever the reason, their presence cowed him. He half smiled and raised a hand in acknowledgment, if not quite in greeting, towards those who challenged him. He then fell silent, as if wondering what might follow. The man leaning out of the window nearest to us sneered the words 'your country' back at Yusef. So bright was the day, and so dark the car's interior in contrast, that the man next to him, in the driver's seat, was visible only in silhouette. The lack of visible facial features made his words appear more threatening. The traffic eased slightly. The minibus advanced. The tension passed. Perhaps partly because of the presence of the television camera, the incident was not going to end in violence.

Later that week, the television cameras were focused first on Sharm-el-Sheikh, in Egypt, and then on Aqaba, in Jordan. The Red Sea, at the centre of the Jews' biblical escape from captivity in Egypt, was the setting for negotiations designed to deliver peace for modern Israel and its Palestinian neighbours. The Roadmap had been formally presented some weeks earlier, on 30 April, to both parties. Mahmoud Abbas had just been sworn in as Palestinian Prime Minister. Abbas was known more usually among Palestinians by the honorific Abu Mazen – so much so that the United Nations Press release that day even referred to him as such.[2] He had been sworn in as prime minister – then a newly created office in the Palestinian Authority – principally in order to provide Israel and the United States with an interlocutor whom they saw as an acceptable negotiating partner. The real authority in the Palestinian Territories remained with Yasser Arafat, but, as the then US Secretary of State, Colin Powell put it, 'we believe his leadership has failed and it was time for new leadership to come forward. We now see that new leadership and we're working with it.'[3] Israel too found the idea of Arafat as a partner for peace unpalatable: an assessment that would remain unchanged for the rest of Arafat's life. He died in the autumn of the following year, 2004. 'At about the same time'[4] as Abbas received the document, it was presented to Ariel Sharon, then Israel's Prime Minister.

There was a wider regional context to this. A year earlier, in June 2002, the president of the United States, George W. Bush, had given 'the first public endorsement by a US president of the goal of Palestinian statehood.'[5] As noted in Powell's remarks above, there was an important condition: the need for the Palestinians to change leaders, at least for the purpose of negotiations. The wider context was the United States' plans to invade Iraq, an invasion that would take place nine months later. As Rosemary Hollis has made clear, Bush's endorsement of Palestinian statehood should have been a 'triumph' for the then British Prime Minister, Tony Blair, who had pressed Bush to act on Israel-Palestine. The condition attached to Bush's endorsement of Palestinian statehood meant it was not so straightforward. Hollis cites a 'confidential Cabinet Office paper of 21 July 2002' making clear that Bush's move was as much about his plans for Baghdad as it was about his plans for the West Bank, Gaza, and Israel, 'The Bush speech was at best a half step forward [...] Real progress towards a viable Palestinian state is the best way to undercut Palestinian extremists and reduce Arab antipathy to military action against Saddam Hussein.'[6] In other words, this drive to solve the Israeli-Palestinian conflict seems to have been part of a means to an end in Iraq, rather than an end in itself.

The formal presentation of the Roadmap prepared the way for the summit meeting which took place in Aqaba on 4 June. Sharon represented Israel; Abbas the Palestinians. Bush joined them. Bush perhaps wondered then whether this really was a new dawn, a moment of great optimism in a dark decade which, early on, had seen the United States shocked and scarred by the attacks of 9/11. Yet he arrived at the summit hailed as a victor. He had, after all, little more than a month before, in front of a banner reading 'Mission Accomplished', announced the end of 'major combat operations in Iraq'.[7] The insurgency in Iraq which was to explode in the spring of 2004, and endure for years with intensity and ferocity, was then unforeseen. Certainly, there was a sense that things might be changing across the entire Middle East region. 'The tyrant is fallen, and Iraq is free,'[8] Mr Bush told service personnel aboard the USS *Abraham Lincoln*. More than a decade later, his words seem infamous for their groundless sense of hope, yet perhaps then they were meant to be remembered as a seminal moment in the remaking – for the better – of the Middle East. Mr Bush's presence in Aqaba suggested that his advisors felt there was enough chance of success to make the trip worthwhile.

For their part, the news media, while not ignoring the difficulties which obviously lay ahead, seemed to echo this optimism. Then, Mr Bush's 'Mission Accomplished' message was taken seriously. His perceived military triumph had delivered him additional diplomatic weight too – and this in an era when the United States seemed to merit the title 'hyperpower' ('hyperpuissance') which the French foreign minister, Hubert Vedrine, had used to describe Washington's position in the post-Cold War world.[9] 'The use of American military power in Iraq has put the Arab world on notice that US diplomacy is more muscular,'[10] wrote Maura Reynolds in the *Los Angeles Times*. Noting that Bush seemed more energetic than he had on a tiring European tour the year before, Elisabeth Bumiller suggested in the *New York Times*, 'One difference is that this time Mr Bush is the victor of the war in Iraq, more in control with far more power to wield.'[11] Nor was such a view the exclusive preserve of the US media. The *Daily Telegraph* correspondent, Toby Harnden, despite having noted that the United States was 'struggling to reconstruct Iraq', suggested that Bush was, 'using victory in Iraq to pursue what amounts to a new blueprint for much of the world.'[12] Describing the picture of Bush flanked by Sharon and Abbas, Justin Huggler in the *Independent* concludes, 'And they would not have been standing here together were it not for Mr Bush's victory in Iraq; a victory that has the Arab regimes desperately moving to cling on to power and reluctant to stand in Mr Bush's way.'[13] Perhaps out of flattery, perhaps in order not to appear to be at odds with this mood of optimism, this idea that 'victory' in Iraq increased the chances of US success in Israel-Palestine, Israeli officials also appeared optimistic. Also in the *New York Times*, James Bennet quoted Dore Gold, an advisor to Sharon, as saying, 'The president of the United States, who has just won a major military victory against Iraq, creates a huge wake in the Middle East even when he is engaged in only the first steps of any kind of diplomatic process.'[14] Ra'anan Gissin, then Sharon's spokesman, is quoted in an article in the *Guardian* in similarly positive vein. 'What came out of the meeting is a reflection of the fact that the US won a great victory in Iraq and there has been a major change in the Middle East – that terrorism is in retreat.'[15] There are, of course, notes of caution. The *Guardian* piece, written by McGreal from the summit, and from which the last quotation comes, is headlined, 'Sharon sticks to script in front of Bush – but the backtracking has already begun'. McGreal's piece goes on to report 'a bizarre twist' in which Sharon's office issued:

> what amounted to a clarification of his speech before he even made it by saying that when he referred to a Palestinian state he meant that one that was demilitarised and that would be the only home for the Palestinian diaspora.

This 'bizarre twist' provided important, sobering, context amongst the praise of the conqueror of Iraq come to deliver justice and peace to the Middle East. It also suggests that Israeli officials came prepared to play a double game with the news media: knowing that Sharon would say one thing, send out one message, his spin doctors, presumably with his knowledge, made sure he was also saying something else too. It suggests, perhaps, that the Israeli delegation knew very well that there were two factors which meant the Roadmap probably would lead to nowhere before too long. Firstly, Sharon's 'clarification', above, which prejudged the outcome in terms which the Palestinians would never accept. Secondly, the Israelis understood the real scale of what lay ahead, and knew that the Roadmap would not, could not, really lead to peace. Perhaps there was another factor, too. Israel did not wish to let down those of its citizens who hoped an agreement could be reached. A couple of days before, I had spoken to a bar owner in Tel Aviv. He had been guardedly optimistic, talking about the need to take the 'first steps' if you want to get to the end of the road. His hope was all the more poignant because his bar had been hit by a suicide bomber, and one of the waitresses killed, a few weeks earlier.[16] Nevertheless, even those correspondents whose newspapers were keen to print the official words of hope were also cautious. The *Daily Mail* quoted Bush's belief that, 'Great hope and change is coming to the Middle East,' but had already noted, some way higher up the story, 'Optimism was dampened within hours, however, when Islamic militants and Jewish settlers condemned the commitments made on each side.'[17] The *Independent*'s Justin Huggler similarly reported that Hamas, 'rejected Abu Mazen's call for the militants to abandon violence, and Jewish settlers demonstrated against Mr Sharon in Jerusalem.'[18] He also tempered his reference, cited above, to Bush's 'victory' in Iraq by observing, 'it could all unravel easily though' – and made clever use of earlier, ultimately unsuccessful, summits which had taken place in other nearby resorts. Reflecting on the location of this meeting, he wrote, 'There were plenty of reminders too on the Red Sea coast here, where the shores are littered with the memories of failed Middle East peace initiatives.' Towards the end of the piece, there is the following blunt assessment, 'All the signs are Mr Sharon is gearing up to offer a state that falls far short of the Palestinians' expectations. Neither side has delivered all that was hoped of them yesterday.' Similarly, the *New York Times* observed that the talks, 'stepped around almost all of the hard details on which the Israelis and the Palestinians disagree'.[19] The accounts of some of the most implacable dissenting voices make interesting reading at this distance. When I was based in Gaza, I used fairly regularly to interview English-speaking senior members of Hamas. At times of heightened Israeli military activity, they would sometimes be in hiding – but usually they were keen to talk to the only member of the international press corps who was resident in the Gaza Strip. The two I spoke to most often were Abdel Aziz Rantisi and Ismail Abu Shanab. Both are quoted in news reports of the summit, Abu Shanab in the *Daily Mail* of 4 June; Rantisi in the *Daily Mirror* of 5 June. Both had less than a year to live. Abu Shanab was killed in August that year; Rantisi survived an attempt on his life the week after the summit in Aqaba. He was eventually killed the following April. Both men died when the cars in which they were travelling were hit by missiles fired from Israeli helicopter gunships. At the meeting with Arab leaders in Sharm el-Sheikh, President Bush had warned, 'We must not allow a few people, a few killers, a few terrorists, to destroy the dreams and hopes of the many.'[20] Perhaps he had in mind men such as Rantisi and Abu Shanab, both of whom Israel killed on the grounds that they were involved in 'terror'. Whatever he had in mind, the deaths of Hamas leaders did ultimately play a role in destroying the dreams and hopes of peace. In the weeks which followed, talk of peace and cooperation was soon laid aside, and the intifada raged again.

A sense that something like this might follow seems to lurk in the references to Hamas's determination not to lay down its arms, and in the settlers' opposition to the idea of giving up their homes on land occupied by force of arms in order to make possible the creation of a Palestinian State. There were questions, too, despite the influence which 'victory' in Iraq has supposedly delivered to him, about whether Bush really understood what he was taking on (many now, of course, would argue that he had no idea what he was taking on in the longer term by invading Iraq). Toby Harnden in the *Daily Telegraph*, for example, writes, 'Critics of Mr Bush say he has insufficient command of detail and is unprepared to tackle the major sticking points such as settlements, the Palestinian right of return and the status of Jerusalem.'[21] Other reporters make similar points, perhaps in less respectful ways. In the *Guardian*, McGreal writes of Bush's stated determination to follow the peace process through, 'Mr Bush said he had promised Mr Sharon and the Palestinian prime minister, Mahmoud Abbas, that he would "ride herd" on what happened – but wasn't sure they understood the expression.' The veteran British foreign correspondent, Ann Leslie, writing in the *Daily Mail*, also alludes to Bush's Texan origins. Before she does so, though, she suggests, 'cynic though I may be, I'm tempted to believe that this time the latest of innumerable peace plans might begin to work.'[22] She then concludes a long and thoughtful piece which combines diplomacy with the views of small shop owners by quoting *Paradise Lost*, and saying, 'Maybe, just maybe, that light is coming at last thanks perhaps to the stupid Texan cowboy.'[23]

Although this book's principal focus is the British and American news media, it is instructive in this case also to consider briefly the response from reporters from the region. The day after the summit, the BBC website published a summary of views expressed in Israeli, Palestinian, and other Middle Eastern newspapers. The story, headlined 'Aqaba under press spotlight',[24] was compiled from a wide range of sources by BBC Monitoring, and, in their introductory paragraph, they did concede that 'there was a wide range of opinion'.[25] Nevertheless, the optimists are certainly allowed to have their say. *Al-Hayat*, the Arabic newspaper based in London, is quoted as saying that the Roadmap, 'represents a big chance for the liberation of Palestine'.[26]

A writer for the Israeli newspaper *Maariv* praised President Bush in terms clearly intended to echo the achievements of Julius Caesar, 'He came, he saw, he dictated. US President George Bush extracted from Palestinian Prime Minister Abu Mazen and Israeli Prime Minister Ariel Sharon big promises, unprecedented commitments from which perhaps there is no going back.'[27] Ten years later, these assessments seem naïve or foolish. It is true that the rest of the press review includes opinions, from both Arab and Israeli media, which question the motives of both the Israelis and Palestinians – depending on the audience they are writing for. One Israeli analyst suggests that 'terror' has been rewarded; an Egyptian newspaper warns that, 'In the end Israel will take the opportunity to breach this peace and occupy Palestinian and Arab lands once more.' Cynical and pessimistic as these latter assessments may seem, nothing has occurred in the last decade to prove them wrong. On the contrary, it is the optimists who must wish that their words, in this internet age, were not so easily found and re-read ten years later. It is the job of the journalist-analyst or the opinion piece writer to try to stand out from the crowd; to say something with a clarity or vision which marks them out from their competitors. It may also be that on this occasion, with a western world, the United States especially, still reeling from 9/11, and a Middle East wounded by the intifada and the invasion of Iraq, those analysts just wanted to offer their audiences some hope. Either way, it did not make for good journalism. At the time, words alone suggested that change was coming. Actions did not bear that out. The passion of the young Palestinian student for his land, and the settler's conviction that his dream was dead, were the reality. The gap between the news reporting from Israel, the West Bank, and Gaza, and the optimism of summit editorials was great, and this division was played out within news organizations. A few days later, a correspondent for an internationally known newspaper complained that his newsdesk had questioned his less-than-optimistic assessment of the Roadmap's chances of success. Was he sure, the editors in London asked? His years of experience reporting the conflict suggested that this could not – not yet at least – been seen as a new dawn. Alan Philps, then the Jerusalem correspondent for the *Daily Telegraph*, says he has 'a strong memory, a very clear memory'[28] of writing the story:

> I had pinned to my noticeboard in my office a series of yellowing bits of paper with various peace plans, and they'd all stumbled at the first hurdle or, in the case of Oslo, second or third hurdle. And I didn't think this one would do any better.

Philps recalls now feeling a sense that he was somehow breaking the rules, that his scepticism meant that he somehow:

> wasn't playing the game. I think the idea was you have a new peace plan and you big it up because it's hope and then comes the collapse. I felt quite strongly about this because this was false hope. This was something concocted in diplomatic chancelleries which wasn't going to get very far. I couldn't see after the horrors of all the bombings that this was going to get anywhere.

On 30 April, when the Roadmap was presented, I had had a call from a BBC news programme asking me to report on the celebrations in Gaza. I could not, I explained, because there would be none. Editors, far removed from the heat, traffic jams, and tension of the West Bank, were also removed from its realities. Almost every journalist to whom I spoke for this book, and to whom I told the story of being asked to broadcast about the celebrations, had the same reaction. They laughed. Their laughter was one of recognition – many of them had found themselves dealing with similar requests. One long-standing member of the foreign press community in Jerusalem suggests a reason why this might be the case:

> Having worked now for papers in Britain and the USA and Canada, it's clear to me that the foreign editors of the media basically follow their foreign ministries' outlook on international affairs. Basically what else are they going to do? You know, you've got to have an awful lot of independent information to second guess the experts at the State Department if you're American, or at the foreign office if you're British.

Therefore, this journalist concludes, that for foreign news editors, 'The starting point is going to be the accepted view of their foreign diplomats.'[29] What consequence does this have for the journalism of the Israeli-Palestinian conflict? If the diplomacy which the news media were following, which they were permitting to set their agenda – at least in part – was itself flawed, then the coverage risks including those flaws. John Pilger is more forthright:

> Much of western journalism is an extension of western power and authority: that is to say, countries are 'covered' according to their usefulness, strategic value, expendability. There are numerous

honourable exceptions to this, of course; but generally speaking, that's been my experience. As someone put it wisely, if the Middle Eastern countries produced only carrots, they would be reported according to the strategic interest in carrot production.

Whether or not one agrees with Pilger's analysis, there is no question that, as Joel Peters writes, 'The United Nations has spent more time discussing this issue than any other international conflict. The region is awash with peace plans and envoys on peace missions.'[30] Furthermore, he adds of a conflict which has defied solution, 'Framing it as a territorial dispute has led to a narrative of ownership and dispossession, with each side denying the rights, claims, and legitimacy of the other.'[31] It was exactly this 'territorial dispute' which the Roadmap sought to address when it was published that summer.

In the same way that, as I argued in Chapter 3, the conflict has commanded colossal editorial attention, it has also, for decades, drawn in countless 'envoys on peace missions'. Most of the plans they have brought with them over the last 20 years and more, since the end of the first intifada, have been based on similar principles. They assume that the 'Two State solution' – where a Palestinian State is created alongside Israel – is the best way to bring a just end to the conflict. The Roadmap was one such plan, and, therefore is worth considering in some detail. The version of the document made public then, in 2003, spoke on its first page of:

> A settlement, negotiated between the parties, will result in the emergence of an independent, democratic, and viable Palestinian state living side by side in peace and security with Israel and its other neighbors. The settlement will resolve the Israel-Palestinian conflict, and end the occupation that began in 1967.[32]

The guiding principle of the Roadmap, referred to in the next paragraph of the document, was 'land for peace' – in other words, the idea that Israel would end the occupation of Gaza and the West Bank (perhaps with exceptions which could be negotiated), thus giving the Palestinians 'land' and seeing in return an end to the intifada. The Roadmap even specified the stages in which the process would happen, the final one, Phase III, foreseeing 'a permanent status agreement in 2005.'[33] As Peters points out in the extract quoted above, the major obstacles to such an approach were the denial by each side of the other's 'rights, claims, and legitimacy'. What the Roadmap failed to address, and what the reporting of the time failed adequately to highlight, was that these rights and claims were, in some cases, based upon notions of land given by God: which is why correspondents at the time identified settlers and Islamists as the plan's most serious opponents. The Roadmap did not include this idea, instead seeing land as more of a purely economic commodity – something to be bought and sold, traded, cultivated, or built upon. Any eventual solution to the Israeli-Palestinian conflict would naturally have to consider land in these terms. Addressing economic grievances is a vital part of ending conflicts where poverty or dispossession is seen as one of the causes of conflict. In the case of the Israeli-Palestinian conflict, this was an incomplete understanding of 'land' and its significance, both at the time the Roadmap was presented, and subsequently. 'Both sides claim to have rights on this land, and they claim that they are the only ones who have the rights on this land, and no side can in any way forego its rights on every inch of territory because it's holy land,' Ephraim Halevy, former Director of Mossad, told a BBC Television documentary, *Israel: Facing the Future*,[34] which was broadcast in April 2013. As Halevy explained, the importance of 'land' in the conflict is not simply economic. It is religious. The land is 'holy', sacred to both belligerents. It could better be understood as 'homeland', which the *Oxford English Dictionary* defines as, 'A person's home country or native land; the land of one's ancestors' – a concept which resonates right through the Israeli-Palestinian conflict. There may be competing accounts of history, and competing interpretations of which law supports which claim. Yet the basis of both Israeli and Palestinian claims is the idea of the 'land of one's ancestors', and this is land given by God. The Roadmap did not address this idea of land as 'homeland', nor as 'holy land'. In fact, the idea of 'holy land' was not even hinted at. Throughout the document, the word 'state', dry and sterile, and without the association of the 'land of one's ancestors', is preferred – perhaps a convenient way of avoiding any echo of the Balfour Declaration, with its favourable view of 'the establishment in Palestine of a national home for the Jewish people'.[35] The Balfour Declaration, although almost a century old, continues to be seen by many Palestinians as one of the causes of their dispossession. Paul Mason, a correspondent for Channel 4 News, was just the latest in a long line of British reporters to suffer admonishment from elderly Palestinians when he visited Gaza in the summer of 2014. His blog post, headlined, 'As a Brit in Gaza, "it's all your fault," is a line I've heard a lot'[36] spoke of his experience being reprimanded for the Balfour Declaration in a region where memories are long, and history fresh in the mind.

So a thoughtful diplomat, drafting the outline of a new agreement, was probably well advised to avoid any phrase which might bring it to mind. 'State' was so much safer, even if, for its exclusion of any notion of the spiritual significance of land, or the importance of religion, it was also incomplete. The word 'faith' occurred only in the sense of 'good faith' (page 1) on the part of the parties as they seek to implement the plan. One looks in vain through the Roadmap for any mention of religion until the very end, where it feels like an afterthought: 'religious concerns' and 'religious interests' appear only in the penultimate paragraph, and are mentioned there only in passing.

As a result, the reporting of the time focused too closely on analysing a proposed solution to the Israeli-Palestinian conflict which largely failed to take into account its religious origins and influences. These were not widely emphasized in diplomatic or journalistic discourses of the time, but they were present. While correspondents at Aqaba questioned Bush's grasp of detail, and reported his cowboy image and turn of phrase, they also hit upon something else which he had brought with him from the United States: his own, Christian, faith. Following his meeting with the Arab leaders in Sharm-el-Sheikh on 3 June, Bush made what McGreal described as, 'an extraordinary invocation of God.'[37] Not realizing that his remarks were being broadcast, Bush said, 'I believe that, as I told the Crown Prince, the Almighty God has endowed each individual on the face of the earth with – that expects each person to be treated with dignity.'[38] It would be fanciful to suggest that Bush sought to solve the Israeli-Palestinian conflict principally for religious reasons, but perhaps his own faith formed part of his purpose. Knowing that he was in the company of representatives of countries (as well as Abbas, Bush met the leaders of Bahrain, Egypt, Jordan, and Saudi Arabia) where faith was, for the majority of the population, a part of everyday life, Bush obviously felt comfortable invoking God in private conversation with them, even if he did not intend his remarks to become public. Leslie, in her lengthy and discursive piece (it ran to more than 2,000 words), did make another reference to Bush's own faith, saying his, 'sometimes naïve belief in the sanctity of democracy is as unshakeable as his belief in the New Testament'. Apart from this, religion was absent then from the diplomatic agenda, and so did not feature greatly in the reporting.

If religion was not part of the Roadmap in anything but the passing references mentioned above, it was also frequently underplayed in much of the journalism of the time. Longer-term factors, such as faith, often struggle to force their way onto daily news agendas. Editors are wary of seeming to seek to give audiences a history lesson, rather than the latest developments. Religion in the Middle East, after all, can hardly be considered new. As noted in Chapter 3, the 'if it bleeds, it leads', rule of thumb for many British newsrooms is a powerful influence. There is nothing fundamentally wrong with this. Editors are putting together bulletins, websites, and newspapers aimed at attracting the attention of busy people generally preoccupied with their own daily concerns. The very word 'journalism', after all, has as its root 'jour', the French word for 'day'. However much there is to be said for the approach taken by the Churchills in their book, discussed earlier, the introduction to which took the reader back to the Bible – that was a book, not a bulletin. As Philps puts it, thinking of the Roadmap time in particular, 'Newspaper articles in the news pages are not the best way for getting nuance across.' During the second intifada especially, including the time of the Roadmap, the deadly cycle of Israeli military raids and suicide bombings, each cited as justified retaliation for the other, made it difficult to find airtime for material which might take a longer view – yet things were already changing. An unexpected announcement by Ariel Sharon in early 2004 provided an unforeseen opportunity.

On Monday 2 February, As Gaza's overwhelmingly Muslim population celebrated Eid Al-Adha, the 'Feast of the Sacrifice' (which remembers Ibrahim's (Abraham) readiness to sacrifice his son in order to obey God's command). Sharon surprised his supporters and his enemies alike by announcing that the Jewish settlements in the Gaza Strip would be evacuated the following year. He was, he said, 'working on the assumption that in the future there (would) be no Jews in Gaza.'[39] The *Independent*'s veteran Middle East correspondent, Robert Fisk, referring to US praise for Sharon's decision, has written witheringly of the number of settlers involved, compared to the West Bank. 'Ariel Sharon was prepared to close down the puny little settlements in Gaza – housing just 8,000 Israelis – and this was a "historic and courageous act".'[40] The Gaza settlers had started arriving in Gaza following Israel's capture and occupation of the territory in the 1967 war, although they themselves spoke of a much older Jewish community which had been there until they were forced to leave during unrest in the 1920s. Sharon himself, in his autobiography, *Warrior*, spoke of his own plans, following the occupation of Gaza, for the location of the settlements, describing them as 'fingers'[41] presumably intended to grip the coastal strip at various strategic intervals. The most contentious of them was Netzarim, situated to the south of Gaza City. The land around the settlements then was cleared to deprive would-be attackers of cover. Netzarim's location meant that this security zone, as the Israeli Army might have called it, made life very difficult for any Palestinian needing to pass nearby. To begin with, Salah al-Din road, the main route through the territory from north to south, was closed here to Palestinians. The effect was to make all travel south of the Gaza Strip's main city difficult, sometimes dangerous, and sometimes, when the Israeli Army decided to divide territory into three and forbid movement between the different parts, impossible. Even some Israelis recognized the problem this presented. The one-time Israeli cabinet minister, Yossi Sarid, called Netzarim not a finger, but 'a bone in the throat'.[42] It was one pronouncement of an Israeli minister which Palestinians were happy to cite. As the intifada continued, even to approach Netzarim at a distance was to take a risk. Shepherds and farm workers might be treated as potential bombers, and fired upon. The residents of Netzarim seemed to know that they were loathed by their neighbours, and unloved by many beyond the region, too. Requests to visit them to hear their views generally met with refusal – until Sharon's decision that they were to leave. Then, they were suddenly keen to be heard.

It would be wrong to conclude that the settlers' views were representative of Israeli society in general. In a sense, they were extremists – willing to put themselves and their families (and as part of their drive to populate the land, settlers generally seemed to have large ones) at risk in pursuit of their ideology. Their answer to suggestions that it was dangerous to live there was that it was dangerous in Tel Aviv or Jerusalem, too. This was, after all, the time of suicide bombers in buses and cafés. Yet not only did the government tolerate them, it actually supported them. Their neat white houses and lawns were protected by the army – although an Israeli officer contact of mine once privately expressed disbelief that anyone could actually want to live there. So in a sense their presence was part of Israel's security policy, a fact which made Sharon's decision to remove them all the more shocking to those who were to be removed. Their willingness to talk to a western reporter created an opportunity to give more context to the coverage of the conflict, to try to get onto the news agenda some of those underlying, longer-term factors that might hold the key to understanding the way people on both sides saw the conflict which the Roadmap was designed to resolve. In the case of the settlers, things were strikingly clear. The idea that their presence was provocative was dismissed as part of an attempt to undermine the State of Israel itself. 'When they say that we don't have a right to be here, they don't mean here Gaza, they mean here in the entire state of Israel. They don't think that the Jews have a right to be in Israel at all,' said Tammy Silberschein, a resident who had come from the United States to live in Netzarim eight years earlier. For the settlers, this was all Israel. In their view, the borders were set by scripture, not the United Nations. 'Being a Torah observant Jew we are taught that this is the Jewish homeland, we have to be sovereign here, and we have to settle all parts of it,'[43] as Mrs Silberschein put it. The interviews I recorded that day were used for a radio documentary, 'The Middle East and Home', which was first broadcast on the BBC World Service in March 2004. The programme also included interviews with refugee families from Rafah, at the Gaza Strip's southern edge. The refugees in Gaza are classed as such by the United Nations because they lost their homes in the 1948 war which led to the founding of the State of Israel. Even then, in 2003, the vast majority of refugees were actually the descendants of those who had fled. Still, the passage of time had not softened their views; the fact that many had never seen the places they called home did not lessen the yearning to 'return' there. I found Naji Abu Hashem standing over a cooking pot on open waste ground. In the autumn of 2003, the Israeli Army had launched 'Operation Root Canal' with the aim of destroying tunnels used to smuggle all kinds of contraband, including ammunition, into Gaza from Egypt. During the initial phase of the operation, 148 'shelters' (houses and other dwellings) were destroyed, according to the United Nations, leaving more than 3,000 people homeless.[44] Mr Abu Hashem was among them. As he leaned over the fire where the pot bubbled, clothes hung on a line nearby – struggling to dry in the damp winter air. Mr Abu Hashem was refusing to leave the area, although his house was gone. The United Nations, which took responsibility for housing and feeding the refugees, was reluctant to rebuild there. They feared that new homes might be bulldozed as the old ones had been. Mr Abu Hashem took the view that, come what may, the land should not be abandoned. In making his point, he drew on the fact that most of the people in the area were refugees from either 1948, or 1967. Where were they supposed to go now? His reason was built on his religion. 'This is my religion tell me to stay here,' he said. 'This is my Palestinian land. This is our land.'[45] His arguments echoed and opposed those of Mrs Silberschein. They seemed to go to the heart of the conflict; they seemed to be exactly those issues which were not addressed in the Roadmap. This was 2004. The Roadmap was supposed to lead to an end to the conflict the following year. Yet how could it, if it chose to ignore these deep-rooted religious beliefs? Of the Oslo Accords of the 1990s, Avi Shlaim has written:

> The declaration was completely silent on such vital issues as the right of return of the 1948 refugees, the borders of the Palestinian entity, the future of the Jewish settlements on the West Bank and Gaza, and the status of Jerusalem. The reason for this silence is not hard to understand: if these issues had been addressed, there would have been no accord.[46]

The same could have been said of the Roadmap a decade later. By all but ignoring faith as a motivational factor, it seemed wilfully to overlook that which it knew it could not address – or at least could only address with great difficulty, and little realistic hope of short-term success. It would be wrong to conclude that this was the only reason for the failure of the Roadmap, and other peace initiatives. For some of those close to the diplomatic process which was then underway in the aftermath of the United States' apparent victory in Iraq, the timing was wrong. The Roadmap came too late. Lord (Michael) Levy, who was then Middle East envoy for the British prime minister, Tony Blair, remembers, 'a Roadmap to nowhere'. He argues that the real chance for peace had gone with the assassination in 1995 of the Israeli Prime Minister Yitzhak Rabin. 'Thereafter I thought every effort was an effort – a serious effort, a well-intended effort – but not really an effort that I thought would come to fruit.'[47]

In the decade which followed, the Roadmap did indeed go nowhere. The sense of hopelessness facing those seeking to promote cooperation between Israelis and Palestinians continued to grow. This was not simply a matter of naïve idealists crushed on contact with reality; rather of knowledgeable, intelligent, and realistic observers seeing no future. Two of those observers, Yossi Alpher and Ghassan Khatib edited the bitterlemons website for more than ten years. In August 2012 (seven years, it might be noted, after the date by which Roadmap foresaw a permanent solution to the conflict), Mr Alpher published on the site an article entitled 'Why we are closing'.[48] In it, explaining the decision to put an end to what had become an important and well-regarded forum for discussion, opinion, and analysis, Mr Alpher wrote, 'There is no peace process, and no prospect of one.'[49] A bleaker assessment from one so well qualified to make one is hard to envisage.

Even the highest-level diplomatic opinion seems now to recognize the changing nature of the conflict, perhaps a factor in the many rounds of negotiations which have failed. Daniel Kurtzer, now Professor in Middle Eastern Policy Studies at Princeton University in the United States, was the US ambassador to Israel from 2001 to 2005: the time of the second intifada; the time of the Roadmap. He had the additional advantage, not always common when diplomatic postings can be relatively short, and involve frequent change, of having been there before. Earlier in a career in the US Foreign Service which lasted almost three decades, he did another posting to Tel Aviv. Kurtzer agrees that religion 'certainly is' playing a greater role in the conflict, but he suggests this is a trend which began in the 1980s – encouraged, at least in part, by a policy through which Israel aimed to undermine its secular nationalist enemies in the Palestine Liberation Organization (PLO).

> During my earlier stint in Tel Aviv, I reported from Gaza about the affirmative decisions that Israel was taking to allow Islamic money to build institutions and provide social welfare, while stopping so-called nationalist money. So we saw it a long time ago that there was the kind of fostering of the idea of Islamism as the antidote for nationalism.[50]

As so often, when states are faced with managing conflicts in the short term, the longer-term effects were unintended. Kurtzer argues that, 'the natural consequence of that of course was, and has been, the growth of religious feelings.' However, over the decades he has been involved in the region, religion's growing influence has not been confined to the increasing power of Hamas in Palestinian politics. On the Israeli side, Kurtzer describes, 'the intoxication of the settlements movement among a certain population – believing that more settlements will, you know, hasten the arrival of ultimate messianic redemption. So both sides are heading in that direction.'

It is a direction in which diplomacy may find itself on unfamiliar territory. While identifying the challenge, one which he believes has roots back in the changing nature of the conflict in the later decades of the last century, Kurtzer continues:

> I think diplomacy has proven so far incapable of figuring out what do about religion. There are some so called Track 2 initiatives – you know, non-formal diplomacy among academics and think tank people – in which religious people are talking to each other, or secular and religious people are talking to each other, or you know, some combination thereof. And some of that will feed into what

the diplomats do, but I haven't seen any success yet in integrating this move towards religion into the diplomacy trying to resolve the conflict. It's a real challenge.

Again, Kurtzer argues that these issues, while growing in significance, are not entirely new. Nevertheless, they have defied conventional diplomatic solution:

> 25 years ago James Baker, to a chorus of real howls, talked about both sides giving up their dreams of achieving all of their territorial ambitions. And of course in a diplomatic sense, he was right. But what he had walked into was exactly this question of territory meaning more than simply where you live, or what field you cultivate. There's some primordial attachment that people have, especially in that region, to the olive tree, to the brook, to the wadi – which diplomacy has not yet figured out how to integrate.

These are the realities which reporting of the Israeli-Palestinian conflict needs to continue to reflect: challenging, difficult, and, it seems, increasingly influenced by religion. For if there were a glimmer of hope of a peace agreement with between Israel and a Palestinian Authority in both Gaza and the West Bank, the same cannot be said of a Gaza where Hamas is in charge – especially where Hamas is in charge of a population further embittered by large-scale Israeli Military operations in 2009, 2012, and, especially, 2014.

> War, that is the animosity and the reciprocal effects of hostile elements, cannot be considered to have ended so long as the enemy's *will* has not been broken: in other words, so long as the enemy government and its allies have not been driven to ask for peace, or the population made to submit.

So wrote von Clausewitz (italics in the original).[51]
Where that will is drawn deep down from a sense of obligation to God and homeland, it may be harder to abandon than that motivated only by desire for land, water, security, and employment. These elements of the Israeli-Palestinian conflict have defied diplomatic solution. They are difficult enough to solve. They are even more difficult to solve when, for sections of populations and political elites, they are reinforced by religion. The Roadmap has been singled out for discussion in this chapter for a number of reasons. Firstly, its principle of land for peace means it

is broadly similar to all the plans aimed at solving the Israeli-Palestinian conflict which have been presented since the first intifada. Secondly, having been launched in 2003, it falls roughly in the middle of the period between the Oslo Accords of the early 1990s, and the present. Thirdly, it was launched after the attacks of 9/11, and was therefore part of the United States' attempts to reshape the Middle East which followed those attacks. As discussed above, however, it also overlooked the importance of faith in the post-9/11 world. As Shindler notes when writing of the early rise of Hamas as a political force in Gaza, 'when the PLO was founded in 1964 it made no mention of God'.[52] Hamas does, of course, see the land between the river and the sea as an entity 'of which no part could be given away under any circumstances'.[53] Combine this with the 'messianic' mission of the settlers, and reporting the Israeli-Palestinian conflict becomes an assignment in which the most ancient ideas are actually the most current and modern.

5
Going Back Two Thousand Years All the Time

Words on a page become pictures in the reader's mind. Different pictures may form in different readers' minds; sometimes the word will remind the reader of a thing or place they know and remember. At other times, the opposite happens. Suddenly the eye sees something concrete which they had previously only imagined from reading: an idea becomes an object. So it was on a late winter afternoon in 2003 when I stood at the top of an Israeli military post at the southern end of the Gaza Strip, overlooking the Rafah refugee camp below. I had been invited there by the spokesman's office of the Israeli Army. They presumably wanted to give me the chance literally to see things from their perspective with a view to informing, and influencing, my reporting of the consequences of their military operations on the people and infrastructure of Gaza. The Israeli fortification was a tall metal fence designed to protect soldiers in their positions behind it. Its construction had involved the clearing of Palestinian houses from the land in front of the fortification, so that no attacker could approach unseen. The demolitions had drawn protests, and, in consequence, deaths. In the three months which followed my visit that afternoon, the Israeli Army would kill two unarmed foreigners, and fatally wound a third. The dead were the pro-Palestinian activist Rachel Corrie, crushed by a bulldozer she sought to prevent from carrying out its work for the Israeli Army, and the British cameraman James Miller, shot dead while filming the destruction of houses near the fence. The third casualty was another activist protesting against the demolitions. Tom Hurndall was shot in April 2003, and died of his wounds in January the following year. Families living near the open area would sometimes flee from their homes at night, sleeping even in the street, for fear that their houses would be knocked down on top of them. It became an increasingly dangerous place to work in as a reporter during my time there, and, in my mind, the fortifications that dominated the area became the 'iron wall' which the early Zionist Ze'ev Jabotinsky had seen as indispensable to protect Jews in Palestine from their Arab neighbours when he wrote:

> Zionist colonisation must either stop, or else proceed regardless of the native population. Which means that it can proceed and develop only under the protection of a power that is independent of the native population – behind an iron wall, which the native population cannot breach.[1]

Jabotinsky presumably did not foresee a physical iron wall around the whole of the 'Zionist colonisation' project, although he must have believed that one had been constructed in certain places. I had always taken his phrase to be a description of a strategy, rather than a physical object – and yet there it was: an iron wall which the 'native population' was powerless to breach.

The other memory I have of that afternoon brings me to one of this chapter's key subjects: journalists' choices, and usage, of language when reporting the Israeli-Palestinian conflict. Israelis – whether right-wing politicians, soldiers, journalists, or ordinary civilians – usually refer to any armed Palestinian as a terrorist. So I was surprised when the Israeli Army officer who accompanied me on the visit to the positions turned to me and then, looking back at the sun-bleached, ramshackle dwellings which stretched out below us asked whether I had met any of the 'resistance fighters'. I was caught completely off guard – puzzled more by the way in which the question was phrased than the question itself. 'Resistance' was a word used only by Palestinians who participated in, or admired, the armed struggle against Israeli occupation of the West Bank and Gaza, and their supporters. To Israel, this armed activity was terrorism. What was it, what is it, for international journalists? The word 'Hamas' means 'enthusiasm' or 'zeal' in Arabic. It is also 'the acronym for Harakat al-Muqawama al-'Islamiyya (the Islamic Resistance Movement)'[2] – yet you will look largely in vain for any reference to Hamas as a 'resistance movement' in English language mainstream journalism. The only exception might be where the word is translated by way of introducing it to an audience – or where the writer is not necessarily subject to the style restrictions which the news media place on their own journalists.[3] Some news organizations, Fox News in the United States, for example, are content to adapt Israel's normal designation of Palestinian armed groups as terrorists. For others, the word is not the tip of an iceberg so much as the most prominent of a count-less number of linguistic pitfalls awaiting the journalist reporting the Israeli-Palestinian conflict. In its entry on 'terrorism', Reuters' *Handbook of Journalism* explains to its journalists:

> We may refer without attribution to terrorism and counterterrorism in general, but do not refer to specific events as terrorism. Nor do we use the word 'terrorist' without attribution to qualify specific indi-viduals, groups or events. 'Terrorism' and 'terrorist' must be retained when quoting someone in direct speech. When quoting someone in indirect speech, care must be taken with sentence structure to ensure it is entirely clear that they are the source's words and not a label.[4]

Further guidance later in the entry exhorts the agency's journalists to, 'Report the subjects of news stories objectively, their actions, identity and background. Aim for a dispassionate use of language so that indi-viduals, organizations and governments can make their own judgment on the basis of facts.'[5] I have cited this guidance at length because it summarizes very well the approach, and rationale, which the objec-tive tradition in western journalism uses in dealing with probably the most controversial word in reporting conflict in general, and the Israeli-Palestinian conflict in particular. Asked about the choices he found himself having to make about language, McGreal replies, 'Certainly the word terrorist was up there. That for me was a very straightforward choice, which is I wasn't going to use it, because it's such a loaded word.' This 'straightforward choice' was one which he found himself challenged to justify:

> I remember appearing on a panel after I'd been living in Israel for several years, in Jerusalem before an Israeli audience, and I was asked 'why won't you call Hamas terrorists?' And my answer was that I was content to call Hamas terrorists provided I could apply the word to Israel's actions as well and I specifically gave the example of the Israeli military's action in Southern Gaza, where effectively it pursued a pol-icy of terror, as far as I was concerned, against the civilian population there, with the sheer scale of the killing and the shooting. And I said if I can call elements of the Israeli army terrorist then I'll call ele-ments of Hamas terrorist and until I can do that I'm not going to use the word.

A colleague working for the BBC Arabic Service once told me that he faced a similar challenge when asked why he did not use the word 'martyr' for Palestinians who died in the conflict with Israel. His reply, reflecting the influence of the BBC's requirements of impartiality, was that, were he to do so, he would have to accord the same status to Israeli settlers living in the Gaza Strip were they to be killed. The example serves to reflect the dilemma faced in using, or not using, the word 'terrorist'. Where most dictionary definitions would offer some variation on the core idea that terrorism is the pursuit of political aims by violent means, I would argue that, in addition, most people understand the definition to include the idea that terrorism is the work of non-state actors. That makes McGreal's logic about Hamas and Israel's killing and wounding of civilians, sound though it seems, susceptible to challenge. McGreal's audience in Israeli, as opposed to Arab, Jerusalem, presumably found it hard to accept – as might any Israeli, or citizen of those countries, including the United States and the members of the European Union, who recognize Israel as a democracy and an ally, while designating Hamas a terrorist organization. Part of the problem with defining Hamas is that while it does have a political leadership formally dedicated to Israel's destruction, and a military wing, the Izzedin Al-Qassam brigades, which seeks to bring that about by force (an impossible objective, of course, given the strength of the enemy it faces in the shape of the Israeli Army) it is also a social movement. Nevertheless, from the point of view of the international news media, Hamas is editorially significant principally as an armed group engaged in military conflict with Israel. To that extent, it is a terrorist organization to Israel, and to Israel's supporters in the media, with Fox News being the most obvious example. Many other British and US news organizations will tend to follow the something similar to the Reuters guidelines, above.

In places, however, those have come under pressure in a post-9/11 world. When, as a correspondent, I reported for the BBC World Service, the word was never used except in contexts similar to those outlined in the Reuters Handbook – that is, when citing a source directly. Because of the nature of radio as a medium, of course, the attribution had to be verbally spelled out in a form of words such as 'what the minister referred to as terrorism' in order not to give the appearance that the BBC was making a value judgement. However, unlike Reuters, which is writing for so many audiences that its impartiality is in part a decision based on journalistic ethics, and in part one taken for commercial reasons. If you are hoping to send your dispatches around the world, you need to find a form of words that will not alienate those who are paying for your service. The BBC finds itself in a different situation. Its audiences may broadly be divided into two. While it is true that, like Reuters and other international agencies, the BBC does seek to serve audiences around the world, it also has a British domestic audience which, in the form of the licence fee, is its main source of funding. Long before 9/11 and the attacks inspired by a militant interpretation of Islam which followed, for example in Madrid in 2004, or on the London transport system in 2005, inhabitants of British towns and cities had experienced a campaign of bombings carried out by Irish Republicans, seeking to end British rule in Northern Ireland. Such attacks were uniformly referred to in the British news media as 'terrorism'. The arrival, therefore, of attacks such as those on London in July 2005 fell into a pre-existing category: if not of motivation, then of civilian experience. This is reflected in the current entry in the BBC Editorial Guidelines on 'Language when Reporting Terrorism'. The entry, choosing as it does examples from the second intifada, when Hamas suicide bombers attacked buses in Israel, and an attack like July 2005, are especially relevant to the point discussed here:

> The value judgements frequently implicit in the use of the words 'terrorist' or 'terrorist group' can create inconsistency in their use or, to audiences, raise doubts about our impartiality. For example, the bombing of a bus in London was carried out by 'terrorists', but the bombing of a bus in Israel was perpetrated by a 'suicide bomber'.[6]

For those news organizations who do not have substantial international audiences, this is less of a dilemma – but, in today's world, these are few in number. Like the BBC, all major British and US news organizations are available to audiences outside the countries where their content is edited. Some actively seek to increase their audiences beyond traditional geographical boundaries, with the *Guardian* and the *New York Times* being two examples which have implemented such strategies with great success. So the distinction between domestic and international audiences which once existed is disappearing, as is the ability to make value judgements – a bombing in London is terrorism, one in Israel a suicide bombing – without such judgements being subject to wider scrutiny. In many cases, audiences are able to see and compare the coverage of two incidents, for example the bombing of public transport, which they might consider as similar or even equivalent, yet which the news organization apparently does not. The widespread use of the words 'terror', 'terrorism', and 'terrorists', in public and political discourse after the attacks of 9/11 made the issue even more challenging to deal with. That presented particular dilemmas for journalists covering the Israeli-Palestinian conflict when, as McGreal pointed out in Chapter 3, the Israeli government of Ariel Sharon strove to present its conflict with the

Palestinians almost as another front in the United States' 'war on terror'. Nor is this tactic confined to that era. In the summer of 2014, as populations of the west and beyond were shocked by what, in effect, were public executions for the internet age carried out by the 'Islamic State' in Iraq and Syria, the Israeli government, then locked in its bloodiest battle with Hamas in Gaza, tried to link their enemies to those atrocities. Then, the Israeli Prime Minister, Benjamin Netanyahu, compared Hamas to Islamic State, calling them a 'branch of the same tree'.[7] At the BBC, whose guidelines are cited above, the need to serve different audiences despite the potential pitfalls of 'implicit' value judgements meant a practical compromise which involved regulations not being observed too strictly. In effect, it seemed to me as one of the Corporation's journalists at the time of the '7/7' attacks, and the second intifada, those value judgements were allowed to hold sway, at least on domestic outlets. Some correspondents seemed to see no reason why they should not refer to bus bombers in London as 'terrorists'. To rein in a reporter for doing something done almost everywhere else in the British news media would hardly have made sense, especially when such judgements must have seemed clear-cut to the majority of the audience. International outlets, on the other hand, especially BBC World Service radio, tended to stick rigorously to their practice, very similar to the one outlined in the Reuters guidelines, of not using the words 'terrorist', 'terrorism', etc., when referring to specific events or people.

While journalistic debates over the use of the word 'terrorist' are relevant to countless conflicts, especially in the post-9/11 world – 'We use the term militants not terrorists almost without exception, that's very standard on *The Independent*', says Macintyre – there are elements of the Israeli-Palestinian conflict which provide particular challenges. Several of the journalists interviewed for this book mentioned, among other linguistic challenges, the description of the barrier separating the West Bank from Israel. 'Is it a wall, is it a fence, is it a separation barrier?' is how Jeremy Bowen summarizes the challenge. Construction began in the summer of 2003, at that time when, as discussed in Chapter 4, the United States' perceived triumph in Iraq had led to the belief, that the Middle East could be remade and when the UK government believed that 'a peace plan for Palestine should be presented as one of the prime objectives of the imposition of a new world order in the Middle East'.[8] The ostensible purpose of the construction of the barrier was to prevent suicide bombers and other attackers crossing from the West Bank into Israel. However, as Ilan Pappe argues, the construction was planned 'with large inroads to ensure that some of the major

Jewish settlements would be on the Israeli side of the divide. For many Palestinians, the territories left to them under the projected "Palestinian State" seemed to be yet another prison camp.'[9] The Palestinians saw it as a land grab; the Israelis a response to a deadly threat which they had every right to counter in that way. For journalists, just the description of something apparently so simple became a difficult linguistic dilemma.

'We had to take a view, while I was there actually, on exactly what the style was for the wall and we called it a separation barrier,' recalls Macintyre. That largely is the form of words upon which most British and American news media seem to have agreed. It is a compromise between the 'security barrier', to which the Israelis refer, and the 'apartheid wall' of which the Palestinians speak. Macintyre remembers one incident where he feels he slipped up.

> Certainly at first you had to check yourself, and I'm sure that once I absorbed something from an Israeli paper without processing it. I think I once referred to the security barrier which makes me blush with embarrassment to think back on it, but that was only once. After a while it just becomes second nature.

'Processing' is a word which describes well the choice of language. Working in a western journalistic culture of objectivity, a reporter covering the Israeli-Palestinian conflict can take little just as it is and report it. That, at least, is the theory. As Macintyre says, until that process becomes 'second nature' where particular words are concerned, there is the risk of what comes to seem a serious professional transgression, the commission of which is cause for a red face. Part of the problem with this particular wall, fence, or barrier is that it is different things in different places: concrete slabs several metres high cut off farmers from their fields in parts of the West Bank; chain link fences snake across the rocky, deserted soil. I remember an afternoon in July 2003 spent in the West Bank town of Qalqiliya, as the barrier was taking shape. I spent it drinking tea with Hassan Harouf, who had a nursery growing fruit and flowers on the edge of town. Huge concrete slabs now overshadowed his greenhouses. Hassan spoke of entertaining 70 different Israeli merchants at his garden table. Those times were gone. 'Now I can't even see the sunset,' he reflected sadly. Harouf's garden had just been cut in half by a wall formed of panels of concrete. They now cast the shadow in which we sat. The coolness on a burning hot summer afternoon was little compensation. For others in the town, the circuitous route to crops, a few hundred metres away, now took two hours through multiple checkpoints. The mayor of Qalqiliya, whose office had been our first calling point when we arrived in the town, had described the barrier as a noose around its collective neck. Certainly, on the map it formed just such a shape. For the farmer cut off from his fields, this must have felt like an apartheid wall – even if, in those early days of its construction, the phrase was not used as widely as it is now. Here, the barrier was a wall, whatever its supporters might have called it. Harvey Morris, writing for the *Financial Times* as the barrier was being built, encountered the dilemma in the form of angry readers' correspondence.

> I wrote one of the early features when they started building the wall and one irate reader of the FT wrote to say it's not a wall, it's a fence, then another reader wrote back in my defence and said if it's a fence how come the photograph to illustrate the piece shows a wall?

Morris's comparison with another long-running conflict serves to reinforce journalists' sense that covering the Israeli-Palestinian conflict brings with it unique pressures.

> Can you imagine if during the Cold War we'd written 'the Berlin fence'? And yet if you look at the actual structure, it's mainly fence and only partly wall, which is the defence the Israelis use for calling it a fence rather than a wall. The slightest word can be loaded.

Sherwood also highlighted the wall/fence as a particular linguistic challenge:

> The phrase which I used to use most of the time was the separation barrier. Because I didn't want to adopt the language on either side. I mean, where it is a wall, I'd call it a wall. And where it's a fence, I'd call it a fence. But I wasn't going to use a generic term to describe the whole thing: the same with settlements, the same with militants, fighters, all that kind of stuff, terrorists. The word that I used to use was militants – you know, I didn't call them terrorists; I didn't call them freedom fighters.

The point here is that in most cases, in many countries around the world, including conflict zones, the distinction between 'wall' and 'fence' might matter little. The fact that a barrier existed – whether to divide, to defend, or to oppress – would be enough to tell the story. Here, though, the normal rules simply do not apply – and any and every word, however simply descriptive it might seem, can come to be seen as controversial. Sherwood says of the use of language in general, 'You try to use language that is politically neutral, but still conveys what you're trying to describe, or what you're trying to say.' Jeremy Bowen accepts that even striving for accuracy is no guarantee of success:

> You've got to be so careful about the terminology you use. Not because you should be worried about offending people because you're always going to offend somebody. It's more about trying to find as accurate a way through it as possible.

This, of course, is true of many international stories; true especially of controversial ones involving armed conflict. Sherwood says, though, that the complexities of the journalism of the Israeli-Palestinian conflict place it in a category of its own for reporters. 'I think it's absolutely another level. All responsible journalists take care about the words they use and what they write but I think when you're writing about the Israeli-Palestinian situation, it is taken to such a high degree,' she says. 'As a journalist when you're there it is actually exhausting because you have this added dimension that most journalists don't have.' Balmer, whose job it was to make sure that the Reuters guidelines cited above were implemented, echoes the view that something is different when a journalist is covering the Israeli-Palestinian conflict. Even someone as senior as he was when he arrived could find it a transformative experience. 'I think that, journalistically speaking for me, that has made me more rigorous than I was when I came here,' he says.

> I certainly think that looking at other stories from other datelines I'm amazed with what they get away with in terms of loose reporting: the sort of stuff that would never be allowed here, because every single word is scrutinized.

This creates a practical problem for journalists covering the conflict. Especially in today's ever more competitive news media world, they are under tremendous pressure to write stories which stand out for audiences who are offered a huge amount of choice. Clear, exciting copy has always increased a reporter's chance of attracting his or her audience's attention. The particular case of the Israeli-Palestinian conflict can make this difficult. For the need to navigate the various linguistic obstacles means that some techniques – such as leaving an audience to assume that something which follows a direct quotation may also be ascribed to the same source – are best avoided. Allowing such assumptions when dealing with such a sensitive story can lead to a lack of clarity over who said what – and accusations of bias. It is therefore best avoided. The result is that a story or script which might flow well as a result of careful crafting will sound or read more clumsily. Any fact or statement, however short or apparently innocuous, needs to be sourced: meaning that stories are held up by phrases such as 'according to the Israeli Army' or 'Palestinian officials say'. Prior to my posting to Gaza, I had been based in Brussels. Writing about European affairs – controversial in their way, especially among some sections of UK audiences – was so much more straightforward than covering the second intifada. Nothing – or at least very little – could be considered a simple matter of fact. In consequence, journalists need constantly to weigh every word even more carefully than they might elsewhere. As Balmer puts it:

> I think this is one of the very few places that I've worked in where every single fact is disputed. I can't think of another environment where you would have apparently quite a straightforward scenario, quite a straightforward situation, and have both sides vehemently disagree with what's going on.

In consequence, differing accounts or interpretations of events often need to appear side by side: something which, Balmer says, can also slow down news stories which are supposed to be pacy and urgent:

> It's very difficult to tell a kind of interesting story that doesn't just become a ping-pong game: one side says this, the other side says that – so stories get laden very quickly with very heavy background.

This is the disadvantage of the phenomenon, which both Sherwood and Balmer identify, whereby journalists raise their standards in order to satisfy the particular requirements of this most challenging of stories. Perhaps because of what she refers to as the 'Jewish hegemony' in the US media, Rudoren seems to feel some of these issues particularly keenly. She shares other correspondents' experience of the difficulty of covering a conflict where even what appear to be the simplest facts are not accepted as such. 'There's a dearth of kind of facts or agreed upon truth,' she says. 'Everything is somebody's version of something. And everything connects back to a contested version of something before and how much context and how much background.'

Rudoren's clear conclusions have grown from a complicated and lengthy process. The main consequence for journalism of this 'dearth of facts' means it becomes all but impossible to find words which work. 'My first lesson about this was very early on,' she recalls of a story she wrote about the city of Hebron, on the West Bank. Hebron features most frequently in news stories because of the presence of 'several hundred Israeli settlers'[10] among a population of some 170,000 Palestinians.[11] 'I referred to Hebron as a disputed city or something.' If the objective language prized in most British and American journalism can be seen as a kind of narrow path of solid ground through a swamp, this was a phrase equivalent to slipping off from where the footing was sure. 'But what I did not know,' Rudoren continues, 'was that "disputed" was what some people – very-pro Israel people – use as a term for the whole West Bank or Gaza, instead of occupied, that is, a less than "occupied" term'. Although Rudoren argues, 'I was kind of trying to use the actual English meaning of the word,' she has altered her subsequent use of the word as a result of the row which followed her use of it on this occasion. 'So there I learned, ok, you avoid the word disputed. I also called it occupied, so it wasn't someone thinking I didn't know it was occupied territory.' Her explanation about 'the actual English meaning' of 'disputed' is illuminating. It strengthens the impression that the Israeli-Palestinian conflict is a unique set of circumstances where facts and language are unable to carry the force they might elsewhere, and that, in consequence journalists face a set of unique challenges.

'Something I wish I'd done differently,' Rudoren continues, on the subject of language: 'I did a long piece this summer[12] about kids who throw stones[13] in the village of Beit Ommar.' The village she refers to is near Hebron on the West Bank.

> And the story was quite harshly criticized by both sides. And most of what people had to say I dismiss entirely; it has nothing to do with the story, it's just their own, what they're bringing to it. But there're just two small things that I feel if I had done it would have undercut a lot of the criticism and it would have been better for me.

At the time of my writing this book, Rudoren's story from Beit Ommar is still available on the website of the *New York Times*,[14] so you may wish to look at it, and see if you can identify the 'two small things' which caused the criticism which followed. Many general readers might not notice those two things; others might not see them as oversights, omissions, or errors. However, anyone with an interest – in any sense of the word – in the conflict might do. On this occasion, plenty apparently did. 'The first is – the story was 700 words – I didn't actually use the word "occupation" anywhere,' Rudoren explains. 'I totally consider the place occupied, I totally get that occupation is what this whole thing is about for these kids. I think I was describing this experience of being occupied but I don't think I used this term.' The version of the story which appears on the *New York Times* website does not include the word 'occupation' in either Rudoren's copy, or in quoted direct speech. However, the story does quote one of the boys featured in the article, ten-year-old Abdullah, as follows: ' "I feel happy when I throw stones on the soldiers," he said. "They occupy us." ' Still, the omission of the word 'occupation' itself is something which Rudoren feels gave her critics 'ammunition' – and, 'seems like it's some sort of conspiracy, like some sort of on purpose thing, to not use this word and it wasn't. And I wish that I'd thought to make sure I used it.'

The second aspect of her article which was criticized was failing to name two victims of a car crash apparently caused by stone-throwing two years before. 'One of the things I think I knew Israelis would question was to make sure that I was clear that sometimes stones kill people,' Rudoren says. 'So I put in examples of where stones had killed this father and baby right near this village I was focusing on.' Rudoren's reason was simple, 'It seemed to me that for an international audience the names wouldn't be that meaningful.' Still, she feels, 'It was not super well thought out. And a ton of people criticized that, like "you're not giving them agency." ' In many respects, Rudoren's decision not to name the father and child who died in the car crash would seem reasonable to most journalists writing, as she was, for 'an international audience'. The audience of a local newspaper or radio station might have known the people killed. Then, surely, they should have been named – but that was not the case here. Editorial convention would suggest the case for Rudoren's decision was only strengthened by the fact that the incident had happened two years earlier – it was not new, so it was not news. Not true, it seems, in the case of the Israeli-Palestinian conflict: leave out their names, the accusation seems to be, and you lessen the importance of their fate. It is perhaps surprising, given the anger provoked by the absence of the word 'occupation', that Rudoren's article was not criticized more for the fact that it nowhere states that the 'Jewish settlements' to which it refers are illegal under international law. Israel, along with its strongest allies around the world, especially in the United States, does not accept this – yet it seems difficult to dispute that the settlements are not built on land occupied in war, as prohibited by the Geneva Conventions. Nevertheless, it could be argued that, as will be discussed in greater detail in Chapter 7, contemporary journalism does actually have a means of addressing this point. In the comments which appear at the end of Rudoren's piece, one of those criticizing the absence of the word 'occupation' also points out that the piece does not 'even (note) that the settlements are illegal'.

Given the deep-rooted religious element to the conflict, descriptions of religious sites are especially sensitive: nowhere more so than in the city both Israelis and Palestinians see as the capital (even if they see it as their own capital, and not that of the others). 'You will be familiar with the whole Jerusalem situation,' says Macintyre. 'We were fairly scrupulous, in saying "the Temple Mount, as Jews know it, Haram al Sharif as Palestinians know it."' This corner of the linguistic battlefield is fought over with particular ferocity. It is here that faith meets history meets ideas of nation. Balmer also identifies the challenge, and the pragmatic, even formulaic, approach that the requirement to follow the narrow path through the swamp can bring. He describes the attitude as 'Well, we've got that onto the wire before' – so there's no reason to make more work by changing it:

> We've got our wording for Al-Aqsa, we've got our wording for the Holy Sepulchre, we've got our wording for Nakba Day, and we're going to stick to it because it's taken years to get something that basically all sides can accept.

He concludes, 'The trouble is with this story that it you put the layer of context which some people seem to demand, you basically go back 2000 years all the time.' Here again, reporters encounter requirements, particular to this story, which would not be such pressing issues elsewhere – even in conflicts where far more people are being killed. As Morris, reflecting some of the points raised in Chapter 3 about the intense attention paid to the coverage of this story, puts it:

> If you're covering the Congo – and there wasn't enough coverage of the Congo – if you write a piece saying, bloodthirsty, drink-crazed gunmen allied to so-and-so yesterday slaughtered twenty innocent civilians, nobody is going to complain. And if they do, your editors

are not going to give a toss. Because it's a long way away, all the people seem to be equally disagreeable.

The Israeli-Palestinian conflict is another matter, he makes clear. 'But if the Israeli foreign ministry ring up your editor in London, it becomes a big case, at the very best you have to justify to your editor that your choice of words was appropriate.' Danny Gold, a correspondent for *Vice News* who, among other Middle Eastern stories, covers the Israeli-Palestinian conflict, says of an assignment to Israel and the Palestinian territories in the summer of 2014, 'I've never gotten as much hate mail in my entire career combined in those three weeks and the weeks following. The level of vitriol was like nothing I've ever experienced before.'[15] Almost a quarter of a century after his first assignment to Jerusalem, Bowen concludes simply, 'You have to grow a bit of a thick skin as a journalist in the Middle East, because people are always going to complain.'

Rudoren's story of the stone-throwers in the West Bank village, and the criticism it provoked, is interesting because it is a case where a story which seemed relatively uncontroversial turned out to be anything but. Aside from the issues of individual words such as 'occupation', there is the wider issue of context. Balmer's experience in his position – Reuters bureau chiefs are both editors and senior correspondents – has led him to conclude that the Israeli-Palestinian conflict requires a level of historical context, 'that other stories do not demand, do not seek'. To explain his point, he draws on an example which combines religion and history:

> It's always a kind of call as an editor where to stop that game. The latest flare-up in Gaza – at what point do you say 'it started there', rather than 'there', rather than 'there', rather than in the time of Napoleon? You've always got to be careful to make that call. If you were silly enough, you could go back all the time to the First Temple, the Second Temple, and beyond.

McGreal also suggests that, for some, to give full context to this story would be to go back millennia, rather than months.

> Context is always difficult. I think it was particularly difficult in reporting this story, because there are people who want to take context back two or three thousand years, and even if you're dealing with Hebron they want to take it back to 1929[16] and every story can become a history lesson. And there's probably not room for

that. And even if you say it once, there's not room for that in every story.

John Pilger agrees on the importance of context, but argues against adherence to what he calls 'a fake objectivity':

> Context is vital. My favourite Orwell quote is, 'Who controls the past controls the future. Who controls the present controls the past.'[17] Palestine is so often misrepresented in the media because it's reported according to the 'rules' of a fake objectivity, not according to the facts and to the rule of law and morality: right and wrong. It's as if the very notion of 'justice' is forbidden. What matters is portraying two grossly unequal sides as equal and calling it 'balance'.

Bowen concedes that, 'BBC impartiality is not perfect. Nothing is.' However, he argues that journalists who become 'polemicists' are no longer journalists:

> Once people think – and I know people think I'm biased in various ways because they write to me and tell me, or tweet it – but once you're seen as a polemicist or propagandist then you cease to be a journalist. You're a polemicist or propagandist.

One of the many challenges which journalists face is that for certain, often vocal and active, sections of their audience, every story should 'become a history lesson'. Bowen, referring to contact with contributors on both sides of the conflict, says such interactions can amount to a request to 'acknowledge my victimhood. And I think that's what people really want. They want you to do that, and sometimes it's clear who's a victim and sometimes it's not.'

Historical perspectives, and national and religious narratives, are all elements in the sense of victimhood felt by both Israelis and Palestinians. Perhaps in that sense, the Churchills' decision, referred to in Chapter 2, to go back to the Bible in their introduction was a wise one. They, though, were writing a book. Journalists working to hourly, daily, or weekly deadlines simply do not have the luxury of that kind of space. That does not mean that they can avoid the issue. Context is indispensable to understanding in most reporting; especially so in the reporting of international conflicts with which the audience may not be familiar. As the Churchills' decision half a century ago suggests, that is not an easy task. 'But then how far back do you go? 1947? 1948? Biblical times? And it's an 800 word story at the end of the day,' is the way that Rudoren sums up the issue. 'When I'm reading the wires, I'm struck by how much context sometimes they'll give. "Israel seized this territory in 1967" like a whole graph explaining 1967, explaining settlements, I generally use less context than that, maybe it's not enough.' This is the syndrome which Balmer strives to avoid to prevent stories getting 'laden very quickly with very heavy background'. As the bureau chief for a news agency, his task is all the harder – especially where aspects of the conflict such as settlements are concerned. The word 'settlement' itself is inadequate to describe what such a place is. While the *Oxford English Dictionary*[18] does give one meaning of the word as, 'The act of settling as colonists or new-comers,' the act of colonization is not one which many readers might immediately associate with the word: especially not 21st century readers, many of whom might be assumed to see colonization as something exclusively negative. Presumably, with their denial that what they are involved in is illegal, the settlers themselves would not welcome such a description. Today (and the examples of usage which that *OED* entry gives are from the 19th century) 'the act of settling as colonists' seems to belong to an era of imperial expansion, not to the current age. The word 'settlement' does not itself convey this. It cannot convey that what are termed settlements in diplomatic documents and journalistic discourse can be anything from a few temporary buildings on a hilltop; to rows of neat white houses and well-watered, closely-clipped lawns, looking like a new housing development on the edge of a British city; to large satellite towns like Ma'ale Adumim, built on the West Bank outside Jerusalem. The English language version of the Ma'ale Adumim municipality's Facebook page describes it as 'a shining pearl in the State of Israel',[19] even though it lies beyond Israel's internationally recognized borders, and on land captured in the 1967 war. How then can one word capture all these different forms of settlements, never mind include their legal, diplomatic, and historical significance? It cannot. Nevertheless, settlement endures as the established word used in most discussion of the conflict. For McGreal, this was not good enough. 'I argued successfully on the paper that I should use the word colonies, and colonize, to describe settlements, because I felt "settlements" was a cleansed word used by the Israelis,' he recalls. 'I used "settlements" on the whole because people recognize what they are,' he explains further. 'But I would use the words colonies, colonization as well because I felt that that was a word that gave full weight to what was happening.'

'Refugee camp' is another phrase which, in the Israeli-Palestinian context, seems inadequate. For the 'camps' which are home to Palestinian refugees from 1948 have grown in the intervening decades into shanty towns. Canvas is only used as shelter when the dwellings in those shanty towns are themselves destroyed, rendering their inhabitants homeless once again. McGreal arrived in the Middle East from a posting as the *Guardian's* correspondent in South Africa. He arrived during the second intifada, and found himself rushing from Tel Aviv airport to the West Bank town and refugee camp of Jenin, accompanied by Sam Kiley, a fellow journalist whom he had known in Africa.

> I said 'Where's the refugee camp? And he said 'This is the refugee camp.' And I went '*This* is the refugee camp?' And that was the beginning of a wholly different experience, because my experience of refugee camps in Africa was of something completely and utterly different.

Like the word 'settlement', the phrase 'refugee camp' has a meaning of its own in the language of the Israeli-Palestinian conflict: making context all the more important. In a sense the refugee camps of Gaza and the West Bank are refugee camps in name only. Time has given them an appearance of permanence because they are made up of houses, even blocks of flats. Yet to suggest that the camps are permanent would be to deny their Palestinian inhabitants both their history, and that which they hope is their destiny. They may not look like camps – there are no tents – but that is what they are. Legally, their inhabitants remain refugees – even as the numbers of those who actually fled grow smaller with each year. Their descendants are proud to describe themselves as refugees, however young they may be, and despite the fact that they have never seen the place they call home. Correspondents can find themselves struggling to keep up. Macintyre concedes that, prior to his arrival in the region he 'had tended to think that a settlement was a few rather bizarre caravans strung together on a hillside, and a refugee camp was a load of tents. There's so much baggage folded in.'

Reflecting this 'baggage' is one of the great complexities of reporting the Israeli-Palestinian conflict. There are other stories, the details of which audiences may not know well. The background to the war in Ukraine in the summer of 2014 is one example. A journalist seeking to explain the causes of the conflict – whether in a news or feature story, or in a piece specifically dedicated to outlining the origins of the war – would need to refer to recent history. Especially for younger audiences today, that might involve a brief explanation of what the Soviet Union was. It should include the fact that Crimea, while geographically part of Ukraine, was formerly politically part of Russia. Where politicians might argue over what significance such historical factors might have today, there is at least, in this case, a sequence of events which can generally be agreed on. That is not the case with the Israeli-Palestinian conflict. While both sides would agree that 1948 changed the region, there is no agreement on the nature of what took place then: liberation and statehood or occupation and expulsion. Pappe, describing teaching a class at Haifa University which includes 'both Palestinian and Jewish students', summarizes this as follows, 'In this very politically charged country of mine, both groups regard history as just another prism through which to view present rather than past reality.'[20] This is one of the key points affecting all the reporting of the Israeli-Palestinian conflict. For here events in history have not simply shaped the present, they are part of the present. That being so, any attempt at writing what happened today is simultaneously, consciously or not, an attempt at writing history, too. Nor is this journalism as the first draft of history. It is journalism as the latest draft of history, as perceived by those who live every day with its consequences, and recorded by those who have come to hear their stories and retell them. In the Holy Land, you cannot write the news without also writing history. 'I think context is particularly an issue in this story because the history is very important. At the very least the history since 1948,' says Macintyre. 'There are many, many things you can't really properly explain unless you give the reader some sort of guide to the history.' In Gaza and on the West Bank, one of the main issues is that of refugees, and their fate and their future. Your contributors – the refugees themselves, in many cases – will expect you to understand their story, even though your audience may not know it. As Macintyre sees it, 'You can't even discuss refugees, without some reference to why there are refugees, and refugees from what, when?' The correspondent who does not arrive in the region with at least a superficial understanding of at least the last century is taking a risk. In my first week in Gaza, I, like Channel 4's Paul Mason, was reprimanded by an elderly refugee for coming from the country responsible for the Balfour Declaration.[21] To the BBC's credit, one of the questions at my interview for the post of Gaza correspondent had been to explain what Balfour was, and what it meant. But what did it mean? My answer was something about its being the first time a world power agreed to the principle of the creation of a Jewish homeland. Yet it meant so very much more than that. It meant a milestone in Zionist history, along the road to the creation of the modern State of Israel. It meant a warning of what was to come for hundreds of thousands of people living where that 'homeland for the Jewish people' was to come into being: a warning that still sounded terrible decades later, when the catastrophe, Al-Nakba, had come, and, in the minds of those who had lost their homes as a result, still overshadowed their everyday lives. Refugees made homeless by Israeli military operations in Gaza would see the loss of their dwellings not only as part of that particular stage of the conflict. Instead, they saw it as part of a systematic attempt to drive them from the land – the latest in a series of attempts which had begun at the birth of Zionism in the 19th century, and continued with Jewish immigration to Palestine in the first half of the 20th century, and, from 1948 onwards, in war. Each of those landmarks meant something else to Jewish Israelis: stages on their road to statehood. That road began with Balfour – and any mention of the name would mean all those different things to the different people who might see or hear the word.

Everywhere these different narratives of the past serve to divide people in the present. It is difficult for western journalists fully to appreciate this sometimes. Where reporters from the United States will be aware of their country's revolutionary history, and those from the UK will identify with episodes of war and triumph in their own country's past, these are events which are recalled at times of national celebration, or reflection. With the exception of the attacks of 9/11, these events do not dominate daily political and public discourse in the way that the last hundred years can in Israel-Palestine. People living surrounded by conflict, or the threat of it, feel the consequences of their history in a way that those living in the more tranquil west do not. Reporters covering the conflict need to try to reflect that. 'Context is always important,' says Sherwood of international reporting in general,

> but in a situation where you have the competing narratives that are so rigidly adhered to by either side, and so much of what each side is presenting is kind of based in what they perceive as a historical claim, I think it's terribly important.

Yet this brings a challenge: Balmer's concern that stories become 'laden very quickly with very heavy background'. Sherwood takes the overloading metaphor a stage further, 'It's very difficult because when you are writing a news story you cannot include…you cannot capsize a news story with a ton of context.' She concludes, 'You have to be realistic about how much you can include in any piece, whether it's a short news story or a long feature.' She describes, in a longer article, the difficulty of sticking to the point, and the need to keep clear of being 'dragged down the avenues of history'.

There are consequences, though, for those reporters who try to take short cuts to avoid these avenues. The 19th-century Russian poet Alexander Pushkin spoke of 'precision and brevity'[22] as being his guiding principles when he turned his pen to the prose of his short stories. It is an excellent way to approach news writing, too – but one which can be very difficult when dealing with the complexities of news and its historical influences. As Morris says, 'You know what it's like writing a 400, 500 word news story.' However, he continues, 'I think the English language press do better than some of their opposite numbers elsewhere. We've got a tradition of tightly pencilling in a bit of background where relevant.' Other journalistic cultures, he suggests, may leave behind the reader without prior knowledge, 'You read the French press or Spanish press on the issue and unless you know the situation pretty well you're not going to follow what's going on.' This is a criticism which readers will sometimes seize upon – ostensibly to help their less well-informed fellows; in practice, to try to exert pressure on reporters in order to promote their own interpretation of events. Rudoren sees such audience members, though they may be the most vocal, as 'this tiny fraction of our readership, and they're the part of our readership that needs us the least', because, she argues,

> they're all getting 17 newsletters about what's going on here, and with 30 million readers on our website, most of them get no information about the Middle East apart from our website, and they don't care about any of this crap, about what this word means.

Rudoren's core point seems to be this: those who seek to hone in on individual words, or who accuse reporters of wilful omission of context, are a minority – and one which probably feels it needs all it needs to know, and that it knows more than the reporters it seeks to castigate. Nevertheless, this kind of constant electronic bombardment can be both trying and wearing for journalists covering the Israeli-Palestinian conflict. This presumably is precisely the intention of those carrying it out: to magnify mistakes in order to shake reporters' self-belief. Sherwood remembers an occasion when, under time pressure, she did not check the number of settlers on the West Bank, thinking that she knew it, but actually, on that occasion, got it wrong. Then, she says, 'the people who spend their lives scrutinizing stories on Israel-Palestine will seize upon this and use it to discredit you, so you have to be really careful. Facts are sacred.'

Those last words are the second half of one of the most famous lines written by the legendary *Guardian* editor, C.P. Scott, whose own association with the early Zionist movement was referred to in Chapter 3. In a 1921 essay which marked both the centenary of the newspaper, and his own half-century as editor, Scott wrote, 'Comment is free, but facts are sacred.'[23]

Yet among her detractors as the correspondent for the *Guardian*, Sherwood highlights particularly the work of an organization calling itself CiF Watch. The 'CiF' of the title is the 'Comment is Free' section of the *Guardian* website, which itself takes its name from Scott's frequently quoted words. CiF Watch's own website says that it is 'Monitoring anti-semitism, and the assault on Israel's legitimacy, at the Guardian and its blog "Comment is Free" '.[24] Sherwood says CiF Watch, 'would write endlessly about me saying I was a rubbish journalist and I was completely biased.' In order to report the Israeli-Palestinian conflict, she says, 'You have to develop a very thick skin, and not make mistakes.' Of his time working in Jerusalem, McGreal says, 'The pressure came from organised groups outside of Israel,' who 'would have pretty well organised mass emailing campaigns and entirely false claims about what you'd said.' Still, he says, 'Until my last year none of it made a difference.' Although he echoes Sherwood's impression of the pressure's effects, 'It makes you make sure you get the facts right, because they pick up on every little fact you get wrong.' In the last year of his posting, McGreal took on a subject which changed completely what had seemed to be a pretty tolerable state of affairs. 'In February 2006, I wrote two very long articles for G2,[25] the magazine, about whether Israel was an apartheid state. That brought the house down.' McGreal was cut off from all cooperation from the Israeli government, and was subject to the 'longest complaint ever to the Press Complaints Commission (PCC)',[26] from Camera, the 'Committee for Accuracy in Middle East Reporting in America.'[27] Camera describes itself as 'a media-monitoring, research and membership organization devoted to promoting accurate and balanced coverage of Israel and the Middle East.'[28] On this occasion, McGreal says, they sent to the PCC, 'about 38,000 words of complaint, which was absurd.' The words, 'included rather amorphous things like I "denied the historic rights of Jewish people, and I had shown contempt for Zionism." These were very weird complaints, and fortunately it got thrown out in its entirety.' His reporting was exonerated, McGreal was left to conclude of the complaint, 'So that was intended to bully, really.'

As will be discussed in greater detail in Chapter 7, the advent of social media has given such complainants far greater opportunities to 'bully'. The mass emails which McGreal described have been added to with endless contributions to social media: aimed either at altering audiences' perceptions directly, or at placing pressure upon reporters so that they can do so. This has added a new dimension to what is a longstanding and important factor in the way that the Israeli-Palestinian conflict is reported: remember the public relations men's attempts to mislead reporters in the early years of the Jewish State; remember Clare Hollingworth's plain-spoken dismissal of Jewish and Arab sources in the late 1940s. Seven decades later, alongside their armed conflict, and their diplomatic battles, the Israelis and the Palestinians continue to set great store by international opinion. In a conflict which attracts the coverage it does, both the Israelis and the Palestinians are keen to try to influence the way it is reported. Such is the importance to Israel of establishing favourable narratives in the international media that it may even be said that Hebrew has a word for it. 'Hasbara' is usually translated as 'public diplomacy' – although this is not entirely adequate. According to Nitzan Chen, the Head of the Israeli Government Press Office (GPO), 'There is no English word. It's either public diplomacy or information, some would even say indoctrination.'[29] Israeli embassies around the world play their role in this 'public diplomacy or information, some would even say indoctrination' in the same way that any embassies would seek to promote the interests and image of its country. They are assisted by well-funded lobby groups such as AIPAC, as noted in Chapter 3, and, in the UK, by the Britain Israel Communications & Research Centre, or BICOM – an outfit which is 'dedicated to creating a more supportive environment for Israel in Britain'.[30] One of the ways in which BICOM strives to achieve this, according to its website, is by, 'Taking British journalists and opinion formers to Israel and the Palestinian territories to learn about the issues first-hand.' Here BICOM's aims coincide with those of the Israeli GPO. International news coverage of Israel, is, Chen says, 'Very important in terms of the *hasbara*, to explain the Israeli policy all over the world.' Perhaps not surprisingly, Chen's approximate opposite number on the Palestinian side, Xavier Abu Eid, uses exactly the same two words to begin his answer about the importance of international media coverage. 'Very important,' Abu Eid says. 'If there's a reason as to why we haven't achieved our right to self-determination, it's because Israel continues to be treated as a state above the law.'[31] Both responses reflect the great importance which is placed upon international opinion. In an era when even indirect talks between the Israelis and the Palestinians break down, it is well understood that, while Israelis and Palestinians might one day have to implement an agreement, it is inconceivable that they could ever reach one in the absence of outside diplomatic help, from the United States in particular. Outside opinion in the shape of news coverage is therefore seen as 'very important'. As Abu Eid says, 'Our people realize that if there is a battle they can win, it's the battle for public opinion.'

Before considering the approaches of Chen and Abu Eid in more detail, it is worth pointing out that they are not exact counterparts. Because of the fractured nature of Palestinian politics, Abu Eid cannot be said to speak for the whole of the Palestinian Territories. His formal role is that of an advisor to the Negotiations Support Unit of the Palestine Liberation Organization (PLO). In effect, he functions as the international press spokesman for the Palestinian Authority, of which Mahmoud Abbas, who is also Chairman of the PLO, is President. Despite attempts during 2014 – attempts which were interrupted by war in Gaza in the summer of that year – to create a working unity government, the Palestinian Authority (PA) has no real authority in the Gaza Strip, which is controlled by Hamas. The PA does govern the West Bank, as far as Israel's military occupation permits. Gaza, though, is separate. Hamas's relationship with the international media is restricted by the fact that, in recent years, Gaza has only attracted widespread international media attention at times of major Israeli military operations in the territory. At such times, Hamas officials tend to go into hiding because their lives are in danger. When I was the BBC's correspondent in Gaza from 2002 to 2004, I used, as mentioned in Chapter 4, regularly to talk to Hamas leaders. The two whom I interviewed most frequently were killed in the months after I completed my posting. Because of those very different circumstances, the authorities on the West Bank and in Gaza cannot be said to have a single strategy for dealing with the international news media. Abu Eid addresses the issue as diplomatically as he can, saying, 'We are a PLO institution and represent Palestinians all over the world not just here.' He concludes, 'Even though it's difficult, we don't have a problem seeing Gaza as part of us, we will always talk about Gaza.'

The biblical story of David and Goliath is often invoked by those seeking to describe the Israeli-Palestinian conflict. The comparison is often presented, as noted in Chapter 3, in terms of the transition which Israel's international image may have undergone: once the struggling small state surrounded by enemies, now the most efficient army in the region with the world's remaining superpower at its side. The resources available to the two sides in terms of fighting the propaganda war for international opinion – that conflict which both see as 'very important' – seem to show a similar imbalance. In terms of human and other resources, that is. Some public relations officials might actually see the Palestinians' underdog role as their greatest asset. As Abu Eid himself says, this is a war Palestinians believe they can win. On consecutive days in June 2014, shortly before the start of Israel's 'Operation Protective Edge' in Gaza, I visited the offices from which Abu Eid and Chen run their respective operations. The difference is instructive. Echoing observations by some of the journalists interviewed for this book about reporters enjoying western luxury in Jerusalem, the Israeli GPO is located in a new office complex adjacent to the Technology Tower which is home to international news organizations such as the BBC, Reuters, and AFP. I had arranged my meeting with Chen through the official dealing with the North American, UK, and Australian press. The GPO's website – 'because media relations count' is one of the slogans which appears in a slideshow on the main page – lists other officials dealing with the press from different parts of the world. In other words, this is an operation which bears comparison with that of the Media Department of, say, the Foreign Ministry in Moscow: in other words, of a country which is a major player on the international stage. For a country the size of Israel, it is a significant commitment of resources. The press operation of the PLO's Negotiations Support Unit, in contrast, is found on the fifth floor of an office building in Ramallah. Unlike the Jerusalem Technology Tower, this is no landmark. I had some difficulty, after arriving by bus at the central bus station in Ramallah, finding a taxi driver who had any idea where the place was located. Even then, the driver I did find had to stop to ask the way. The landmark was not the office building itself, but a better-known building across the street. Abu Eid is frank about the relative lack of resources.[32] 'The Israelis can offer things we can't,' he says. 'Some reporters get invited for helicopter tours. We don't even have a helicopter for the President!'

Perhaps because of the importance which they place upon international news coverage, neither Chen nor Abu Eid claim to be especially pleased with what they get. This, of course, is probably in part a tactic: suggesting publicly that coverage was all that you hoped for would hardly demonstrate great public relations skill. At one point in our interview, Chen was sharply critical of the more than 300 journalists accredited to his office. Asked what he thought of the coverage of Israel, he replied, 'I don't want to make generalizations because some people are very professional and very unique, see the facts before they write the story. But,' he went on, 'the majority are lazy.' Asked why he said journalists were lazy, Chen explained:

> They are lazy in the sense that they won't wait until they have all the resources, all the material to write a story. They will research 60% of material. Before you wouldn't write a story until you knew 100% of the facts. Now it's more like 70%. They won't wait until the IDF gives them a response, until I give a response.

Despite his rather dim view of the majority of the reporters accredited to his office, Chen denies that he ever tries to put pressure on journalists:

> No. Absolutely not. I was a journalist myself for 25 years. I know that it will never, ever succeed to put pressure. I know that sometimes when people tried to put pressure on me the result was exactly the opposite. It's not worth it.

Critics of the Israeli government would counter that perhaps they don't need to. After all, in McGreal's case the 'bullying' came from organizations not associated with the Israeli government – not formally, at least. As will be discussed in Chapter 7, there have been reports – which Chen denied – that Israel has a contingent of social media activists seeking to promote its views online. Certainly, Israel's attempts to influence opinion in conventional media have been well documented – all the way back to the PR men in the early days of statehood. They continue – aided by carefully chosen phrases based on detailed research – as the *Independent*'s Patrick Cockburn discussed in the context of the conflict in Gaza in the summer of 2014.[33] The Palestinians also have their lobby – Morris describes what he sees as large-scale 'very unquestioning support' in the west for the Palestinian cause – but Abu Eid still points to his people's relative lack of resources, 'We don't have the tools the other side has,' he argues. 'The main tool we have is the moral way of our cause.' He does not seem convinced of that tool's efficacy. When asked whether he is frustrated with foreign journalists' coverage of the conflict, he is unhesitant, 'Certainly. We need years of work still to show them that we are human beings and equals.' Echoing some of the points which reporters themselves made (discussed in Chapter 3) about life in Israel, Abu Eid suggests that international journalists are seduced by the life they can lead:

> Most foreign reporters live in Israeli areas, they don't live here so they end up going to Israeli bars and Israeli cinemas. We can't offer the

same Western style of life that they would like. So they normalise the situation whereby they end up saying, 'It's true they violate human rights, it's true they build settlement – but they cannot be that bad look at the play they have on in the theatre.'

This connection to the west has further implications. During the second intifada, Palestinians would sometimes complain that stories about Gaza and the West Bank were reported in live broadcasts from (Israeli West) Jerusalem. The reason: the international TV companies, including the BBC for which I then worked, had their own studios there from which they could go live at a few minutes' notice. The effect on the audiences, as the Palestinians saw it, was that all stories had to go through Israeli territory, both physically, and editorially. Added to this was the fact that Israeli officials, in the immediate aftermath of any incident of major violence, would sometimes appear at the studios of international news organizations without the prior knowledge of the editorial staff in the bureaux. It may be that on some occasions they had been invited by producers in London who were yet to communicate this to their colleagues in Jerusalem – at least, that was the story which officials sometimes gave. It may also be that they simply turned up because they knew it was an important part of their job to get Israel's point of view across – whether or not, at that point, they had been invited to share that point of view. Again, the Palestinians could not compete. The western TV companies did not have equivalent facilities in the Palestinian territories – with few exceptions, they did not have resident correspondents in the Palestinian territories – and getting a live TV transmission from Gaza or Ramallah took time and money. In this respect, Israel's technical and cultural connection to the west may well have delivered it more favourable coverage. Palestinian officials see that system enduring until today, and, among western media, single out the Associated Press for criticism. 'In the office the vast majority are Jewish Americans or Israelis, some of them serving in the Israeli army,' suggests one Palestinian official. 'Would anyone accept that a Palestinian fighter from Al Aqsa brigades to be a reporter for the AP?' Israel, and its international allies, would no doubt take offence at such a comparison; many Palestinians, and Arabs, would no doubt agree with the official that it is a valid one.

Given Palestinian concern about some AP coverage, it is also appropriate to mention a major controversy between the PA and AP in the aftermath of the 9/11 attacks on the United States. On that day, the AP carried a report datelined 'Nablus, West Bank' and headlined 'Arafat says he is horrified by terror attacks in U.S., but Palestinians celebrate in the streets'.[34] The despatch described about 3,000 people coming onto the streets of Nablus to give out sweets (as the report noted, a traditional celebration) while armed men fired shots into the air. As is often the case with major news agencies, there was a cameraman there to take video footage, too. Those pictures were not distributed, and a stills photographer at the scene heeded warnings not to take pictures either. According to an AP report[35] about what followed, Yasser Arafat's cabinet secretary said that the PA could not 'guarantee the life' of the cameraman if the footage were broadcast. Mindful of their international image at a time when even America's critics were expressing sympathy and condolence for the attacks on the World Trade Center and the Pentagon, Palestinian officials clearly realized that the airing of pictures of celebration would show them in an appalling light. Their response to the problem hardly does them credit, either.

This is an extreme example of the pressures which journalists sometimes come under in covering the conflict. It is perhaps noteworthy that, although the threat was made against a western organization, AP, it was made against a Palestinian freelance on assignment for that organization. Unlike others working for international news organizations, he did not have the option of leaving (as a Palestinian, his movement even on the West Bank was severely restricted). It is not this book's focus, but the conditions for Palestinian journalists are often immeasurably worse – representatives as they are of a people party to the conflict.[36] For international journalists, as this chapter has discussed, the pressure is that of processing information under time pressure, and sometimes in danger: knowing that armies of critics are waiting to rubbish your efforts. Aside from those who have a particular axe to grind, the general audience, it appears, is often left confused. Despite all the efforts which journalists take to provide context in the Israeli-Palestinian conflict, one study of British TV audiences suggests, 'they felt that journalists assumed a level of knowledge or understanding which they did not have'.[37] One member of a focus group quoted in the study's findings said, 'There's no depth to it – television news more or less covers anything superficially.'[38] McGregor-Wood, with his experience especially of working for US TV news, echoes this – concluding of the complexity of the Israeli-Palestinian conflict, 'There are so many historical strata that each inform how people behave today. News reporting is inadequate to the task, particularly television news reporting.' Nor is this a problem confined to broadcast news journalism. Rudoren points out that, where context is concerned, 'It's a struggle because I think you risk losing readers if you go too far back. So you have to pick the meaningful context.'

This is part of the problem. The truth seems to be that journalism alone is inadequate to the task of explaining the Israeli-Palestinian conflict yet, conversely, the best journalists may – as will be argued in Chapter 6 – understand it better than anyone else. Rudoren's concern about losing readers is a widely held one. As a news producer on a commercial TV channel in the UK, I worked for a wise editor who implored us to remember we were writing for 'Mrs Scroggins in Rochdale'. She has countless counterparts, back to William Randolph Hearst's telling his reporters to write for the cable-car driver on the early shift,[39] and probably much earlier. A full understanding of the complexities of the Holy Land requires more than dipping into daily news reporting – but daily news reporting is most people's primary source of information. For that reason, for all its faults real and imagined, it plays the leading role in how people, diplomats included, view the Israeli-Palestinian conflict. Given the restrictions placed upon most of those involved, foreign policy makers included, journalists' perspectives are perhaps the most complete.

6

The Ambassador's Eyes and Ears

They had such certainty, such determination, and such faith that God and history were on their side. Travellers to the Middle East are often struck by the heat, and the starkness of the light. Yet in winter, in the hills of Jerusalem and the West Bank, it is cool, wet, and even sometimes snowy. That day was damp. It was January 2003. Israel was preparing to vote in a general election which would return Ariel Sharon as Prime Minister. I had gone to do a story on settlers on the West Bank. In those days, the months before the presentation of the Roadmap, the United States' efforts to bring peace to the region were a significant, if secondary, theme of the coverage of the Israeli-Palestinian conflict. Everyone between the River Jordan and the Mediterranean seemed strongly to suspect, even to know, that the United States and its allies were going to attack Iraq, and remove Saddam Hussein from power. Then, the future of Iraq and seeking a resolution to the Israeli-Palestinian conflict were seen in British and American diplomatic circles as two parts of a wider approach to the region as a whole. The talk was of whether the road to Jerusalem went through Baghdad,[1] or vice-versa – in other words, would the establishment of liberal democracy in Iraq (spoken of in those days as an achievable policy goal) lead to wider change in the region, which would include a resolution of the Israeli-Palestinian conflict, or should the west first seek to solve that conflict, and thereby demonstrate that it had the interests of everyone in mind, and was not just intent on invading Iraq in order to secure oil supplies? London and Washington, although both committed by then to the invasion of Iraq, were not united in their views of the wider region. As Rosemary Hollis says of the then British Prime Minister, Tony Blair, and his team, they, 'advocated peacemaking on the Arab-Israeli front both as an end in itself and to facilitate addressing the Iraq issue'.[2]

Those high-minded discussions of strategies, none of which was successfully implemented (with the exception of the removal from power of Saddam Hussein), seemed distant that day, though. The future of the settlers would be one of the harder issues to resolve if peace were to be achieved. It was impossible to imagine the Palestinians agreeing to any long-term solution while Israeli settlers remained on the West Bank in such large, and growing, numbers.[3] A report by the United Nations' Office for the Coordination of Humanitarian Affairs (OCHA), published in 2007, also noted that, 'Most of the settlements deeper into the central West Bank are located on hilltops affording them a commanding presence over surrounding Palestinian communities.'[4] Whatever might be discussed in Aqaba or Sharm-el-Sheikh later that year, the people of the settlement I visited that day, Itamar, were clearly not expecting to go anywhere. It might be argued that then, in 2003, the settlers of Gaza might have felt the same way – and they proved to be mistaken. The residents of Itamar though, come winter rain or summer heat, remained there – unmoved by what went on around them. Like the description in the OCHA document, Itamar was on a hilltop, near the West Bank city of Nablus, which the settlers knew as Shechem, the biblical city which they believed was located there. It was wet. The rain fell hard. Four days earlier, it had been so heavy that we had had to abandon filming after an hour. This was a return trip to complete what we had been unable to do then. Two things struck me about the settlement: firstly, the calm, and apparently fearless, determination of the head of the settlement's yeshiva, or religious seminary, as he quietly surveyed the rocks and hills around him, assault rifle slung across his back; secondly, the poor conditions in which the settlers lived. Most of the homes were prefabricated cabins, shabby and providing little protection against the damp cold of winter. This was no Mediterranean dreamland of the kind immigrants might hope to find in Tel Aviv. Even the hated settlements of Gush Katif in Gaza seemed like a seaside paradise in comparison. It could be dangerous, too. In March 2011, a Palestinian stabbed to death five members of the Fogel family, who lived in Itamar.[5] The decision to come to Itamar had evidently been taken on for reasons of faith, not reasons of comfort. This determination can only be understood by those who encounter it in person. Reporters covering international news encounter all sorts of people motivated by all sorts of ideas. The unshakeable faith which inspires some parties to the Israeli-Palestinian conflict seems almost without parallel around the world. While John Pilger sees the conflict as being essentially about 'land, and resources such as water', he also notes the role of religion:

> How important is religion in the Palestine conflict? Of course, it's extremely important. The illegal Israeli colonists – known as 'settlers' – justify their theft of Palestinian land with reference to the Old Testament. I've met many of them and confess I am often at a loss when confronted by such zealotry. That said, the essence of the Palestine issue is land, and resources such as water. Taking land, piece by piece, was the political strategy of the early Zionists who themselves could be secular. On the Palestinian side, religion has clearly played a part in making Hamas into a cohesive governing, social and fighting force – yet here again, land and social justice are the overriding issues.

So for all the miserable weather and other obstacles encountered in travelling to Itamar that day (four days earlier, returning from our largely fruitless filming trip, we had been detained at an Israeli Army checkpoint, and only allowed on our way after our Israeli producer had had a shouting match by phone with a local commander), I was in a privileged position. I was in a privileged position not because of the view which this vantage point offered of the craggy hills of the West Bank in winter, although I did find that impressive. I was in a privileged position because of my metaphorical view of my surroundings, rather than my physical one. Just a couple of days before, I had been in Gaza – seeing rain similar to that which now fell on the rocks on the slopes around, making them shine a little in the dullness of the wet winter day. There, in Gaza, in the flatness of the coastal plain, the water had caused streets to flood, and made more miserable the lives of refugees sheltering under roofs not fit to keep out the rain. In the space of a few days, I had seen both places, both peoples, and heard their differing views. My Israeli government press card, combined with my British passport, had allowed me to make a journey off limits to the vast majority of Israelis and Palestinians. Then, even during the intifada, some Palestinians were allowed to leave Gaza for work. There were still casual day labourers, although their lives were made increasingly miserable by the very time it took to leave the territory, and by never knowing when suddenly the crossing might close. Other Gazans got permission to leave for other reasons, although those who wanted to leave for business, study, or personal reasons were generally forced to do so through

Egypt rather than Israel. Israelis had once travelled relatively freely to Gaza and the West Bank. If they did so during the intifada, it was more often in army uniform and protected by the hard shells of armoured vehicles.

Now the separation seems all but complete. At Qalandiya, the main crossing between Jerusalem and the West Bank, Palestinians who are resident in Jerusalem, or who have permission to travel there, are still able to come and go. The same is not true for Israelis. A huge yellow sign written in Hebrew, Arabic, and English warns that it is illegal for Israelis to cross onto the West Bank (settlers have their own crossing points, and do not come this way). Yet Gazans, now under a state of siege, live in total ignorance of the lives of Israelis living just a short distance from the fence and fortifications which confine the Palestinians of Gaza to their scrubby, stiflingly overcrowded coastal strip. Where once there might have been some form of cooperation – perhaps in the form of car repairs done more cheaply in Palestinian areas (this is now expressly forbidden by the yellow sign of Qalandia) – now there is none. The two peoples are more distant than ever. Their ignorance reinforces their enmity. So while some dissenting voices, such as those cited in Chapter 3, may suggest that journalists come to cover this conflict because it is a 'five star war' – there is another, much more significant aspect to their presence here. Journalists are able to gain a perspective denied to almost everyone else involved: including those diplomats and policy makers whose job it is to seek a solution.

'I'm in a unique position even compared to Palestinian and Israeli colleagues, because I can travel round and speak first-hand to people on the ground,'[6] says Yolande Knell, the BBC correspondent with responsibility for covering the West Bank and Gaza. 'It's a privilege and an illustration of the disadvantage that people are up against here.' Such are the restrictions placed on Palestinians' ability to travel to Israel or to other parts of the Palestinian Territories, that Knell offers the example of a friend on the West Bank telling her, 'It's easier for me to go to Malaysia than visit my uncle in Gaza.' Knell concludes that there is a wider, more worrying, conclusion to be drawn from the fact that she is one of the few people able to move throughout the region with comparative ease. 'As a journalist this is an incredible advantage, but when you relate it back to the context it's quite alarming that I should be one of a handful of people moving around freely.' In other words, she is able to acquire knowledge and experience which, if there is ever to be a peace agreement – might be useful to the Israelis and Palestinians – but which they cannot currently hope to get. This, Knell argues, is particularly true of the people of the Gaza Strip:

> because it's such a young population so many from Gaza have no concept of what Israelis are like because they've never met any first-hand. They've grown up without ever meeting an Israeli. It's completely bizarre. They have no comprehension of what an Israeli might be like, or the diversity of Israeli opinion that might exist.

In the absence of any opportunity to appreciate varying shades of Israeli public opinion, Knell suggests that for the people of Gaza, Israelis are 'just "the Jews" '. Yet while they are clearly able to understand that both Palestinian and Israeli public opinion includes a variety of views, diplomats are no longer in the position they once were to observe shifts in that opinion – at least where Gaza is concerned.

Israel has launched major military operations against the Gaza Strip on three occasions since late 2008, causing thousands of deaths and injuries in the process. In the summer of 2014, during 'Operation Protective Edge', the Israeli Army even sustained casualties on a scale which might not normally be considered politically acceptable. Yet despite the territory's obvious importance, despite what one might imagine to be the pressing importance of taking action to reduce deaths, injuries, and the destruction of property, the European Union's and the United States' labelling of Hamas as a terrorist organization means that they are unable to talk to them. For the United States, the territory has in addition long been a perilous proposition. In October 2003, three people travelling in an American diplomatic convoy were killed when their vehicle was blown up by a roadside bomb. They were reported at the time to have been going to Gaza in order to interview applicants for scholarships to American universities.[7] Following the attack, the United States understandably stopped sending diplomats to Gaza, 'for about a year', remembers the then US Ambassador to Israel, Dan Kurtzer.[8] Subsequently, as Kurtzer remembers, United States diplomats did start going back again – but a combination of the political and security situations which followed means that was relatively short-lived. 'I think for a while we did. But I think we're not for the last three or four years – maybe even since Hamas took over.' Hamas took control of Gaza in 2007, after emerging victorious from an armed conflict with Fatah (the Palestinian movement of which, until his death in 2004, Yasser Arafat had been the leader). That conflict became, in effect, a Gazan civil war. It had been simmering for years. In 2002, a blood feud between prominent supporters of the two factions[9] boiled over into armed conflict before cooler counsel prevailed and the situation calmed down. A major factor in this was the time: the height of the second intifada. The intensity of the conflict with Israel then meant that the fighters of Hamas and Fatah could be persuaded that their interests were better served by making common cause. That changed after Israel dismantled its Gaza settlements in 2004, and Hamas won elections in the territory in 2006. Fatah, with which the majority of Palestinian Authority officials in Gaza identified as supporters, if not actual members, was reluctant to cede power, and the armed conflict followed.

Hamas's victory presented diplomats – especially United States diplomats – with an almighty headache. While Washington had since 1997 considered Hamas a terrorist organization,[10] and the European Union had followed in 2003, this had mattered less while the Palestinian Authority were in control of both the West Bank and Gaza (in control, at least, within the confines of Israel's military occupation of those territories). Now, with an organization with which they were prevented from having any contact – publicly at least – in charge of Gaza, they would struggle even more with their lack of information. It was not always so. Prior to becoming ambassador, Kurtzer had a previous diplomatic posting to Israel, in the 1980s. Gaza was one of the areas he covered. Then, he was able simply to get in a car and go. 'I would take a self drive, wander around, talk to people in coffee shops, on the beach. You learn things that way not in individual meetings.' It is quite impossible to imagine that an American diplomat could do anything of the sort now, or could have done at any time since 2000. Now that such easy access has long been a thing of the past, Kurtzer concludes, 'Our sources were very dry and they became even drier.' Kurtzer's approach may even then have been unusual. As Alan Philps recalls of his early years covering the conflict, 'One of the things I learned very early on was that the policy makers – the American ones – even before 9/11, and the great worry about terrorism, didn't get out much or meet people. They were in a bubble.'

If that was true then, it has only become more so. A combination of security risk and adherence to foreign policy edicts, such as bans on 'talking to terrorists', means that, in the Israeli-Palestinian conflict, diplomats' access to information can be inferior to that enjoyed by journalists. That is not true in every case, of course. Diplomats, especially from the United States, have access to Israeli government officials in a way that reporters can only dream of, even in a country like Israel, which is keen to make officials available to help with *hasbara*. As one longstanding member of the foreign press community in Jerusalem puts it:

> Diplomats have access to stuff I don't. They get information on political insecurity and other issues. So it's not like they're completely unaware. The issue that I have with them is that an awful lot of their information comes from people like me.

One is reminded of Clare Hollingworth's conclusion, in the 1940s, that diplomats 'obtain their information from the press'. To illustrate the point, the correspondent tells the story of the aftermath of the bombing of the US diplomatic convoy in Gaza in 2003 – when he was one of a number of journalists offered a briefing at the US embassy on what had happened.

> I remember once being in a briefing with Dan Kurtzer because there'd been an incident in Gaza, maybe the attack on the American convoy. And I asked him the latest, he told us, then when we asked how we should attribute it he told us he was reading from the Ha'aretz website.

In his interview with the author for this book, Kurtzer confirmed that he was relying on the source this reporter describes. Today, it is impossible to imagine that an American diplomatic convoy would enter Gaza, but, were there an incident in the territory involving a US citizen (aid worker, UN employee, activist, or journalist), then the US diplomats in Tel Aviv, Jerusalem, or anywhere else, would be similarly in the dark. This is not an especially new situation. Tom Fitzalan Howard, who was British military attaché accredited to Israel for three years from 2000, remembers the first intifada as a time of increasing safety restrictions placed upon diplomats by their own governments. As the Palestinian uprising against Israel continued, Fitzalan Howard suggests that only military attachés of a few countries, including Britain (a number of journalists interviewed for this book mentioned Fitzalan Howard's willingness to travel to the Palestinian territories) were permitted to head out to areas which might be considered hazardous. Aside from them he says, 'no one moved. So the only briefings the other embassies got on the military nature [were] from the standard visits or briefings by the IDF, who showed you what they wanted you to see.'[11] Fitzalan Howard, with the support of his diplomatic superiors (as a serving army officer, he was 'paid by the Ministry of Defence' but his 'line manager was the ambassador in Tel Aviv') was encouraged by the then Ambassador, Sir Sherard Cowper-Coles, to be his 'eyes and ears':

> I had the freedom to travel anywhere. It caused the Israelis some angst. They didn't like it, but there was nothing they could do about it. We had a diplomatic vehicle – they could stop it but they couldn't search it. They could delay us for ages, but you've just got to put up with that.

Certainly, I remember from personal experience his willingness to travel to Gaza, especially in the aftermath of the deaths of the two British citizens, Tom Hurndall and James Miller, who were killed by the Israeli Army in the territory during my posting there as BBC correspondent.[12]

The situation for European diplomats, depending on the country, is less stark than it is for representatives of the United States. Some Europeans do travel to Gaza from time to time – but they are not able to talk to the authorities in charge of the territory, not officially at least.

Lord Levy, who was Middle East envoy for Tony Blair during the latter's time as British Prime Minister said in an interview for this book, 'I can assure you that there's been contacts with Hamas on the q.t. (i.e. secretly) from people that feedback to the British Government for years.'[13] Sir Jeremy Greenstock was British Ambassador to the United Nations at the time of the Iraq War. Publication of his memoir, *The Costs of War*, was banned – apparently because of critical revelations about the decision making which led to the invasion of Iraq in 2003. As Martin Bright and Peter Beaumont wrote in the *Observer* at the time, 'The decision to block the book until Greenstock removes substantial passages will be interpreted as an attempt by ministers to avoid further embarrassing disclosures over the conduct of the war and its aftermath from a highly credible source.'[14] A fluent Arabist, Greenstock has, since 2006 and in retirement from the British Foreign Office, had a close interest in the Israeli-Palestinian conflict. This has included contacts with Hamas. He insists that he has, 'known of no requests from either the American or the British or any other European government for people like me and quite a few others who have had contact to carry on any messages or to do any diplomacy.' This leads him to conclude that, 'those contacts have been pretty limited, actually'.[15] He believes that the British have observed the ban on talking to Hamas, because the British government:

> had to be able to deny that truthfully. They pick up all sorts of things from people who do talk to them. So they get information on it. But

there is no direct conversation that would produce a relationship or capacity to negotiate.

Sir Sherard Cowper-Coles, British Ambassador to Tel Aviv from 2001 to 2003, concurs, saying of the suggestion that there might be contacts between the British government and Hamas, 'At the moment? I think it's highly unlikely.'[16] That lack of contact means that journalists' meetings with representatives of Hamas gain a particular value because of their rarity. As Simon McGregor-Wood points out, reflecting on his own reporting trips to Gaza, 'Once you're there as a foreign reporter it's crucial that we speak to everybody.' This is an area in which journalists, because of their access, have an advantage over diplomats. 'It makes our ability to report the comments and ideas of those in Gaza all the more important,' he suggests. 'The political officer at the British consulate in East Jerusalem is going to be interested in those reports because he can't talk to those people himself.' Chris McGreal draws on his own experience as a correspondent to explain what it is that diplomats are missing. 'We all know that as a reporter if you're sitting in your office in Jerusalem it's very much harder, even when you can get everybody on the phone, than it is to be there, and see it with your own eyes, and to have that human interaction,' he says. 'That's the value, you are a witness, you pick up on things, you see things that you wouldn't otherwise see that lead you down paths that you wouldn't otherwise pursue.' In other words, it is not just the information itself which is lost, but the ability to act upon it, to consider in greater detail ideas which come up during the kind of unstructured visits to Gaza which Kurtzer recalls from the 1980s. Harriet Sherwood remembers diplomats asking her about Gaza on her return from the territory. 'Diplomats and politicians don't spend much time talking to ordinary people,' she feels. 'So they were quite hungry for that information, and because I used to talk to Hamas officials and they are banned from doing that, they would say "who've you seen, what are they saying?"' For some journalists, this might present something of a dilemma. I remember being rather cagey about the information I would share with diplomats when I was resident in Gaza. After all, you are there to gather information for your news organization and its audiences, not for one government or another. I decided on a policy of only repeating what was already in the public domain, even if I chose to phrase it differently. Sherwood's conclusion seems to have been similar. She says she shared, 'nothing that I wasn't writing about but,' she adds of the diplomats who talked to her on her return, 'they are interested in speaking to journalists who are spending time in Gaza, for sure'. When asked whether he feels that journalists are sometimes better informed than diplomats, Crispian Balmer makes a similar point, 'In some ways, yes,' he agrees, 'particularly down in Gaza. I often find that diplomats want to know what's being said when I come out of Gaza.' Asked if he feels that journalists have the edge as far as information goes, Greenstock admits, 'Sometimes.' Drawing on his extensive experience of diplomacy, he argues that, 'it's always sensible to have access to potential enemies or difficult groups if those groups have reasons to make relative judgements about where they place themselves in the future'. He explains:

> Governments are unwise totally to restrict themselves to not talking to enemies or terrorists or groups – if those groups have relative judgements to make. I think there's no point talking to absolutist groups like Al Qaeda or ISIS. But Hamas is not like ISIS and Al Qaeda.

While some journalists are dismissive of diplomats' first-hand knowledge of certain aspects of the conflict, diplomats are more, well, diplomatic, about the way their relationship with reporters works. According to Greenstock, journalism and diplomacy are 'two sides of the same coin'. He suggests that, 'In seeking to portray what is going on we're very similar, diplomacy is more proactive in trying to influence events in a country's interest, whereas journalism should be more objective but is often influenced by editorial policy.' While here one might remember Jodi Rudoren's reflection, cited in Chapter 3, on 'Jewish hegemony in the media', it is also interesting to note that correspondents also describe a separation between news coverage and opinion. The *Daily Telegraph*, for example, is known for its conservative political outlook. However, 'The reality of the *Telegraph* is much more complicated than it looks,' Alan Philps recalls of his time on the paper. 'Bunch of lefties really. The ideologically sound stuff tended to be written by a coterie of people who wrote the op-eds, and the foreign desk was left to its own devices.' Greenstock further observes that, in the case of the Israeli-Palestinian conflict, both correspondents and ambassadors find themselves subject to similar pressures. 'The Israelis are very active for instance in trying to influence journalistic sources as well as diplomatic ones. So we both have to respond to that. There's a very strong crossover.' Coincidentally, Kurtzer's choice of phrase to begin to explain the relationship between journalism and diplomacy is exactly the same as that used by Greenstock, 'two sides of the same coin'. He elaborates, 'Both seek to understand what's going on on the ground. Journalism is more about the here and now, diplomacy tries to add value to reporting,' but he adds, 'One doesn't exist without the other. In diplomacy we focus a lot of attention on "open source information", that's not just from journalism, but from diplomatic contacts, speeches and the like. There's a synergy with the two.' Asked if, as the correspondents cited above suggest, journalists are sometimes better informed than diplomats, Kurtzer replies, 'Sure. That's where the synergy comes in. As a diplomat you foster relationships with journalists not just to convey the views of your government, but also to learn what they know that you don't or can't know.' Reflecting on his own career since his retirement from the US diplomatic service in 2005 (he is now Professor of Middle Eastern Policy Studies at Princeton University) he goes on:

> I've seen it from the other side since coming into academia. I've met with people from Hamas and had the paradoxical situation where I've told people from the embassies where I've done it that I'm about to. And they say please don't, because it's against our policies, but if you do please come and tell us what they say. In a sense I'm acting as the journalist.

'Please don't...but if you do please come and tell us.' Kurtzer's view 'from the other side' seems to have confirmed to him what he already knew – there are areas outside diplomats' knowledge which lie within journalists' knowledge. Most of the journalists interviewed for this book seemed also to agree that they had better access than diplomats to certain groups: Hamas in particular. While it is true that diplomats have better access to government officials – Donald Macintyre echoes the view of the correspondent quoted above when he says that, 'It was easier for the Consul General to ring up major players' – that seems to be where their superior information ends. Few current or former Jerusalem correspondents seem to value diplomats as sources. Macintyre, for example, goes on, 'We probably did see more on the ground, and didn't face anything like the security restrictions.' Speaking of US diplomats in particular, he says, 'It always amazed me that American diplomats after the second intifada were still unable to go to the West Bank – they weren't able to go to Gaza at all – and they weren't able to go the West Bank without some kind of security escort.' Balmer draws similar conclusions, feeling that journalists are better informed, 'particularly down in Gaza.

I often find that diplomats want to know what's being said when I come out of Gaza.' While he recognizes that 'Diplomats do have instant access to certain people that we don't have,' he also says 'I think diplomats are in more of a corner than journalists as to where they can and can't go. I think the American diplomats have a difficult time going to the West Bank.' In contrast, journalists, he argues, 'are free spirits, independent observers. And can see and do things at a quicker rate than many diplomats.' Jeremy Bowen suggests that even when diplomats do get out and about:

> They don't sit around and talk to regular people. If they go to a refugee camp it's with security and they meet the mukhtar, they bring them tea, watch a display by the local children and they leave. It's like a royal visit.

For McGreal, the restrictions placed on diplomats for security and policy reasons meant that they:

> were out the loop a lot, I would occasionally find them useful on something specific but I didn't spend much time with them, no. And that included the UN people. I would make the effort, go and chat to them, but were they primary sources? Almost never, unless there was a very narrowly focused, specific story.

Nowadays more likely to be working on a crime novel – his central character is an elderly West Bank schoolteacher turned detective – Matt Rees says of the time when news and features were the focus of his writing:

> I never had a particularly useful relationship with diplomats here. I never cultivated relationships; I'd interview them here and there so I don't think they got much out of me, but they would benefit from building contacts with journalists. I think the other way around, it's only useful for a quote almost.[17]

John Pilger, who, among countless other assignments, has reported on the conflict for more than four decades, is even more dismissive when asked about his relationship with diplomats:

> I try to have no 'relationship' with them. This doesn't mean I keep my distance; I'll listen to what diplomats say, knowing that much of what I'll be told is a line, or outright disinformation. Rare exceptions

aside, whenever I read in a newspaper 'diplomatic sources' or 'intelligence sources', I turn the page. It suggests a journalism that is not journalism at all: more an echo, or a cypher.

At this point, the two-sided coin seems to split down the middle. For while both journalists' and diplomats' objectives may coincide up to a point, they inevitably diverge. Journalists may seek to change things as part of their reporting, but it is the diplomats who must finally formulate the policy, and see it to completion. In order to do this, they need what Greenstock calls the 'relationship or capacity to negotiate'. Journalists and their sources need a relationship which, depending on a number of factors ranging from personality to political conviction, can range from loathing to sycophancy. They do not need a capacity to negotiate anything beyond access to their sources. In a sense, therefore, the diplomats' finding themselves cut off from direct contacts with Hamas seems even more short-sighted – however one might view the organization. No reporter who prized a professional culture of objectivity would consider trying to tell the story of Gaza without referring to Hamas's aims and motives. Yet diplomats in Greenstock's phrase 'seeking to portray what is going on' are asked to do so without even having direct contact with some of the most important protagonists.

The way that diplomatic missions are structured further compounds this sense that the diplomat's view of the Israeli-Palestinian conflict is an incomplete one. Diplomats are accredited either to the Israeli government, or to the Palestinian Authority. The institutions of most of the former are based in Jerusalem, but because (with a few exceptions) Jerusalem is not internationally recognized as Israel's capital, the embassies are in Tel Aviv. Governments, though, also have representations to the Palestinian Authority: Consulates based in East Jerusalem, on the grounds that the Palestinians hope one day to make that the capital of a Palestinian State, or in Ramallah. The result is that there are two diplomatic missions dealing with the two sides in the Israeli-Palestinian conflict. The way that their responsibilities are divided means representatives of the same country end up with different perspectives on the same situation, but neither has an overview. 'It's an absurd way to conduct business,' argues Kurtzer:

> Both in the 80s and my tenure as ambassador the embassy in Tel Aviv I covered Israel and Gaza, and the consul in Jerusalem covered

the West Bank. That was even stranger in some ways – but at least allowed the embassy to have some texture in its understanding of the Arab-Israeli dimension. They were talking to Palestinians under occupation.

However, after Israel withdrew its settlements from Gaza in 2005, the 'disengagement', as it became known, that changed, as Kurtzer explains further:

> Shortly after the disengagement in 2005, Gaza was transferred to the consulate which concluded this split between the embassy and the consulate. And it did exacerbate the problem. In a sense, the embassy reflected what it heard from Israelis, and the consulate what it heard from Palestinians, and left it up to Washington to make sense of that situation. And you never want to leave it to Washington to make sense of anything because they're too busy. That's the point of embassies.

One is left to conclude that the effect of the diplomatic status quo is that diplomacy is at best hampered in, at worst prevented from, performing its key task: providing governments and policy makers with the information they need to take decisions. Not only that: the diplomats' incomplete picture leaves them unsure of what is happening around them. Journalists notice this. As Balmer puts it:

> the big difference is that the diplomats are divided into those who cover Israel – and are based in Tel Aviv – and those who are in East Jerusalem. The journalists here cover both sides and meet people from both, and have a global view. I'm often quite surprised how limited the diplomats' vision is of what's going on in the other camp because they seem to be frightened of stepping on the turf of their colleagues up or down the hill. It causes a tension when trying to release joint statements.

One journalist I spoke to talked of 'a difference between the consulate in Jerusalem and the Embassy in Tel Aviv – maybe a result of geography. So I was much friendlier with the Jerusalem people than the Tel Aviv who, I felt, were quite wary of the media.' Harvey Morris says that the British diplomatic representatives who were in Tel Aviv and East

Jerusalem at the same time as he covered the region, 'talked to each other'. However, he goes on:

> Other countries, as I understood it, had very bad relations between the two. Tel Aviv tended to adopt an Israeli perspective and Jerusalem tended to adopt a Palestinian perspective. So journalists who inevitably endeavour to cover both sides, and also just talked to ordinary people on both sides – in some respects this gave them a better picture than the diplomats had.

Greenstock suggests that there is a difference between the British system, and that of the United States. In contrast to Kurtzer's argument that, 'You never want to leave anything to Washington', Greenstock says that in the British system, 'The unification happens in London, the analysis happens in London, and it's what in the end the foreign secretary or the Prime Minister think with all the advice available to them that unifies policy.' As part of that process, 'the Consul General in Jerusalem and the Ambassador in Israel see each others' reports and will disagree with them where they disagree with them. But they're both reporting in a unified system to London.' He defines the difference between the UK and US approaches as follows, 'The Washington system is competitive, whereas the British system is cooperative.' This seems to have been Lord Levy's impression, too. His role as an envoy meant that he was outside the normal structures of a Foreign Office or State Department so, he says:

> When I did the Israel side I would stay with the ambassador, when I did the Palestinian side I would stay with the Consul General in Jerusalem. I would go on one section of the visit with the ambassador, the other section with the Consul General and because I could be under the radar screen I often got them together to discuss the visit.

Aside from what he describes as the 'freedom – flexibility is a better word' of the role that enabled him to do this, Levy also points out that British diplomatic missions:

> would see all the cables from all our other postings as I did, so true, it's not the same as sitting in a meeting and experiencing the atmosphere, but by seeing the cable one gets a feeling of everything going on.

Cowper-Coles feels that the system worked well, especially in the circumstances where Israeli political and public opinion counts for so much. He remembers of his time as Ambassador:

> We did joint reporting telegrams from the Consulate in Jerusalem and the embassy in Tel Aviv. We constantly exchanged visits. We knew that the reality is if you want a peace settlement you've got to take the Knesset with you. Israel is a democracy for better or worse, you've got to work with Israel. So we did try to be as joined up as we possibly could.

Nevertheless, the way that the information can be treated once it reaches London serves as a reminder of the influence of domestic political opinion. Even after the 'unification happens in London' as Greenstock puts it, a Whitehall source suggests that:

> there's always a difference between the Foreign Office and Number 10, where inevitably the Prime Minister is conscious of the power of Israeli sympathisers in the business community, people who fund both major political parties, the respective Friends of Israel in the house, and that's a consideration that does weigh on the mind of almost every Prime Minister. So they try to be very even handed, just as it weighs on the minds of the editors of publications that have a wide circulation in the United States.

This observation about editors echoes Greenstock's regarding the pressure to which diplomats and journalists are both subject. Fitzalan Howard, perhaps offering further insight into what the Whitehall source calls 'the power of Israeli sympathisers', remembers part of his role as Defence Attaché involving briefing ministers and officials who came out from London. Once their trips were over, Fitzalan Howard recalls, 'All of them at the end of their tour would write a letter back, thanking everybody, saying they understood the position much more clearly, and we waited to see what's going to happen now. And we waited.' Cowper-Coles adds a further note of realistic pragmatism. If Fitzalan Howard reflects now on the lack of political will to address Israeli settlements in particular, Cowper-Coles reflects on the lack of British international political power. Despite having served at the top level of British diplomacy in the Middle East, he has no illusions about the limits of the influence wielded by the country which once ran Mandate Palestine. 'Britain is a very minor player in all of this. The only outside player who really matters is the United States, and there I'm afraid the pressure of domestic politics make it all very difficult.' Asked for his view on whether Tony Blair, in his capacity as Middle East envoy for the Quartet (the United Nations, the United States, the European Union, and Russia), is still well placed for his international role, Lord Levy also makes a similar point:

> the politics are going to come from Washington. And they're going to really hold the cards, as well as both sides. But has he had a role as a conduit, in helping the economics on the Palestinian side? Yes, he has. Ultimately will he be able to achieve anything? No.

Given these verdicts, the view that the division in United States diplomacy may be 'an absurd way to do business' is obviously of greater consequence than if it were the case with another country's diplomatic missions. The Israelis and Palestinians are divided enough without representatives of those governments who have committed themselves to seeking a solution also taking sides. Then there is the question of the extent to which, even when they are frank and full, accounts of the situation in the region can actually influence policy. Diplomatic dispatches from the time of the second intifada, seen in the course of this research, can be pretty blunt. One describes of the Israeli Army's 'heavy-handed approach,' adding that 'the damage to the Palestinian civilian infrastructure has been deliberate and severe – often to serve as punishment.' Israel is accused of 'taking measures that in most societies would not be acceptable in the 21st century'. There is particular criticism of Ariel Sharon. 'Our ideas of balance and fair play are shaped by the assumption that the Israeli government is working for peace and a responsible state actor. Sharon has arguably put us in the wrong on both counts.'

The diplomats' incomplete picture is rendered even more so when one takes into account the lack of access which some have to important protagonists such as West Bank settlers, or members of Hamas. There are, of course, significant areas in which diplomats are better informed than journalists. Firstly, there is the point made above that diplomats have far better access to government officials than do journalists. Secondly, it would be wrong to suggest that all reporters based in Israel – and while there are some, like Knell, based in the Palestinian territories, they are very much the exception – spend vast amounts of time travelling to the tougher parts of Gaza and the West Bank. As Xavier Abu Eid puts it, 'Not all journalists are the same. Some are very committed to Palestine, and others love the glamour of Tel Aviv.' This is an issue on which there is less than total professional solidarity. 'It's the Americans that are the worst at this,' suggested one journalist I spoke to, saying that correspondents of some leading publications, 'very rarely go to Gaza. I think it's wrong.' Diplomatic missions do at least have representatives accredited to the Palestinian territories. If, however, they do not actually travel there frequently, then they cannot expect to be fully informed. It may be that their main task is to understand and to influence political elites: officials, ministers, prime ministers, presidents. How can they do that, though, how can they know the questions to put to those elites if they have not spent at least some time gathering views in the West Bank market place, in the West Bank settlement, or in the coffee shops and on the beach in Gaza, as Kurtzer says he did in the 1980s? A journalist who has visited West Bank settlements like Itamar knows the determination of their inhabitants to stay, whatever the political climate. To a diplomat, the buildings and portable shelters appear as sites on a map, sites which can be moved when the time comes. If you do not see the zealous determination of the people who reside there, there will be a greater part of it you cannot understand. Policy makers' task may be to develop strategies, and that of journalists to dig out details. The former cannot successfully be done without taking some account of the latter – especially in a conflict as complex and complicated as this. On a visit to Hebron, on the West Bank, in 2007 after he had left office as British Prime Minister, Tony Blair reportedly admitted that he had been 'shocked' by the discrimination which Palestinians suffered there. While 'shocked' is the word pulled out of Macintyre's report from that day,[18] it does not appear in a direct quotation in the piece. Nevertheless, it is instructive that the same headline is still available on Tony Blair's own website,[19] seven years after the event. Mr Blair's critics would argue that he has hardly acted upon this shock during his years as a Middle East peace envoy; even his supporters might wonder if things might have been different had he had such an understanding of West Bank realities during his time as Prime Minister.

If diplomats may stay away from the details, the daily life, of a war zone, then there is one area in which they do have superior knowledge to that of journalists: the sphere of their own activity. Here too, because of the nature of Israeli politicians' relationship with the news media, the Israeli-Palestinian conflict is rare, if not unique. As a correspondent based in Gaza, I would naturally read as much of the Israeli press as possible: the two main English language publications *Ha'aretz* and the *Jerusalem Post* (this was before the days of the online 'Times of

Israel'), and 'Israel News Today': a digest of the Hebrew language press. All had one common factor which was new to me: the detailed, apparently verbatim, leaks of top-level meetings. These could be either the weekly Israeli cabinet meeting, which took place on Sunday, the first day of the Israeli working week, or meetings between Israeli officials and high-level visitors. Kurtzer describes this as 'the norm' in Israeli political life, recalling a conversation he once had with Ariel Sharon, who was Israel's Prime Minister during Kurtzer's posting as US Ambassador:

> He told me once that he decided to call a break midway through Sunday cabinet meetings, so as to allow people to go out and do their leaking in an organised way rather than walking in and out of the meeting. He was only half joking. That's Israeli politics.

Obviously aware of the porous political culture in which he was to work, Kurtzer says he tried to make his position clear from the start.

> I told Sharon as soon as I arrived that if he ever saw anything that looked like it was leaked from me he should know that it wasn't true; that I would talk to the press about American policy and provide an American viewpoint.

Kurtzer says, before adding of Sharon, 'He smiled like he didn't believe me.' This unusual aspect of the relationship between journalism and diplomacy came to affect Kurtzer's approach to his work.

> It would affect how you would say something. You would be thinking about how it would look when leaked. What you couldn't control is how it would look if it leaked incorrectly, which often happened. Then you just had to do damage control.

Kurtzer says of his time in Israel that the prime minister's office was not the one which leaked the most. However, he describes another minister from the time as 'a serial leaker, it became a problem with some of our discussions'.

Cowper-Coles knows the difficulty well. In preparation for a meeting in 2002 at which he says he had been instructed by the then Foreign Secretary, Jack Straw, to protest against conditions in the occupied territories, Cowper-Coles went, with Fitzalan Howard, to look at the situation on the West Bank.

What I saw was pretty shocking. I remember a checkpoint in the North of the West Bank where the Israeli army was deliberately making the Palestinians walk through some muddy fields, get off the road into a field of mud. And I remember going to checkpoints where the Israeli soldiers spoke, not Arabic, not English, not Hebrew, all of which I spoke, but Russian.

In other words, a language of which very few Palestinians, especially those travelling on foot in rural areas, might have been expected to understand even the basics – although during my time in Gaza, I did encounter some Palestinians who spoke Russian, in consequence of having received university scholarships to the Soviet Union. I also encountered Russian-speaking soldiers in the Israeli Army, keener to talk to each other in that language, than in the language of command. Permitting them to order Palestinians about in a language which Palestinians did not understand seems calculated to confuse and humiliate. That certainly seems to have been the effect in this case. Armed with the information and impressions he had gathered on his trip, Cowper-Coles recalls that he then:

> said to the Israelis in a private meeting in the ministry of Defence in Tel Aviv with the administrator of the territories. I said 'You're in danger of turning the occupied territories into the largest detention camp in the world if this carries on.'

Cowper-Coles insists that his remarks were motivated by his being as 'a friend of Israel' and 'someone who spoke Hebrew'. Still, he later discovered, 'the Israeli Foreign Ministry had a note taker there. And I think they thought this would embarrass me.' The remarks were leaked to the Israeli press, and from there reported around the world. A major scandal blew up, with the Simon Wiesenthal Centre, an organization famous for its work to track down Nazi war criminals, even suggesting that Cowper-Coles had used the phrase 'concentration camp' – he had not – and demanding his recall. McGreal's report from the time[20] quoted British officials as saying that 'on instruction from London the ambassador had conveyed concerns' about the conditions imposed upon Palestinians, and about the conduct of some Israeli soldiers. In the pre-Wikileaks era at least, diplomats could generally rely upon these kinds of remarks to remain private: unless, apparently, they were made in Israel. As will be discussed in Chapter 7, the increasing importance of social media as a means of newsgathering and distribution has changed the rules everywhere, not just in Israel, as have the possibilities offered by the internet and mobile technology. While there have probably been leakers as long as there have been diplomats, they have never had the ability to leak material as Julian Assange and his associates did until the age when massive amounts of information could be copied onto small, portable media, and made available online to an audience around the world. Much diplomatic activity has traditionally been conducted away from the media, with journalists only fed information (and frequently misled) as part of a process of news management, or kept in the dark entirely. The initial stages of the Oslo process were an example of this. Kurtzer's experience of the advantages or otherwise of holding talks away from the news media has led him to conclude that there are 'two extremes'. Speaking in the summer of 2014, weeks after the latest round of peace negotiations between Israel and the Palestinians had foundered, despite the best efforts of the United States Secretary of State, John Kerry, Kurtzer elaborated:

> One, John Kerry tried to follow these past 9 or 10 months, was to provide nothing to the media and expect the two parties to provide nothing. It led to serious speculation which was mostly wrong and contributed to development of public opinion which was not supportive of the process.
>
> The other extreme is to do a Woodrow Wilson, open covenant, which also doesn't work. Diplomats need a certain amount of privacy to think out loud and convey ideas. The right mix would be talks kept relatively private whereby the parties are open on background or to be quoted by name to prepare the public for what will emerge from the negotiations themselves.

Greenstock suggests that, 'in today's world even in non-democratic countries you've got to bring public support with you because if you lose that you lose the power of your legitimate position'. He also refers to Kerry when he argues for a degree of confidentiality in negotiations:

> In my mind there are proper reasons for keeping diplomacy confidential. The fact that it's going on might be public with Kerry, but the detailed stages you're going through need to be protected in certain circumstances, because revealing them would affect the responses of one side or the other.

Cowper-Coles draws on his later experience in Kabul when he says, 'you do need a sustained private engagement, and one of the things that most upset me as ambassador in Afghanistan was America's unwillingness to engage seriously in private discussions'. He supports this contention by pointing out that, where there has been success in negotiations between Israel and the Palestinians – such as at Camp David, or in the Oslo process – it has happened away from the media spotlight. Such breakthroughs 'have been made when people are put together and kept together for sustained periods with the media not present. The media may be at the perimeter fence, but they're not inside the room.' Kurtzer's second 'extreme' is, he says, 'to do a Woodrow Wilson, open covenant, which also doesn't work.' Here – not surprisingly given their shared backgrounds in the establishment of global diplomacy – he seems largely to agree with the views of Greenstock and Cowper-Coles.

> Diplomats need a certain amount of privacy to think out loud and convey ideas. The right mix would be talks kept relatively private whereby the parties are open on background or to be quoted by name to prepare the public for what will emerge from the negotiations themselves.

Desirable though that may be, there is a question to what extent it is possible today. While Israel's may have been exceptionally leaky as political cultures go, social media and digital technology which enables the access to, and distribution of, large caches of confidential documents, have changed many aspects of journalism, diplomacy, and the relationship between the two. What has remained constant is the sense that while, as discussed in Chapter 3, this is the ultimate story for journalists, it is also the ultimate challenge for diplomacy. Kurtzer says, 'Every serious Secretary of State during my time as a diplomat – during my time, and after – has come to that conclusion.' He observes:

> They all start out saying, 'I don't want to touch this thing, I'm going to get burned,' then they end up being where James Baker was at the end of his tenure where he joked around with us that 'when I come back in my next life I want to be an Arab-Israeli specialist.' There is a sense that this is the Rubik's cube that remains to be solved and that's the allure to a Secretary of State: the 'I can do this' when my predecessors did not.

Any attempt to solve this greatest of diplomatic puzzles will require diplomats to consider carefully their relationship with the media: this is likely to be a mixture of openness and cooperation, spin and secrecy. Selecting the proportions and quantities in which these elements can best be combined has become all the more complicated in an age where neither journalism nor diplomacy has the control which once they did over what is made public.

7
Social Media: A Real Battleground

They had been missing for ten days, and, it would later be suggested, had already been dead for some time – although their deaths were not officially confirmed until more than a week later. Those first deaths would be followed by over 2,000 more that summer, most of them Palestinian civilians in Gaza. It was Sunday evening, 22 June 2014. I had just landed at Tel Aviv airport, and was on my way by car to Jerusalem. I was heading for a hotel on the eastern side of the city, so the driver took a route through the rocky hills of the West Bank, especially dry then in the cloudless days of midsummer. At the time, the international news agenda was dominated by the growing conflict in Ukraine. Editors' eyes were turned away from the West Bank, yet it was there that the charges were being laid for the next explosion of bloodshed in the Israeli-Palestinian conflict. At that stage, the story was this: three Israeli teenagers – Naftali Frenkel and Gilad Shaer, who were both aged 16, and Eyal Yifrach, who was 19 – had disappeared while hitch-hiking home from a yeshiva, or place of religious study, in a West Bank settlement. They had not been heard of since. Naturally, fears were growing for their safety. It was possible that they had been kidnapped for ransom, as a soldier might have been. It was more likely, even at that stage, that they had been killed. The next day, in fact, the website Mondoweiss, drawing on Hebrew language comments on social media, reported 'speculation that Israeli authorities believe one or more of the boys is dead – speculation that has appeared in print'.[1] It was though, at that stage, only speculation – and while the teenagers remained officially missing, rather than dead, a massive Israeli Army and police operation was launched on the West Bank. As with any such case in the modern, digitally connected world, a social media campaign was launched to try to raise public awareness. The hashtag on Twitter was #bringbackourboys.

It was an early development in what was to be a long and intense social media battle lasting all summer. I had read about the teenagers' disappearance before leaving London, and now I spoke of it with the driver who was taking me to Jerusalem. Israel had blamed Hamas for the abductions,[2] and in, in a telephone call with Mahmoud Abbas, the Israeli Prime Minister Benjamin Netanyahu also 'warned Mr. Abbas over the Palestinian president's recent reconciliation accord with Hamas, which Israel's government has called unacceptable'.[3] It was this element of the story which seemed to exercise my interlocutor. For he saw the whole episode as an attempt to undermine what was potentially a significant development for Palestinian unity. A couple of weeks earlier, after seven years of division following Hamas's 2006 election victory in Gaza, and what was in effect the civil war between it and Fatah which followed, Abbas had sworn in a unity government. The new government did not contain any Hamas members, but it did have Hamas support. Palestinians I spoke to in East Jerusalem and on the West Bank in the days which followed were deeply sceptical of Israeli claims that Hamas had abducted the missing Israelis. To have done so was to have given Israel a pretext for the kind of security crackdown which was now under way. In any case, ran the argument, if Hamas had actually taken the Israelis, they might well have chosen to announce it as a means of demonstrating their ability to do so. At that stage, no one could be certain what had happened to the teenagers, but the Israeli operation on the West Bank had already led to hundreds of Palestinians being detained. By the time the announcement was made, on 30 June, that the bodies of the three hitch-hikers had been found, Israeli security forces had killed five Palestinians, and detained some 400,[4] in the course of their search. The Palestinians I spoke to that week were filled with a sense of foreboding that the incident was going to end badly. So were the Israelis I met. Yet their interpretation of what had happened seemed largely to follow the Israeli government line that Hamas were to blame. It seemed to unnerve them. This was an Israel in which the violence of the second intifada, if not a distant memory, was at least in the past. Travelling from Jerusalem to the West Bank later in the week, I found the relatively relaxed atmosphere at Qalandia checkpoint a great contrast to that which I had known as a reporter a decade earlier, when tension and confrontation were the norm. Now the abduction of hitch-hikers in the West Bank had brought back a hint of that sense of vulnerability which had disappeared along with the armed guards and metal detectors which used to stand at the entrance to every West Jerusalem restaurant and café during the first years of the new century.

The deaths of the Israeli teenagers, when they were confirmed, also confirmed their compatriots' fears – and drew a violent response. A few days later, a 16-year-old Palestinian boy, Mohammad Abu Khdair, was abducted and killed – apparently burned alive.[5] In the weeks which followed, Israel and the armed Palestinian groups fought in Gaza – a conflict in which more than 2,000 Palestinians, and more than 60 Israeli military personnel[6] (an unusually high number for Israeli Army casualties in Gaza) were killed. Eventually, in September, Israeli forces killed two Palestinians, Marwan Qawasmeh and Amer Abu Aisha, who they said were the killers of the hitch-hikers.[7] By that time, Hamas had conceded that it was responsible for the deaths.[8] The contradictory interpretations of the way the original incident – the disappearance and death of the three Israelis – were mirrored in what followed once the conflict escalated. Israelis and Palestinians – aided in large numbers by their respective advocates and apologists around the world, irrespective of whether those supporters had anything valuable to contribute – fought a parallel media war on Twitter and other social media. Israel's operation, which it named 'Protective Edge', eventually came to a halt at the end of August. The tension did not entirely subside, but burst out in other areas. East Jerusalem saw clashes in October – one flashpoint being the killing of a Palestinian suspected of having shot a 'far right Jewish activist',[9] Yehuda Glick, who had led a campaign for Jews to be allowed to pray at the compound which contains the Al-Aqsa mosque. As during any incident when Palestinians confront Israeli security forces, many Palestinians were detained – some of them teenagers. In response, Palestinian activists took to Twitter to demand their release. Among the hashtags they used was #bringbackourboys.

Since the Arab uprisings of early 2011, social media has played an increasing role in the politics and conflict of the wider Middle East. That has been especially true in the Israeli-Palestinian conflict. Harriet Sherwood, who returned to Gaza to cover the Israeli military operation in the summer of 2014, concluded of her time on that assignment, 'If you want to know what's happening, it's on social media first, before any other news outlet, so it's essential to be monitoring Twitter all the time.'[10] This is how the journalism of the Israeli-Palestinian conflict has evolved: while eyewitness reporting remains of paramount importance, it is no longer sufficient just to be in one place. With social media, and Twitter in particular, you have simultaneously to keep an eye on what is going on elsewhere, too. This was always the case with reporting on armed conflict: correspondents always needed, where possible, to have an idea of what was going on in the wider area around them. They might be missing something important nearby; there might be danger heading their way. Yet traditionally checking on that meant relying on talking to others you might meet by accident or design; making occasional phone calls. Now the reporter has information literally in the palm of his or her hand – glancing down at the screen of their mobile phone even as they wander around a war zone gathering material. There seems to be something exceptional about the Israeli-Palestinian conflict, though. As Jeremy Bowen recalls of the start of large-scale hostilities in Gaza in the summer of 2014, 'As soon as the Gaza War started, I stick out a tweet and I've got about 500 retweets straight away. There seems to be that extra resonance. The story can go from nothing to a lead like that.' While noting that the need to tweet adds to a correspondent's already long list of commitments on a big story, he also sees it as a bonus, 'Sometimes with TV there's not enough time to get everything in, so I use Twitter to try and get in some of these softer sides of life. I think it's value added.' Social media had been a part of the Israeli-Palestinian conflict since it came into being. Following 'Operation Cast Lead' – an Israeli military campaign in Gaza in late 2008 and early 2009 – there were reports that both the Israeli Army and Hamas's military wing had warned those in their ranks against using social media for what doing so might give away to the enemy.[11] This was different. Sherwood found Twitter 'essential' this time because of the wide range of sources it offered to add to what she was seeing and hearing around her. 'And a lot of that isn't from journalists but people in Gaza who are tweeting what's happening in real time. It's incredibly useful.' Crispian Balmer echoes this, pointing out the rapidity with which Twitter has made itself an indispensable part of newsgathering and distribution. 'When I came here 4 years ago I was aware of Twitter, but it wasn't any more than that. Now I can't conceive of a world without it.' For agencies, this has not been an entirely welcome development. Balmer says of the new reality, in which the Israeli and other official sources are 'tweeting aggressively':

> In a way they risk undermining our business model of speed, accuracy, receiving and disseminating information. Now they can put out the news directly. I think people still do look and wait for Reuters, AP, BBC flash. I think it makes it more important for us to put context in the stories.

To illustrate his point, he gives the example of the Israeli Army commemorating the anniversary of the 1967 war by tweeting news from their archives. One such tweet was a report of Israeli warplanes bombing Damascus. But this came at a time, in the summer of 2013, when there was growing speculation that western air forces might be preparing to attack targets in Syria as a means of influencing the outcome of the civil war there. As a result, Balmer says, 'some not very bright energy traders moved markets on it, based on the tweet, at a moment where fears of an attack on Assad were heightened'. There was a comical side to this, as it appeared from Balmer's experience when he drew to the Israeli Army's attention what had happened, but also a potentially serious side, too:

> I called the IDF to get comment, and got laughter. Then I realized that it was actually quite serious – that they are playing with economic and financial forces that they are not necessarily aware of. It said '67' on it, but if you're not reading the signs as the markets can do, they just latch on to a few words and go.

It was not the only misjudgement which the Israeli Army has made on social media in recent years – illustrating the hazards lurking in the new media world for all its users, even those, like the Israeli Army, who have arguably taken the national idea of *hasbara* and employed it as a weapon in information war. It was as part of this strategy that the Israeli Army decided, in October 2013, to have a day during which Twitter users could put questions to them using the hashtag #askIDF. Here too, it turned out that they were playing with forces they were 'not necessarily aware of'. They had not learned from the experience of other organizations which tried something similar, with less than the desired results (the story is told in British public relations circles of an upmarket shop which invited Twitter users to share the reasons why they liked that particular retailer – one response apparently suggested it was because there were no poor people there). Perhaps predictably, many of the responses were critical, or mocking – frequently referring to child and other civilian casualties of Israeli Army operations. The New York-based Palestinian poet and activist Remi Kanazi satirized the whole venture when he tweeted, 'Is it demoralizing when multi-million dollar Israeli PR initiatives are thwarted by Palestine solidarity activists working for free? #askIDF.'[12] Unsuccessful though this may have been, the Israeli Army, like all organizations seeking to influence news coverage of their activities, knew that it had to continue. In a time when the Reuters bureau chief cannot conceive of a world without Twitter, all PR-conscious governments, armies, and companies have to have a Twitter presence. The Israeli Army even has a 'Commander of the IDF social media activities' in the shape of Lieutenant Colonel Peter Lerner, their spokesman for the international news media. The earlier description is taken from his Twitter profile, @LTCPeterLerner – a capacity in which he was busier than ever during the Israeli military operation in Gaza 'Protective Edge' in the summer of 2014.

Even before that campaign was launched, and during the #bringbackourboys Twitter campaign referred to above, it was clear that social media, Twitter in particular, was altering forever the way that political communication worked in the Israeli-Palestinian conflict. 'It's an important change,' said Xavier Abu Eid. He went on, however, to describe the limits of social media's influence. They might cover issues or events the mainstream media would not; they would still benefit from being picked up by mainstream news organizations:

> Social media has a very important effect in terms of being able to show reality even though a paper may not write about it. However they need the paper to write about it. A tweet is not going to change the world.

It has changed journalism, though. As one long-standing member of the international press corps puts it, 'It revolutionized everything.' For better, in the case of availability of information, for worse in the sense that it shortened even further the time to consider the kind of complex issues which characterize the reporting of the Israeli-Palestinian conflict – a time which was already compressed by the advent a couple of decades earlier of 24 hour television news. When even Reuters sees social media as a threat to their business, those who seek to influence public and diplomatic opinion know they need to be there. Since the creation of the state, Israel and its supporters have always had an extensive and efficient public relations network – remember the complaint from the Information Department of the Jewish Agency for Palestine about Clare Hollingworth's 1948 coverage. In the social media age, they have proved just as efficient at exploiting those platforms, or at least trying to – the #askIDF day being an example of where things did not work as well as was planned. In terms of more successful use of social media, certainly where monitoring and refuting negative opinion is concerned, media reports[13] – as well as the sheer scale of the number of tweets and posts – suggest the involvement of the Israeli government. The Head of the Israeli Government Press Office (GPO), Nitzan Chen, admits that there is an effort to organize social media contributions, but that this is, he says:

For big events only. We only have two or three people that look after it on a regular basis, but it's not our main issue. The Prime Minister has his own new media staff but again just to respond and show what he wants to say. The government doesn't hire anyone to fight on social media.

An apparently well-sourced story published on the website of the *Jerusalem Post* some months before my conversation with Chen suggested that the scheme was much more extensive and ambitious than Chen described, and also stated, 'The plans have received the direct approval of Prime Minister Binyamin Netanyahu.'[14] Any army that appoints a 'Commander' of 'social media activities' obviously treats its communications policy extremely seriously, and obviously considers social media a very important part of that communications policy. Perhaps the fundamental question, especially in the light of the negative part of the #askIDF experience – something which even the slickest spin doctor would probably have found it impossible to avoid – is this: what are the possibilities and limits for social media to influence the reporting of contemporary armed conflict? Does the very democratic, participatory nature of Twitter and Facebook mean that any statement can always be countered, that any message will inevitably be diluted? If so, why should governments and armies bother with Twitter? Won't their tweets always end up as opportunities for their critics and enemies to abuse them? To consider this in the context of the Israeli-Palestinian conflict in general, and in the context of 'Operation Protective Edge' in particular, it seems useful to look at some tweets, and the responses to them, in detail.

At 1.30 pm on 27 July 2014, with the campaign in Gaza coming towards the end of its third week, the Israeli Army's main Twitter account, @IDFspokesperson, put out a tweet which said 'The simple truth. Retweet.'[15] Below the 'simple truth' caption was a graphic, divided into two parts. The left showed a building, apparently a civilian house, apparently in Gaza, with an armed man in silhouette at an upstairs window, and with rockets launching from the roof. The house was shown in section, and below ground there was a cellar containing a cache of shells and rockets. On the right, there was a plain black background with white shapes apparently representing the fractured masonry of a ruined house. At the top of the graphic, a caption, crossing the line which divided the 'before and after' pictures, read, 'Why did this turn into this?' At the bottom of the graphic, a further caption said, 'Because Hamas uses civilian homes for military purposes.' 'The simple truth':

Chapter 5 demonstrated that there really is no such thing in any discussion of the Israeli-Palestinian conflict – but obviously the purpose of an army's Twitter feed is to convince, not to discuss. The response in this case was predictable. While the tweet was retweeted 1,485 times,[16] presumably by people who agreed with it, most of the responses were not supportive. They ranged from the simple and direct 'shut the fuck up' (@mcsole); to a reference to civilian deaths which the Israeli military had caused, 'Ah yes, the idiocy of @IDFspokesperson strikes again. Making cartoons with menacing little men to justify evaporating children on beaches?' (@Mario_Greenly); to an attempt to turn the cartoon's message back on itself, 'I think you guys forgot to include women & children on bottom floor' (@Pol_Sec_Analyst). Perhaps most interestingly from the point of view of considering the coverage of this stage of the conflict was this response, 'no they don't and the world's journalists in Gaza have told and shown us your lies' (@corleydavid). The Israeli Army had tried to open a front in the new media war, only to face a suggestion that old media, in the form of 'the world's journalists', had already undermined their message to the point that it was not credible. So why would they embark on it, and risk a repetition of the less than successful #askIDF experience?

There is a distinction to be made here; a distinction which helps to define the need or otherwise for governments, armies, indeed any combatants or their supporters, to use social media in time of conflict. The #askIDF day was launched at a relatively low point – October 2013 – in the conflict. The Israeli Army were not involved in any unusual major military operation. Their forces were continuing to occupy the West Bank, but that had been so for almost half a century. There was nothing of the scale of 'Operation Protective Edge', or even 'Cast Lead'. So this might be termed a 'media war of choice'. The Israeli Army had no need to set itself up for abuse and ridicule, and should have known – perhaps did know – that it would end up doing so. Presumably the person behind the idea would point to the positive responses which resulted from the initiative, such as people asking how they could best offer their support to Israel, and argue that it had all been worth it. On this occasion, though, the Israeli Army could have avoided the attacks by not embarking on a social media war of choice, which was certain to provoke the responses it did. It is beyond belief that the Israeli Army's PR team did not realize this – although perhaps they did not realize the extent to which it is impossible to keep control of the message on social media, whether you are a supermarket, or an army. They might also argue that drawing out certain comments – such as those emphasizing the civilian casualties which result from Israeli Army operations – did give them the opportunity to address and refute those views. The fundamental point, though, is that this was a social media war of choice, and one which the Israeli Army might have been better advised to avoid.

The social media war fought during 'Operation Protective Edge' was different. In terms of modern communication policy in time of conflict, this could be termed a media war of necessity. With correspondents making frequent checks of Twitter even while they were out reporting, the Israeli Army had to have a presence, had to put across their point of view as forcefully as possible, even if one consequence was a torrent of obscenities and more subtle attempts to subvert the message they were seeking to spread. In terms of a media strategy to run in parallel with the military campaign, this seemed sound. An absence from Twitter would surely have been seen almost as an admission that the tweets alleging war crimes, such as the deliberate targeting of civilians, had a point. Just as an army has to accept casualties in conflict, so, in our century, its public relations department has to accept that its message will be abused and ridiculed. A realistic media strategy will accept that abuse, as an army must reluctantly accept that some among its soldiers will be wounded or killed. Yet in terms of a media tactic within that media strategy, it is harder to see the purpose behind the 'Hamas house' graphic. It must be assumed that those who retweeted it to show their support did so largely to Twitter followers who would probably have agreed with it anyway. In tactical terms, did the Israeli Army's social media team really believe that particular graphic would yield a net benefit, deliver a net advantage in the media war, once the mocking and cursing had been taken into account? Yes, the graphic did seek to promote one of the Israeli Army's and Israeli government's core messages: everything realistically possible was being done to minimize the number of Gazan civilians killed during the operation. 'The enemy uses the residents of Gaza as a human shield and inflicts disaster on them. The responsibility for harm to the citizens of Gaza lies on the shoulders of Hamas and Israel regrets every harm to them,'[17] the Israeli Prime Minister, Benjamin Netanyahu, said on 13 July, when the operation had been underway for about a week. The 'Hamas House' graphic was clearly an attempt to make exactly the same point in a different way, on a different platform, for a different audience. Tactically, especially given the responses, it arguably did not work so well. The Israeli Army was content to show what happened to a house once its missiles struck it. This gave its critics an opportunity to mention once again the number of women and children who had been killed during the course of 'Operation Protective Edge'. Leaving aside the tactical effectiveness or otherwise of the 'Hamas House' graphic, the fact remains that this was a social media war of necessity. The Israeli Army, and the Israeli government, simply could not afford to be absent from the global public space where their actions were being so extensively criticized. Their bitterest enemies, on the other hand, were forced to be absent. Two Twitter accounts – @qassamfeed and @Qassam_Arabic – belonging to the Al-Qassam Brigades (the military wing of Hamas) were suspended, and remained so for months afterwards. The lack of any Hamas presence in English is so complete, in fact, that a search of Twitter in November 2014 for 'Hamas' actually brought up the Israeli Army Twitter account as one of the first suggestions under 'people'.[18] If they were considering their social media strategy to the same extent as the Israeli Army obviously was – possibly unlikely given that almost all Hamas officials were in hiding for the duration of Israel's assault on targets in Gaza – they might still not have been too concerned. In addition to the kind of criticism of the Israeli Army's action discussed above, the scale of civilian casualties was constantly communicated by tweets from Gazan medical staff, journalists, and others. Combined with the fact that Hamas's unprecedented ability to launch rockets at targets deep inside Israel (while almost all of them were intercepted by Israel's 'Iron Dome' missile defence system, the danger was seen as great enough for some international airlines to suspend flights into Tel Aviv airport at the height of the conflict[19]), this will presumably have made Hamas feel that they scored media war successes both as defenders of victims (civilian casualties in Gaza), and as a credible military force. Whether Israel's message that they had no choice but to destroy civilian lives and property was a winner is open to debate. The increased range of Hamas's missiles demonstrated that Israel had a point when it said it was facing a real threat, a point which was slightly weakened by the fact that the rockets were not the best, while 'Iron Dome' is state of the art. Israel's claims to be taking every possible measure to avoid civilian casualties, though, are not as easy to accept as the 'Hamas House' graphic would have Twitter users believe. Anyone who has spent any time in Gaza during an Israeli military operation, as I have (although never during anything on the scale of 'Protective Edge') knows that civilians often have nowhere to seek safety. Whereas in many conflict zones, civilians will simply flee once they feel they cannot take any more, heading for other regions, or even other countries, the people of Gaza are trapped like fish in a barrel. If they happen to be someone seen as a terrorist, too bad. The killing in 2002 of the head of Hamas's military wing, Saleh Shehada, is an example. In order to kill Shehada, Israel dropped a 1-tonne bomb on the house where he was staying – also killing more than ten civilians in the process.[20]

During 'Operation Protective Edge' though, there were occasions when the Israeli Army did order civilians to leave areas which they were planning to attack. Many of them, short of options of places which might provide the safety they sought, headed for facilities, such as schools, operated by the United Nations, particularly the United Nations agency for Palestinian refugees, or UNRWA. Yet not all found they were safe even there. On 30 July 2014, as the fighting in Gaza raged, a school in the Jabaliya refugee camp was hit by shellfire. The attack killed at least 16 people. They had gone to the school in the hope that it would not be a target. At the time of writing, November 2014, the source of the shelling remains unclear, although as the UN Secretary General, Ban Ki-moon said at the time, 'All available evidence points to Israeli artillery as the cause.'[21] Ban Ki-moon's verdict on the incident, 'The world stands disgraced,' became a headline as media organizations[22] focused on one of the more terrible incidents of a terrible conflict. As UNRWA spokesman, Chris Gunness found himself fielding countless requests for interviews right throughout 'Operation Protective Edge' – but this particular incident stood out as one where the constraints involved in the diplomatic use of language were severely stretched. 'There are moments,' Gunness says, 'such as when the Israeli Army shelled our schools, where we feel like the conventional UN style guide does not adequately express the profound sense of moral indignation that we wanted to wake the world up to'.[23] He sees Ban Ki-moon's choice of words as an example of such a time – a time when conventional diplomatic talk will not suffice. 'At times like that,' Gunness explains, 'we take a conscious decision to use the language which is outside the purview of the UN style guide. Such as when we talked about "The world stands disgraced".' Gunness also sees the scale of the Israeli Army's operation in Gaza in the summer of 2014 as unprecedented 'certainly since 1967', noting that, 'I think it's fair to say for Gaza that the Secretary General and other senior world figures talked about the disproportionate conduct of hostilities and I think that's another aspect in which one could say it was unprecedented.'

Journalists, and spin doctors and spokespeople to an even greater extent, are often warned not to become a story themselves. Doing so, the conventions of political communication hold, detract from the message or the person which you are seeking to promote. It was in this unprecedented atmosphere of violence and bloodshed in the summer of 2014 that Gunness broke this rule – albeit, as he said later, unwittingly. In the

aftermath of the shelling of the school, and presumably exhausted emo-
tionally and physically from fulfilling a demanding role at a distressing
time, Gunness gave an interview to Al Jazeera. The interview finished,
he burst into tears – not knowing that he was still going out on air. The
video, widely available on the internet,[24] shows him saying quietly 'My
pleasure,' as if acknowledging the presenter's thanks for doing the interview. He then begins to weep. A colleague appears in shot and places
a comforting arm on Gunness's shoulder, before the camera pans away
to his office wall so that Gunness is no longer visible. 'I didn't mean to
do it. The interview was over,' Gunness said three months later. He feels
that part of the reason he did break down is linked to Al Jazeera Arabic's policy of showing 'graphic depictions of suffering' which would
not usually appear even on Al Jazeera English, the channel on which, as
a native English speaker, Gunness more frequently appears, 'So I saw
on the monitor in front of me things that I would never see before
an interview and as the interview started – it was live – I already felt
moved beyond belief at the appalling suffering,' he says. 'I just about
got through the interview,' Gunness explains, although watching the
video later, obviously with the knowledge of what is going to happen,
you can tell that he is upset:

> and then I break down, but the camera, because they brought it to
> my office, kept rolling without telling me. They then sent it back to
> Doha without my consent and it was then broadcast every hour on
> the top of the hour for goodness knows how many times. It wasn't
> actually during an interview.

Given the vitriolic nature of some of the social media discussion of
Israel's military operation in Gaza, it is hardly surprising that, after he
had appeared on television in tears, Gunness received his share of abusive messages on Twitter (a quick internet search will give you a taste if
you are interested). Nevertheless, he talks of strong support from senior
colleagues, and also of, 'emails from everywhere, including on the Israeli
side, saying, "That was one of the most memorable moments of this
conflict, because it was the moment in which the world realised that
the indignation was genuine." I have no regrets whatsoever.' So while
he may apparently have broken one of the golden rules of public relations, Gunness feels that his show of emotion demonstrated a depth of
feeling which was anything but false – whatever his detractors might
claim. The incident may also have been a factor in Gunness's growing presence on social media: Twitter, as noted above, being the key

battleground in the media war which raged alongside the military conflict. 'I think that the Gaza war was a watershed in terms of our use of social media. The number of people following me on Twitter went up by over 30 thousand during the Gaza war,' Gunness said in his interview for this book, 'And many of those are opinion formers, and journalists.' As noted above, this was a media war of necessity – any party to the conflict, United Nations agencies included – had to have a social media presence. Gunness is convinced that this is of particular value because, he argues, 'there's something much more democratic about social media which isn't related to the traditional power structures within the media business'. He echoes reporters' reflections on ownership and how it affects content (remember Rudoren's phrase, 'Jewish hegemony in the media', cited in Chapter 3) to support his point. 'When you're looking at the old media you've got to look at who owns the *New York Times*, where is the *Jerusalem Post* coming from, who owns Al Jazeera. Then you start looking at how big business and power interests are inter-related with the politics around the narratives.' Gunness sees in social media an opportunity to bypass these traditional media power structures. 'The great thing about social media is there is a kind of egalitarianism about it,' he says. 'There's a democratic quality. It's one person, one vote in a very meaningful sense.'

That 'democratic quality' does not mean that some people are not singled out, as Gunness himself discovered in the summer of 2014, during 'Operation Protective Edge'. One of his tweets encouraged reporters to contact a surgeon treating wounded in Shifa Hospital, Gaza City's main medical facility. Israel's Ambassador to the United Nations, Ron Prosor, responded by demanding, in an open letter, that Gunness be suspended. Prosor argued, 'Mr. Gunness has demonstrated an ongoing pattern of anti-Israel bias. He has abused his position to promote incitement against Israel and present a one-sided view of reality.'[25]

The 'one-sided view of reality' is a charge which can be levelled at many parties to this conflict. Social media has facilitated the free expression of opinion; they have also facilitated the free expression of abuse. The internet has provided journalism with many new benefits, as well as challenges. In Sherwood's opinion, for example, the *Guardian* website now compares favourably with a printed newspaper as an outlet for her work.

To me, whether or not something appeared in a newspaper with a decline in circulation in the UK ceased to be relevant. If I wanted to do something and thought it was important, I would do the story and it would be published. So that was great, it was very liberating in that sense.

In other senses, it was less so. While a news organization can, through moderation, retain a degree of control over what appears on its website – 'Most of the articles we don't open to comment on Israel-Palestine, for obvious reasons,' says Sherwood – the same is not true on social media. 'On Twitter, of course, any time I write anything there's a whole torrent of criticism and often abuse,' she continues. 'I tend not to read it because you can get demoralised by it – or futile engagement with people who aren't interested in having a rational debate, they're just interested in scoring points.' As a result, she says, 'I find that to fight through the wall of criticism to find the people who actually do want to have a discussion would take me forever. I think it's a shame. Social media around Israel-Palestine has become a real battleground.'[26]

Most of the correspondents interviewed for this book seemed to agree, with Danny Gold describing 'a ton' of abuse on Twitter. 'Every now and then I get frustrated and engage,' he says, 'and down the road the vitriol comes out.' He does not feel this is the whole picture, just the dominant one. 'But I got a lot of support from both sides too,' he says of his experience of reporting from Gaza during 'Operation Protective Edge' in the summer of 2014. 'It's just drowned out in the sea of vitriol and racism.' Jodi Rudoren sees some aspects of journalism in the internet age – such as being able to stay in touch with the news by mobile phone – as ubiquitous where international reporting is concerned. 'We all really benefit from that, to be free, you take everything with you in your pocket,' she says. 'The flipside of that, of course, is the increasing speed.' That increasing speed has meant instant deadlines where once deadlines only fell daily, at fixed times. As Harvey Morris observes of his lengthy reporting career, 'The key thing that the internet has changed from the perspective of a writer is that you can't get away from the desk.' The result is that heading off in search of depth or detail on a story has become harder. The newsdesk will always want to know where a reporter is. 'The days when a reporter might be able to spend three days in Gaza really finding out what's going on,' he says, 'are gone – because you get down there, a bomb goes off, and they ring you up and just want coverage of the bomb. So that sort of reflective stuff that you could do before is more difficult.' This transformation in the nature of reporting is hardly unique to coverage of the Israeli-Palestinian conflict. Rudoren says that the journalist's experience here is not like elsewhere. 'I think what's different about this place is the

toxicity of social media,' she argues. 'I think that in a lot of places journalists are finding that social media is a tool and they can really engage
with readers and engage with sources and have a productive engagement.' Reporting the Israeli-Palestinian conflict is different. 'That's all
but impossible here, because it just gets hijacked by extremists who just
want to use you as a platform to say their own piece.' Yolande Knell
describes similar experiences, including 'a lot of abuse'. While she says
she has used Twitter a lot while reporting from Egypt, the messages she
has received while covering the Israeli-Palestinian conflict have made
her, 'much more reluctant to use social media, even though the BBC
encourage us to use it more, and presenters follow us on social media,
I tend not to tweet much here'. The experience has led her to draw
a distinction between what happens on social media, and the content
she contributes to more traditional platforms, 'I'll save my words and
strength for my proper, official broadcasting which people have more
of a right to monitor – and complain about if we don't get it right.'
Working as she does in a round-the-clock media world, Knell argues
that, 'When you've finished work you don't want to be woken in the
middle of the night by your phone buzzing with abusive messages.'
In one sense, this is just the continuation of an old trend by new media:
remember Clare Hollingworth's reporting being criticized in the letters
pages of the 1940s. In the early years of this century, the BBC bureau in
Jerusalem would receive abusive fax messages and telephone calls. Email
soon became another way of seeking to influence reporting by abusing
the reporter. When I was based in Gaza, I used regularly to receive unsolicited emails from a BBC listener in North London (I know because he
included his personal address in his messages) criticizing my reporting.
What has changed is the ability of the abuser to interact directly on the
medium, in the case of Twitter, where the reporter is working – and the
sheer number of people who are able to do that at the same time. Abu
Eid seems to have a degree of sympathy for journalists. 'Now there is
a lot of harassment against reporters and against officials on Twitter,'
he says.

> As officials, it's part of our work, but when it comes to reporters, a
> few years ago if you wrote a story you would get some letters, but it
> would not be that two minutes later your Twitter account has 200
> people writing. It's very personal.

There are two other incidents from the reporting of 'Operation Protective Edge' which are worth mentioning for what they say about the way

that social media, and Twitter in particular, have come to play a role in the reporting of the Israeli-Palestinian conflict. Both involve correspondents working for US-based news organizations being reassigned following material they posted on social media. The first concerned the CNN reporter Diana Magnay, who, in a tweet, described as 'scum' Israelis cheering as they watched from a nearby hill missiles hitting targets in Gaza.[27] The second involved the NBC correspondent Ayman Mohyeldin, who was close to one of the most notorious incidents of civilian deaths of the entire Israeli operation: the killing of four boys playing football on the Gaza beachfront.[28] After he had posted details of what he had seen on Twitter, and then broadcast them, Mohyeldin was taken off the story.[29] While there is nothing new in news organizations deciding to redeploy reporters as a consequence of a controversial story, the way in which these two incidents unfolded belonged very much to the 21st-century media world. When a reporter broadcasts live, the only editorial control is to end the broadcast. When a reporter tweets, the only editorial control – aside from guidelines established in advance – is retrospective, or, to put it more plainly: too late.

As new technology has affected newsgathering and distribution, and relations with audiences, it has also affected political communication – particularly the way journalists and diplomats are able to talk to each other. 'There is no longer "off the record"', NATO's former spokesperson, Jamie Shea, told a conference audience in 2013.[30] His observation was a reflection on the ubiquity of devices connected to the internet, and the immediacy with which they can publish material which can then be seen around the world. 'It's changed in so far as there are no off the cuff remarks any more,' says Dan Kurtzer. 'At any point you could be recorded having dinner or lunch by someone at the next table. You can be photographed and videoed and put on YouTube.' However, he adds, 'It has not changed the nature of formal diplomacy.' Jeremy Greenstock agrees that 'The world is much leakier, and the public, through the media and also directly, are much better informed. But,' he adds, 'diplomats in governments, and agencies find ways of keeping information from the public and conducting conversations that are not revealed. So I wouldn't agree with Jamie that there's no such thing.' So while digital technology may have been a factor in changing the way that diplomats approach their task, it has not altered formal diplomacy, according to Kurtzer, and, according to Greenstock, informal diplomacy, has had to become more cautious. 'It's much more difficult but diplomats find ways of having private contacts with difficult interlocutors just as they did in previous years, it's just that much more difficult in an open age.' This, he feels, is indispensable. 'Diplomacy would lose something if it didn't find ways of having private talks,' he argues. 'I've done it myself. You don't record it, you don't put it anywhere hackable, you keep it in a restricted space, or you agree not to record it.' In the post-Wikileaks, post-Edward Snowden world, diplomats are compelled to be more cautious. Sherard Cowper-Coles says that caution even extends to communications within ministries. 'Some minsters in London don't want open and honest reporting, because it creates problems elsewhere in Whitehall. They're worried about leaks,' he says. 'I was told when I was in Afghanistan to not report private and inconvenient American criticism of the British Army's performance in Helmand because it upset the MoD, and the Foreign Office needed good relations with the Ministry of Defence.' Greenstock's characterization of ours as an 'open age' is useful for an understanding of the way diplomacy has had almost to reappraise its relationship with the news media, and the public domain. 'In today's world, even in non-democratic countries, you've got to bring public support with you – because if you lose that, you lose the power of your legitimate position,' he says. It has never been easier to make information public, and at the same time it has never been harder to keep it private when you do not want it made public. For journalists, this is an example of changing technology both bringing benefits, and taking possibilities away. Diplomats may be more cautious than once they were, worried about leaks or private conversations appearing on YouTube. Even diplomats themselves have to be careful about what they are committing to email. Different parts of the diplomatic service, and armed forces, keeping things from each other is nothing new; their moderating their own internal communications, because of the ease with which these can reach unintended recipients, is new. 'The problem is these days any email can be forwarded. There is always a risk of leaks,' observes Cowper-Coles. For journalists, especially when they have acquired sensitive information, there are the challenges of protecting it until the time is right, and protecting the source who supplied it. When I was the BBC's correspondent in Gaza, I was warned by some Palestinian fellow journalists always not only to switch off my Israeli mobile phone when talking to members of Hamas, but also to remove the battery. It was widely believed that the Israeli secret services could both track you from your phone (true, I imagine), and also listen to what you were saying (I cannot say whether or not this might have been true). In the light of what we have learned in the intervening decade about intelligence agencies' ability to eavesdrop, such measures seem laughably inadequate. I did, on at least one occasion, end a telephone conversation, arranging with my interlocutor to meet to continue it outside in the street. The subject was a meeting with the Hamas leader, Abdel Aziz Rantisi, who was then in hiding after Israeli attempts to kill him. The meeting went ahead, although I often wondered whether the Israelis learnt of it from subsequent media stories reporting it, or whether they knew anyway, and just decided not to strike. If a man on Israel's target list, a Hamas leader who had been in hiding for months, suddenly invited journalists to a meeting, why did the Israeli military not seize the chance to try to kill him?

A different but related question came back to me in the summer of 2014, during 'Operation Protective Edge', as I worked on this book. On Wednesday evening, 6 August, the Israeli Prime Minister, Benjamin Netanyahu, spoke to the international news media. 'I expect, now that the members of the press are leaving Gaza, or some of them are leaving Gaza, and are no longer subjected to Hamas restrictions and intimidations,' Netanyahu said, 'I expect we'll see even more documentation of Hamas terrorists hiding behind the civilian population, exploiting civilian targets. I think it's very important for the truth to come out.'[31]

As it sought to promote its version of events – and to try to make the reporting of 'Protective Edge' focus on stories other than the massive loss of Palestinian civilian life and property – Israel did its best to discredit foreign journalists. In Netanyahu's remark, the approach was to patronize them – suggesting that they had been subject to pressure which they had been unwilling, or unable, to withstand. The tone is almost one of fake sympathy. However, with the exception of one specific case – discussed below – there seems little evidence that international journalists were subject to 'restrictions and intimidations'. If anything, the opposite seems true. Donald Macintyre, who returned to Gaza in the summer of 2014 to cover the conflict, reports almost no contact with Hamas representatives, never mind pressure from them. 'In fact,' he says, 'actually my impression is that Hamas people – political officials – were staying not exactly underground but out of sight most of the time.'[32] Sherwood 'totally and utterly' rejects the suggestion that Hamas were somehow in a position to apply pressure to international journalists. 'I didn't speak to a single Hamas person in the two weeks that I was there,' she says. 'And I don't know anybody who came under pressure. This is something that really suits the Israeli narrative because what it is does is to cast doubt on the veracity of our reporting.' Gold recalls 'a lot of hubbub about us getting threats and not feeling safe' but, on the specific subject of pressure coming from Hamas, is very clear, 'I didn't experience that.' He does add that, having been warned by a fixer 'you're not going to get an honest answer', he did not 'push too hard' in terms of asking people what they thought of the fact that Hamas was in charge in the Gaza Strip – but that is separate from the idea that Hamas was seeking to intimidate reporters. If anything, international journalists wanted better access. Jeremy Bowen says that, while reporting the story, he would have welcomed greater contact with Hamas 'but they're all hiding'.

> They had a spokesman who hung out at Shifa hospital. And he was very much a spokesman. He didn't tell us what to do. If we went out to areas that had been bombed, spoke to Hamas on the ground, street level Hamas people, they weren't telling us what to do either.

The fact is that – as I remembered from not seeing Abdel Aziz Rantisi when he was in hiding – members of Palestinian armed groups often make themselves scarce when the territory is under attack. They, after all, are prime targets. During the second intifada, even members of the official security forces would be cautious (as many of them had ties to the armed groups fighting Israel, this was hardly surprising). One night in December 2002, as an Israeli military helicopter – apparently looking for Palestinians wanted by Israel – hovered over the central area of Gaza City where I then lived, I watched from my balcony as two Palestinian policemen tried to hide under bushes in a children's playground I which lay across the road from my flat. Recent and more distant experience, therefore, tend to suggest that Netanyahu's words about 'restrictions and intimidations' were, as Sherwood concludes, part of a wider attempt to 'cast doubt on the veracity' of international reporting. During Israeli military operations in Gaza, members of Palestinian armed groups – including high-level political representatives – are simply not in a position to try to manage or control the activities of the international press. They tend either to be hiding, or fighting. In the communications battleground of summer 2014, when the Israeli Army circulated the 'Hamas House' graphic on social media, there was a concerted attempt by the Israeli military and political establishment to suggest that the international news media were reporting what they were as the result of pressure from Hamas. There is little or no evidence to support such an interpretation: Netanyahu's expectation of 'even more documentation of Hamas terrorists hiding behind the civilian population' was not borne out by what followed. Nor could the Israelis, despite suggestions that they would, produce reporters who had been intimidated. Sherwood tells of the Israeli government press office announcing a news briefing 'where they were going to produce two foreign journalists who were going to give an account of the pressure they'd come under from Hamas'. In the end, it did not take place. 'The day beforehand they said they were going to postpone it, it's never been rescheduled,' Sherwood explains. 'We've never known the identity of these people, nobody had ever come forward and said publicly "I was put under pressure." '

This might be a relatively minor detail were it not for the contention, at the very highest level and in public, that the international reporting of 'Protective Edge' was deficient because of Hamas pressure. As mentioned above, there is one specific case which merits further discussion. This is the issue of whether international journalists were deliberately failing to report the fact that members of Palestinian armed groups were launching rockets from civilian areas – as claimed in the 'Hamas House' graphic. 'Part of the answer is fear', suggested a page on the Israeli Foreign Ministry website.[33] A report from the Indian news organization, NDTV, was frequently mentioned in this context. There is, for example, a link to it from that Israeli Foreign Ministry webpage, which purports to chronicle 'Testimonies from Gaza and Hamas intimidation of foreign journalists'. The NDTV report,[34] by Sreenivasan Jain, begins with Jain describing something 'very, very, unusual' taking place in what he calls an 'abandoned plot of land' next to the hotel where he and his colleagues are staying. The compelling commentary which follows, over pictures of activity apparently going on under a small shelter or tent, tells the story of a rocket being prepared and eventually fired. Jain and his colleagues then head outside, before he says to camera that he and his colleagues have been 'asked by people not to go to the location' from which the rocket has been launched. The reason given is not because they have been threatened, but 'because it has been rightly pointed out to us that there could be immediate Israeli retaliation'. Jain does say in his commentary that the 'it also establishes something which Hamas has always been accused of, that they actually use densely populated civilian areas to fire their rockets'. This will hardly surprise anyone who has spent time in the Gaza Strip. It is the nature of the territory that much of it is 'densely populated civilian areas'. As Bowen says, 'I think they were firing from populated areas. Everywhere is populated pretty much.' However, he also specifically made the point that he 'saw no evidence of Hamas using people as human shields – and by human shields I mean forcing them to stay in a place so they can fire from there'. One is therefore left to conclude that many of the accusations which Israel levelled at international journalists during 'Operation Protective Edge' were designed, as Sherwood put it, to 'cast doubt on the veracity' of their reporting. During my research for this book I did hear stories, which I have not been able to confirm, that some photographers decided not to circulate pictures of damage which may have been caused by a misfiring Hamas rocket, rather than incoming fire. The source for these stories described them as 'hearsay' and, even assuming they are true, need to be considered in context. No armed group – established army or otherwise – wants the publication of anything which can compromise their own security. When I was in Gaza during the second intifada, there were a couple of incidents where camera crews, having heard an explosion, arrived on the scene of what were euphemistically called 'work accidents'. This usually meant that something had gone wrong at an illicit bomb-making factory – a place which would obviously not seek media coverage. This would be the same with almost any army or armed group. Israel, after all, would probably not have wished to have its artillery filmed because of the civilian casualties they were causing. Again, this accusation feels much more like an attempt by the Israeli government to undermine the credibility of international reporters because the coverage reflected poorly upon Israel's military and its political masters. It is an echo of Nitzan Chen's assertion that the foreign press accredited to his office are 'lazy'.

'Operation Protective Edge' followed the collapse a few months earlier of the latest United States-led attempt to restart a diplomatic solution to the Israeli-Palestinian conflict. As Cowper-Coles observed in the last chapter, the US is 'the only outside player who really matters'. Absent Washington's engagement, it is left to journalists and diplomats to observe and chronicle what happens until an attempt at a solution can be made once more. Their accounts will inform the next set of would-be peacemakers. Yet in the summer of 2014, the diplomats were absent. It was left to the journalists – and, increasingly, through social media, to anyone else in Gaza – to tell the story of what happened there. That is why the reporting of the Israeli-Palestinian conflict takes on such great importance: parties to the conflict seek to influence it because they know it may in turn influence third parties, such as activists and policy makers. When, as after 'Operation Protective Edge', there is no international diplomacy, journalism takes centre stage – and the belligerents want to make sure their versions of events are included in the account.

8
Holy Land

It was astonishing how silence could fall. Gaza City was overcrowded, and the climate meant that, most of the year round, a lot of daily life was outside. Constant car horns – taxis drumming up business, drivers greeting friends or cursing incautious fellow motorists – meant that the noise often seemed as if it would never stop. It drifted in through the open windows of my apartment; drifted up to my office in a high-rise building near the city centre. Some of the first Arabic phrases I learnt to recognize were the cries of fruit sellers calling out from their horse-drawn carts as they made their way along the street below, their shouts sometimes supported by tinny sirens. Yet at certain times the city fell still: on winter evenings, especially when an Israeli attack was feared; when the time came to break the daily fast during the month of Ramadan; on Friday mornings, as the people of Gaza rested from their week's work, and, in many cases, prepared to go to prayers. When prayer time came, the loudspeakers of mosques across the city and beyond broadcast the muezzin. Because it was Friday, there followed sermons, and the preachers' words seemed to compete with each other as they too came out from the loudspeakers across the town. Some Fridays, I would be preparing to leave Gaza City to spend the weekend in Jerusalem, perhaps after catching up with some editing in the superior facilities of the BBC's bureau there. As nightfall approached in Jerusalem, the sound of the siren, audible for all, was heard across the city, announcing the start of the Jewish Sabbath. The sounds of Friday sermons and the start of Sabbath came to represent for me the way in which religion punctuated the lives of the two peoples amongst whom I was then living: their distinctiveness, and geographical distance, small though the latter might have been, emphasized their division. Nor was the separation just physical. As discussed in Chapter 5, settling on a version of events which is beyond challenge or dispute is one of the greatest tasks facing journalists reporting on the Israeli-Palestinian conflict. Sometimes, it proves impossible.

On the evening of Monday 20 October 2003, Israeli military helicopters fired missiles at a target in the Nuseirat refugee camp in the centre of the Gaza Strip. It was the latest in a series of strikes launched that day, some from warplanes. The missiles which hit Nuseirat killed seven people – at least, that is the number of dead bodies which arrived in the local morgue following the attack. Beyond that, it was impossible to determine what had happened. The Israelis said that their soldiers had killed two armed Palestinians in a gun battle at the fence which separates Gaza from Israel. The missile strike had been aimed at a car carrying the dead Palestinians' comrades, fleeing the scene. The story from Nuseirat was quite different. Most of those killed had died after the initial strike. A crowd had gathered to see what had happened – this was common after attacks in Gaza – and the helicopter had fired a second missile at the onlookers. According to a reliable local journalist, the bodies in the morgue all resembled those of civilians. None of the Palestinian armed groups issued statements hailing their 'martyrs', as would normally have been the case when one of their number was killed fighting the Israelis. One of the dead, a doctor, turned out to have been a cousin of a Palestinian journalist, Seif Shahin, whom I knew as a fellow member of the Gaza press corps. My Palestinian BBC colleagues were going to visit the family to pay their respects, so I decided to go with them. As far as the visitors in the traditional tent set up for mourners outside the family home were concerned, this had been a missile sent to kill civilians. As far as the Israeli military were concerned, it was aimed at 'terrorists', who had got what they deserved.

An experienced correspondent can usually read between the lines of conflicting accounts to a sufficient extent to write a short story about what has happened. This time, especially as the incident came in the midst of so many others, it was all but impossible. The two versions of events agreed on practically nothing except that Israeli helicopters had fired missiles, and that some people had been killed. My suspicions, and experience of reporting on similar strikes, led me towards one interpretation – but the facts which I could establish were not sufficient to draw a definite conclusion. The task was further complicated on this occasion by the fact that the Israelis produced video in support of their version of events. It showed a street, empty save for the car which was the target, and the car travelling along the street and being hit by a missile. Because the pictures were taken from overhead, and the buildings which lined the streets had low concrete roofs – covers for shops' merchandise, and shade from the sun – protruding from their first floors, some Palestinians suggested that the civilians killed had been sheltering under these, and were therefore invisible from above. In any case, there was no way of knowing for sure what the video actually showed. So in terms of a news story, there were the bare bones of a 'what', a 'when', 'where', and a 'how', next to nothing on the 'who', or the 'why'. The story soon passed; the individual deaths lost to all but the friends and families of the dead, in the stream of others which went before, and which followed. The experience of reporting it stood for something larger, though – which is why I have discussed it here. For the Israelis and Palestinians disagree fundamentally not only on interpretation of their shared history, but actually on the facts of their shared history – and they do so to an extent that they can perhaps not be said to have a shared history, but rather two different histories. These contradictory narratives have, in recent years, been added to further by the babel of voices on social media; they have been further reinforced, on both sides, by an increasing unwillingness to consider other points of view. This may partly be a consequence of the absence of a political or diplomatic process to address the Israeli-Palestinian conflict, never mind to seek to bring it to an end. In an age where governments seem to place increasing emphasis on getting their message across in the news media, especially in times of war or conflict, spin seems to have become almost as important as policy. Benjamin Netanyahu's decision, discussed in Chapter 7, to criticize and patronize international journalists reporting 'Operation Protective Edge', is an example of this. Yet there are limits to how successful this can be. Lord Levy, reflecting on the way that Israel came out of 'Operation Protective Edge' in terms of international opinion, suggests:

> You can have the best PR, and Bibi Netanyahu's a big PR guy, but you cannot stop what the eyes see, and what the world saw in Gaza, when your counterargument is 'look what they would have done, and wanted to do'.

Israel did try to make this point by emphasizing the danger which the 'terror tunnels' – the underground passages dug by Palestinians for the purpose of moving or hiding men or materiel, or even for launching attacks – represented to its security. Levy suggests that the 'what they would have done' – that is, speculating on the consequences for Israel had their troops not engaged in fighting with Hamas, and their 'Iron Dome' missile defence system not afforded protection – is 'a potent argument as well'. Given, however, that 'regrettably what happened in Gaza did happen. So you've got to be pretty good at manipulating that story.' It is questionable whether Israel was 'pretty good' on this occasion. Not content with seeking to undermine the international press corps, in the weeks which followed 'Operation Protective Edge', Netanyahu also tried to persuade the world that ISIS and Hamas were 'branches of the same poisonous tree'.[1] Such an approach seemed to fool few: it was mocked even in Israel, with one columnist for the liberal daily newspaper, *Ha'aretz*, suggesting that such statements made the administration of US President Barack Obama look upon Netanyahu 'as a used car salesman'.[2] Another Israeli 'big PR guy' – to borrow Levy's description – also faced some of his toughest moments during 'Operation Protective Edge'. Mark Regev, hailed by the Huffington Post at the time as the 'world's best spinner',[3] was thought to have come off second best in an encounter with Jon Snow, presenter of Britain's *Channel 4 News*. Snow himself was also in the news, at least where coverage of 'Operation Protective Edge' was being considered, for his own broadcast after he returned from a reporting trip. Giving a detailed account of the number of children killed and wounded during the Israeli assault on Gaza, he said, 'We have to know that in some way we actually share some responsibility for those deaths, because for us it is no priority whatever to stop it.'[4] This intervention divided journalistic opinion, with other respected veterans of the reporting of armed conflict, such as the BBC's David Loyn, arguing against such an approach.[5] Such events – the 'world's best spinner' being stumped; a respected leading British broadcast journalist appearing to leap off the sacred fence of impartiality – almost gave a sense in the summer of 2014 that 'Operation Protective Edge' was a kind of turning point, a new level in the ferocity of the Israeli-Palestinian conflict. Certainly, it was the worst fighting in Gaza since the 1967 war which brought the territory under Israeli control. In fact, it followed a pattern of Israeli military campaigns of previous years: unprecedented only for its scale, and for the fact that, despite huge loss of life, in the short term, it neither led to a resumption of negotiations, nor even the prospect of one. Instead, it led to lengthy speculation about who had emerged stronger from the brief and bloody war: your answer to that question probably based upon which of the competing narratives you were minded to give more weight.

Unwilling, or unable, to appreciate the other's point of view – and having long despaired of persuading their enemies of the validity of their narrative – the Israelis and Palestinians instead concentrate on speaking to their own people, and to sympathizers around the world.

Even in an age of social media, journalism remains at the heart of this process: the first draft of history is still the first draft of history – even if a contradictory history exists on the other side of the security fence, barrier, or apartheid wall, depending on who is selecting the description. For the differences of language, like the differing accounts exemplified by that 2003 missile strike on Nuseirat, like the commemoration of deliverance or disaster in 1948 are all elements of these contradictory Israeli and Palestinian narratives. Always present in the enmity which those narratives reflect, and now growing in significance, is religion – as those journalists covering the conflict over longer periods cannot fail to notice. 'I think religion does underpin everything here, and I think people of take quite a lot of comfort and relief in the idea that well, this: I'm part of this struggle that God endorses, I'm fulfilling Allah's wish or whatever,' as the *New York Times'* Jodi Rudoren puts it. 'You can't understand the motivations without understanding religion,' adds one long-standing member of the foreign press community in Jerusalem. 'It causes people to send their children out to kill themselves and other people; to set up an encampment on a hillside surrounded by people who hate them because they believe that God gave them that right. It's a huge motivation.' This is in contrast with the west where, he argues, religion 'is like being a moderate football supporter – you're interested for a couple of hours a week. Religion here is people's lives.' Yolande Knell highlights this last point, too. 'Europeans, because we've become less religious as a continent, it's something people tend to forget when they come here,' she says. This presumably makes it harder for journalists, and their audiences, fully to understand the nature of the Israeli-Palestinian conflict – although Knell draws a distinction between 'less religious' Europe, and the United States. Her time in the US, where she took a Master's degree in Middle East studies and US foreign policy, left her with an impression of an 'evangelical Christian lobby' which was solidly 'pro-Israel'. The presence of this lobby, and its possible effect on Washington's foreign policy, is not this book's principal focus, yet it could be argued that it represents a further religious factor in the Israeli-Palestinian conflict. As Knell concludes, 'We often forget about it. They haven't lost touch with their religion in the way that a lot of Western Europeans have.'

Ever since the Balfour Declaration, with its endorsement of a 'national home for the Jewish people', and especially in the Mandate period where it would not have been correct to speak of 'Israelis', international diplomatic and journalistic discourse has referred to faith. It could not be otherwise – even if, as I argued in Chapter 4, documents such as the

Roadmap have not paid due attention to it. The whole Zionist idea is based upon an idea of 'return', as enshrined in modern Israel's 'law of return'.[6] As such, it draws on Biblical ideas of the land between the River Jordan and the Mediterranean Sea being the home of the Jewish people. These have become an integral part of Israel's own story from pre-state times. Moshe Dayan writes that his own parents had not been persecuted in Russia. Rather, they decided to emigrate to Palestine in the early 20th century because 'the place for a Jew was in the Land of Israel'.[7] That lack of persecution was hardly the experience of later generations of European Jews, faced with a merciless, mechanized, attempt to exterminate them. Even though they came for sanctuary, their choice of destination had a spiritual side, too. After all, as the newspaper reports in Chapter 1 of ships arriving from in Haifa during the late Mandate period show, the British authorities were hardly minded to offer a warm welcome to those who tried to come to Palestine. On the Palestinian side, their drive to 'liberate' the territory of Mandate Palestine, after the creation of the State of Israel, was led by the largely secular Palestine Liberation Organization. Gradually, that has come to change. Simon McGregor-Wood says that religion has 'become much more important', contrasting his first impressions of the Palestinian Territories, when he arrived shortly after the turn of the 21st century, with the transformation which followed. 'It felt like a secular society. There were always religious places, Hebron, Gaza. But in the course of the near decade I was there, with the rise of Hamas, religion and various shades of Islamism became more important.' Philps goes back to his own arrival in the region in the early 1980s, when he encountered the PLO in Lebanon. 'When I first met the Palestinians in Beirut they were very secular, in 1982. There were Christians in the PLO HQ,' he remembers. 'So I always thought of the Palestinians as secular. That changed, Hamas appeared.' It would be wrong to conclude that Hamas's rise to prominence, and preeminence, in Gaza at least, is simply the result of some massive surge of Islamist feeling among the Palestinian people. The reasons for Hamas's success are complex, and are discussed in more detail below. Nevertheless, their increase in influence and power over the last quarter-century, since Hamas was founded in 1987, is a fact which has influenced the way that the Israeli-Palestinian conflict has evolved: not only in the way that one side conducts its struggle, but also in the way that enemies seek to portray each other. Reflecting on his time covering the second intifada, McGreal suggests that, 'The suicide bombings in particular were seen by the Israelis as driven by Islamic fanaticism rather than something to do with the context of a the conflict for a state.' In consequence, he says, suicide bombings, 'allowed the Israeli narrative to say "they just hate us because we're Jews", and it's got nothing to do with democracy and freedom.' He has observed a transformation in the Israeli Army, too. 'On the other hand, the military is being increasingly taken over by people saying that land was given to them by God, and the occupation wasn't about security, occupation was about rights.' In his near decade in Jerusalem, McGregor-Wood sensed a similar transition in civilian life. 'I noticed that Jerusalem became a much more religious city. Ultra-orthodox populations continued to grow, the smart liberal secular Israelis have all left.'

This is precisely the kind of trend which often eludes elucidation in daily news coverage. Yet it needs to be reflected if audiences are to understand what is happening. The diplomacy aimed at ending the Israeli-Palestinian conflict, such as that diplomacy is, concentrates on a two-state solution. If that is ever to come to pass, those promoting it will have to find a way to overcome, or at least somehow bypass, that idea that occupation is 'about rights' – that is, Jews' right to ownership of all the land between the river and the sea. 'We all have lands that "God" or our fathers gave us. Didn't Queen Mary Tudor of England die with "Calais" engraved on her heart? Doesn't Spain have a legitimate right to the Netherlands?' asked Robert Fisk in *The Great War for Civilisation*. 'Every colonial power, including Israel, could put forward these preposterous demands.'[8] If anything, this feeling among settlers on the West Bank seems to have become stronger since I stood on that rainswept hilltop in Itamar more than a decade ago. In recent years, some settlers have carried out what they have come to call 'price tag' attacks on West Bank Palestinians and their property. The attacks are so-called because they are designed to teach Palestinians living on the West Bank that their presence carries a price. Danny Gold's 2014 story for *Vice News*, 'Radical Young Israelis and the Price Tag Attacks: Rockets and Revenge',[9] told the story of Moriah Goldberg, a young woman who had just been released from jail. She had served three months after refusing to carry out the community service to which she had been sentenced for throwing rocks at Palestinians' cars. In the report, she tells Gold that the Palestinians' living on the West Bank 'makes them guilty'. The land, she argues on the basis of the Torah, 'belongs to us'. 'You look these people in the eyes, otherwise rational people, and you see them convinced that they have God's permission to hurt other innocent people just because they are different,' Gold says. His conclusion echoes John Pilger's confession, quoted in Chapter 6, that he found himself, 'often at a loss when confronted by such zealotry'. 'You see that on both sides of this conflict,' Gold says. 'That's almost more disturbing than seeing bodies and crying people at a morgue. These people are entirely convinced. And there's no way to get through to them.' West Bank settlers may not be representative of Israeli society as a whole, but their presence is one of the main obstacles to the creation of a Palestinian state. The fact that their 'zealotry' has been tolerated and encouraged by successive Israeli governments means that it has become a factor in policy making. They may not represent mainstream opinion, but they influence government. While, as noted in Chapter 2, the 1967 war was a seminal moment in Middle Eastern history, one which continues to influence the realities of the region today, not all its consequences were clear. While correspondents such as James Cameron and Winston Churchill captured that sense that things had changed for good, the complete nature of the change has perhaps become apparent only subsequently: as David Hirst suggested in Chapter 3, the 1967 war 'was clearly a landmark in the rise of Islamism in the region, you couldn't see it at the time but it clearly was'. Jeremy Bowen, himself the author a book, *Six Days*, on the 1967 war, makes a similar point about the role that the consequences of that conflict have played in shaping the situation in the present day. 'Now what's changed is that it is a religious conflict now – the growth in religious Zionism,' he says. 'There was always religious Zionism from the beginning, but it got kick-started when they suddenly had the West Bank to colonize.'

The way that the religious influence has grown in both Israeli and Palestinian society since represents a special challenge for reporters. It is one of the contextual factors which it can be hard adequately to reflect in daily coverage, and yet it is at the 'core of the conflict', as Knell puts it. Donald Macintyre says 'It's obviously incredibly important. Very important. It's quite a sort of hard question to unpack. It's probably more important than we allowed for, or that I allowed for.' Nevertheless, he adds, while there is among journalists a 'natural tendency to see everything in purely political terms. On the other hand, I'm also slightly resistant to the idea that everything can be explained in terms of religion.' Other journalists interviewed for the book agreed. Balmer says of religion in the Israeli-Palestinian conflict, 'I suspect it's becoming more important because religion in this region in general has.' He continues, however, 'I don't think that at the core of the conflict religion is the determining factor, I think it's land, refugees, borders and security, and religion is clunked on making it more difficult to resolve.' Sherwood too is cautious about ascribing too much significance to religion alone. 'It seems strange to say in a situation where Jews and Muslims are fighting over land but I never felt that religion was *the* defining thing.' As noted above, it would be wrong to suggest that Hamas's rise to power was simply the result of a surge of religious feeling among Palestinians. In Gaza during the second intifada, there was widespread discontent with the Palestinian Authority, and with the senior members of the PLO who were its leaders. This discontent was rarely voiced publicly, principally because such criticism might have been judged to undermine national morale at a time of intense conflict with Israel. Therefore, it generally took the form of jokes about the poor state of the roads (the suggestion being that development money earmarked for spending on repairs had been misappropriated by corrupt officials), or disgruntled observations about the size and opulence of seaside villas belonging to people in the PLO's senior ranks. In a religiously conservative territory such as the Gaza Strip, some of Hamas's success must indeed be due to the support of devout Muslims; the fact that they were not the PLO, and therefore seen as less corrupt, may however have been a stronger factor. As Sherwood says, of the year when Hamas's electoral success led eventually to their taking over control of the territory (after what was in effect a civil war with Fatah the following year), 'There were all sorts of reasons for Hamas's victory in 2006. I don't think it was a big Islamic surge that led to them winning the elections.' As Macintyre bluntly puts it, 'Fatah were seen as thieves who haven't achieved anything. There were some other factors. Hamas made headway with publicity that they'd driven Israel out of Gaza.' This is not a phenomenon confined to Gaza in the last decade. Jeremy Greenstock observes a similar decline in Fatah's popularity on the West Bank, 'because it's such an incompetent, corrupt and, from time to time, brutal administration – with the help of the Israelis in the security brutality'.

While the increase in the influence of faith in both Israeli and Palestinian politics cannot simply be explained as some kind of mass religious revival, it is real. Whether or not religion lies at the core of the conflict, or has come to the fore because of a more complex set of global political circumstances, both diplomats and journalists interviewed for this book agreed that its role is growing. Harvey Morris even suggests 'there is a danger there you could end up with a fundamentalist Israel and a fundamentalist Palestine'. Lord Levy is cautious, and not especially optimistic:

> Religion is playing more of a part, on both sides. Now, whether that is a catalyst for something more positive, or more negative, thus far regrettably it seems to have been the catalyst for something more negative rather than positive, which I find very worrying.

Some journalists question whether diplomats following the Israeli-Palestinian conflict are fully aware of the possible consequences of this shift. Drawing on his experience of encounters with Israel's religious right – and referring to the 1995 assassination of the then Israeli Prime Minister, Yitzhak Rabin, by an Israeli opposed to the peace process – Matt Rees suggests that diplomats:

> just draw a line on a map, and live behind the line on the map. You give people money for refugees. You give them money for this. You compensate strategically for this. They don't have a clue about that. They don't see why someone would kill the Israeli Prime Minister because he's going to give up the land. I see why he did it. Because I've spoken to a lot of people who have the same perspective.

His views echo the points raised in Chapter 6 about whether diplomats, given their inability – and, in some cases, reluctance – to travel to certain places and talk to certain parties to the conflict, really have a complete understanding of the challenges which must be overcome if there is ever to be a durable solution. Certainly, Balmer has gained the impression from his contact with diplomats that the question of faith in the conflict is not a priority. 'I've never had a conversation with a diplomat here where religion has come up bar a shaking of the head at extremism, of the ultra-Orthodox Jews and the Salafis,' he says.

Dan Kurtzer, while conceding that 'diplomacy has so far proven incapable of figuring out what to do about religion', suggests that there is no prospect of an end to the conflict without its being taken into account. 'It has to be addressed,' he says, even if it is not necessarily the first stage. 'The question is kind of chicken and the egg. What's going to come first? I think I still come out on the side of resolving what we can resolve of the territorial, political, governance issues.' Later, though, he foresees a stage, 'in which you deal with the narratives, the religious feelings, you get people to do activities together that change people's minds.' Sherard Cowper-Coles offers a slightly different perspective. Addressing the question of whether religion is playing a greater role in the Israeli-Palestinian conflict, he responds:

> It is. But religion is a symptom not a cause. These things are driven by the alienation of people in Gaza, the failure of the Palestinian Authority to be seen to be representing all Palestinians and within Israel a polarisation of politics, disillusionment with the peace process, a fear and loathing of the Palestinians and Arabs. Religion exploits

and feeds and expresses that. But religion isn't the cause, it's the symptom.

In this respect, he sees it as a challenge for diplomacy only

> up to a point. The great thing about religion is that it's irrational. It's born of fear and prejudice, and if you can address the sources of that fear and prejudice, then you find that the religious reasons that tell you that Gaza is an inalienable part of Eretz Israel disappear overnight.

To support his point, he draws on an example of a major change of heart in another conflict with a strong religious element:

> We saw in Northern Ireland the late Ian Paisley at one stage in his career telling his parishioners that the Pope was the anti-Christ, and in the end sitting down rather jovially with Catholic leaders. Those beliefs are irrational and in a way they are easier to address than other beliefs with are more rational and based on a sort of master plan to acquire someone else's territory or what else it might be.

Cowper-Coles's analysis suggests that there is the prospect of further change. After all, if, as the people interviewed for this book generally agreed, religion is playing a more prominent role in the Israeli-Palestinian conflict, why could its influence not diminish once again? Greenstock agrees that religion is becoming more important, with significant qualifications. 'The answer is yes. But I would put it a different way,' he explains. 'Political trends are becoming more identity-driven as the world gets freer and more open, and globalization intrudes in economics and communications and information in particular,' he suggests. In consequence, Greenstock argues, 'the world divides up into smaller units for two reasons. One, people feel that their true personal or close or tribal identities are being threatened in a global world where everything is flowing everywhere.' The second effect of this 'era of greater freedom', is that:

> people are more inclined to go back to the human default setting of identity which is tribal. So we see it as religion breaking out everywhere, but it's part of the geopolitical trend that a strong identity should seek its own space to govern or have a community run in the way it wants.

It may be then, that religion has come to greater prominence because of a particular set of current circumstances which include, on the Palestinian side, Fatah's failure to achieve Palestinian statehood, and the corruption, real and perceived, which has plagued the Palestinian Authority. Greenstock's argument about people seeking to go back to a 'tribal' identity in response to uncertain times is also persuasive. Bowen, while saying that 'this is a religious conflict now', also observes that, 'People in the end go in for religious solutions because other ones haven't worked.' This could apply equally to Israelis denied peace with their neighbours, and, in consequence, denied security, as it could to Palestinians denied statehood. Where secular politics have failed to achieve national ambitions, two peoples for whom religion is such an integral part of identity might well be expected to fall back on faith. Then there is the view that religion is being used by the protagonists in a national-territorial conflict to add legitimacy to their causes. AP's Dan Perry argues, 'Even religious settlers in Hebron sometimes don't frame the issue as being religious in a theological way. They're using their religion to justify actions they've taken in what is a national/ethnic dispute. They're saying "God gave Hebron to the Jews." ' Whatever the relative strength and influence of factors such as these may be, whatever the extent to which the growth of religious feeling may be new, perhaps temporary, and perhaps reversible, faith is nevertheless a permanent factor in the Israeli-Palestinian conflict: a factor which diplomacy has been reluctant or unable to address, and a factor which journalism, especially within the confines of daily news, has not always adequately reflected. It is one of the contextual factors which can be very hard to cram into a short news report, or even a longer feature, where a reporter does not have the space to 'go back two thousand years all the time'. Part of this has to do with the idea of land almost as a spiritual commodity, the 'primordial attachment that people have, especially in that region, to the olive tree, to the brook, to the wadi – which diplomacy has not yet figured out how to integrate' which Kurtzer described in Chapter 4. This attachment itself may be primordial, but the failure of the Israeli-Palestinian peace process over the last two decades and more has come to expose it to the extent that it almost has the characteristics of a new discovery. It is one of the factors of which the Roadmap, and other, similar plans based upon two states, and land for peace, failed to take account. For this is not a conflict which can be solved, in Rees's words by 'giving money for this', or 'compensating strategically for that'. There is a further change underway which makes that less likely than once it might have been: a change which affects journalism just as much as diplomacy.

As I argued in Chapter 3, one of the reasons why the Israeli-Palestinian conflict is covered to such an extent is foreign policy. The United States, as a superpower both during the Cold War era, and after it, has invested colossal diplomatic time and other resources into making peace between Israel and the Palestinians. Washington's colossal efforts have attracted editorial resources in their wake. The unpredictable situation in the Middle East as a whole – and the fact that prospects of peace between the Israelis and the Palestinians are scarce, to say the least – mean that diplomatic realities are changing, too. While Sherard Cowper-Coles's contention that, 'The only outside player who really matters is the United States,' remains persuasive. Who else, after all, has the will and the wherewithal to lead an attempt to take on this 'Rubik's cube' of international diplomacy, as Kurtzer describes it? Nevertheless, Kurtzer also says:

> There's no question that fatigue has set in with respect to the Arab-Israeli conflict and the resolution process. Of course, Senator Kerry injected life into this again. When a Secretary of State or foreign minister decides that he's going to focus on an issue then the bureaucracy will follow suit.

The unsuccessful end to John Kerry's attempt, in 2014, to inject life into the process once more means that the bureaucracy will not necessarily continue to function in anticipation of further renewed diplomatic initiatives. As Kurtzer sees it, 'They're probably very quick now to dismantle that infrastructure because they have other callings, Isis, or Syria, or Iran negotiations. There's fatigue and desire to escape from this headache.' Nor is the headache as simple as the challenges which lie before anyone seeking to end the conflict. In a changing region, it may be that that changing attitudes to the United States have placed a question mark over the extent of Washington's influence – or at least over its willingness to use that influence. Kurtzer sees a shift from a time when, 'the Arabs would say to the United States "We know you're biased, we know you favour Israel's position, but you're the only party we believe can make Israel take the risks necessary for peace."' That hard-headed acceptance of the reality of US foreign policy has changed, Kurtzer believes, apparently with reason.

> I think the Arabs have become more persuaded that we're not ready to do that; that even though we may be the only party that Israel at

the end of the day will trust, the politics in Washington, and the flow of U.S. policy, is not going to push Israel to accommodate the risks of peace.

This echoes Cowper-Coles's reflection, cited in Chapter 6, that the pressure of domestic politics in the United States makes progress more difficult. Kurtzer wonders whether

> this idea of the US as negotiator – notwithstanding that bias – may be coming to an end. I don't know what you do when the US is not seen as a third party. Who else is going to be there that in a sense can do that work with Israel that's ultimately going to be required to get Israel to move?

In a world where, he argues, 'governments have become less able to handle the complexity of events' Greenstock says:

> the Americans are having to come to terms with the fact that their comfort areas of twenty or thirty years ago no longer deliver the same results, and yet they're reluctant to change because they were cock of the walk in that previous era, and don't want things to change.

Similarly to Bowen's conclusion that, 'People in the end go in for religious solutions because other ones haven't worked,' Greenstock observes that, 'the greater the misery, the greater the pressure, the more you're imprisoned by circumstances and the occupation the more inclined people may be to go to their god to seek relief'. He adds, however, that, 'even if religion has intruded into those politics you still have to interpret the politics'.

That, of course, is one of the core duties both of journalists and diplomats in any international arena, and the Israeli-Palestinian conflict, in that sense, is no exception. In an age when the conflict is seen as a diplomatic 'headache', from which even Washington's seasoned practitioners seek relief, new approaches may be needed successfully to achieve that. For more than two decades, international diplomacy, led by the United States, has pursued an end to the Israeli-Palestinian conflict based on the idea of a two-state solution. While the creation of the Palestinian Authority might be seen as a small step towards achieving that goal, the PA is known for its shortcomings – such as the corruption mentioned above – and has no 'authority' at all in the Gaza Strip, an important part of any eventual Palestinian state. In practice, Israel remains in overall control of most of the West Bank, and settlers such as Moriah

Goldberg are able to make Palestinians' lives a misery. The sanction which Goldberg received for her attacks was rare, and not especially severe. While she and others who share her beliefs remain on the West Bank, convinced that it is land given to them by God, there seems little prospect of any settlement based upon the borders which Israel was generally accepted to have in 1967. So Yossi Alpher's 2012 conclusion, quoted in Chapter 4, that 'There is no peace process, and no prospect of one,' has been proved prescient by what has happened since. In fact, his words seem wiser than ever.

Between the presentation of the Roadmap, in 2003, and Mr Alpher's pronouncement in 2012, much changed. Hamas took over Gaza. Jewish settlements were removed from that territory, only to continue to expand at a great rate on the West Bank. In a document published late in 2012 by its Office for the Coordination of Humanitarian Affairs, the United Nations said that, in 2011, the settler population was estimated at over 520,000.[10] The document also said that the annual average rate of growth during the preceding decade was 5.3% (excluding East Jerusalem), compared to 1.8% for the Israeli population as a whole. The same month, December 2012, the European Union reiterated its view that Israeli plans to expand settlements, 'would seriously undermine the prospects of a negotiated resolution of the conflict by jeopardizing the possibility of a contiguous and viable Palestinian state and of Jerusalem as the future capital of two states'.[11] The scepticism of those reporters who questioned the Roadmap has been justified by what followed. The reporting of the Israeli general election of early 2013 perhaps reflected that to the extent that it sought out, and listened to, the voices of the new religious politicians whose influence was growing. One example was David Remnick's piece for the *New Yorker*, which that magazine promoted on its cover as 'the emerging religious right'.[12] Remnick's principal interview was with Naftali Bennett, of the Jewish Home Party. Bennett's assertion that, 'The land is ours',[13] and that there is no distinction between land within Israel's internationally recognized borders and land in Gaza or on the West Bank,[14] could just as well have come from Tammy Silberschein – the Gaza settler quoted in Chapter 4 – so many years earlier – only now they were views not of the fringe, but on the edge of the mainstream, and coming from a man who apparently has ambitions to be Israel's Prime Minister. His party may not have made the impact which some predicted in the 2013 election, but Bennett did end up as Trade Minister. At the time of writing, January 2015, he is spoken of as a possible Defence Minister in the next Israeli government.[15] So the enforced evacuation of settlements from Gaza in 2005 perhaps seemed like a setback for the settler movement at the time, but it has flourished since. Moreover, as David Newman has written:

> the scenes which accompanied the forced removal of the 7,000 settlers of the Gaza region in the summer of 2005 are seen as being no more than a small prelude of what could be expected if a similar scenario were practised with respect to the entire West Bank settler population, and could potentially lead to levels of violence between settlers and soldiers which the government is unable to manage.[16]

One has only to recall the determination of settlers such as those in Danny Gold's report, or those whom I met at Itamar more than a decade earlier, to see how convincing such a scenario seems. Even supposing a future Israeli government were minded to remove the settlements from the West Bank – something which seems inconceivable in the foreseeable future – the practical challenges and political costs of trying to achieve that make it unrealistic. That being the case, it is indeed difficult to see how a Palestinian state can ever come into being – and the EU concern that settlements could 'seriously undermine the prospects of a negotiated resolution of the conflict' reads like what it is: diplomatic understatement.

With the two-state solution facing such colossal obstacles, both the diplomatic challenge, and the longer-term story for journalism, are changing. Religion, whether the rise of a latent, underlying cause of the Israeli-Palestinian conflict, or a phenomenon born of disaffection with failing secular politics, is combined with the power of history and narrative. The West Bank settlers cite the Bible to support their claim; Palestinian graffiti demanding an end to the Israeli occupation are accompanied by spray-paint drawings of Mandate Palestine. At this level of national narrative, a state based on the West Bank and Gaza will not suffice. Reflecting this kind of reality in daily news is a major challenge, for all the reasons pointed out in Chapter 5. Documentaries occasionally get the chance, with the programme *Israel: Facing the Future*, referred to in Chapter 4, an example. A decade after the presentation of the Roadmap, and years after it lay rusting on the scrapheap of diplomatic breakdowns, the former Israeli intelligence chief, Ephraim Halevy, referred in his interview for the programme to 'holy land'. Halevy's remarks were prefaced by a script line from the BBC reporter, John Ware, which suggested that the, 'growth of religious ideology on both sides of the conflict', had led him to this conclusion. In consequence of this being 'holy land', Halevy argued, 'no side can in any way forego its rights on every inch of territory'. Halevy's choice of words was highly significant. 'No side *can*', he said. So this is not a matter of choice, in which case the word 'will' might have sufficed. It is a matter of obligation, perhaps even of destiny. It cannot be otherwise: 'no side can'. This idea of the land between the River Jordan and the Mediterranean being 'holy' is one of the reasons the Israeli-Palestinian conflict is set apart from other diplomatic and journalistic challenges around the globe. Religions are in conflict in many parts of the world; nowhere else are they in conflict over the actual places sacred to Judaism, Islam, and Christianity. That helps to explain why it is a story so many reporters want to cover; why secretaries of state have come to see it as a 'Rubik's cube' of international diplomacy. In a diplomatic and journalistic world much preoccupied with the rise of Islamic State, and while considering the role of religion in the Israeli-Palestinian conflict, there is a further point to make about the nature of Hamas – especially in the light of Benjamin Netanyahu's suggestion that they and Islamic State, or ISIS as he preferred to call them, were 'branches of the same tree'. Greenstock disagrees:

> I think there's no point talking to absolutist groups like Al Qaeda or ISIS. But Hamas is not like ISIS and Al Qaeda. And as an ex-diplomat I've talked frequently to Hamas at the top political level of their leadership and governments can learn from those sorts of contacts.

To support his view, Greenstock points to the difference between statements for media and public consumption, and the demands of managing the practicalities of a conflict: in this case, 'what is said in public to demonise an organization doesn't necessarily reveal everything that goes on in having to handle that organization. How did the prisoner swaps happen for instance?' Based on his experience of interviewing him, Bowen also argues that the Hamas leader, Khaled Meshaal, is 'an incredibly subtle political mind' and 'not a thumping, bearded religious maniac'. Bowen's experience of covering the whole region, especially since the Arab uprisings, has also led him to conclude that:

> Among Palestinians – unlike among Iraqis and Syrians and people who've lived under long dictatorship – there are no blank slates there for Jihadis to work on. People are more aware, they're more political, aware of different groups and subtleties. And don't follow simple slogans quite as easily.

So while Islamist groups around the world often cite the injustices in Palestine as a reason for their own actions, Islam plays a different role in the Israeli-Palestinian conflict, where it is combined with a high level of political literacy, and an awareness of the huge challenges involved in the struggle for statehood. Islam seems to be playing an increasingly powerful role, though – just as Judaism is in Israeli politics. As long as the West Bank settlers use scripture to justify views others – Israelis as well as non-Israelis – see as irrational and extreme, the kind of compromises needed to bring about a two-state solution seem impossibly distant. Greenstock says that diplomats do understand that

> with those sorts of Israelis it's extremely difficult to think that there will be a comprehensive settlement because each of them, the Palestinians and the Israelis, actually want to own all the land. Because they think it's theirs and has been theirs for thousands of years in particular periods.

This is combined with the challenges inherent in the land being not just an economic and agricultural commodity – important though those are – but also a spiritual one, as mentioned above. Greenstock argues that diplomats are aware of this, but concedes that it may not have received adequate attention. He says:

> I think the land is extremely important and diplomats who understand the depth of the problems here know that. But the Oslo Madrid process, and the Roadmap, never really treated that with the seriousness that it should have done – or we would have taken the diplomatic approach to negotiations down a different route.

This may, in the future, be necessary if negotiations are one day to succeed. While the perfect solution to the conflict – with peace, justice, and security for all clearly does not exist – there may yet be some kind of solution if the 'painful compromises', so often referred to at the start of ultimately fruitless negotiations, can one day be reached. For the nearer future, the conflict shows signs of becoming harder to solve, not easier.

In the autumn of 2014, in the aftermath of a summer of bloodshed in Gaza, a series of incidents in Jerusalem suggested a new, religious, departure in the conflict. At the end of October, Yehuda Glick, a United States-born rabbi, who campaigns for Jews to be allowed to pray at the Temple Mount/Noble Sanctuary in Jerusalem, was shot and wounded as he left a conference dedicated to the campaign.[17] His suspected attacker,

Moataz Hejazi, was shot dead by Israeli police shortly afterwards.[18] Less than three weeks later, two Palestinians killed four worshippers in an attack on a synagogue in West Jerusalem before being shot dead themselves.[19] Writing in *Ha'aretz* the following day, Amos Harel described the attacks as, 'a religious and ideological act, stemming from a deep hatred of Jews. It was an attack on a clearly religious target, carefully chosen for maximum shock value.'[20] It is difficult to disagree with the conclusion. West Jerusalem in 2014 was not the West Jerusalem of the second intifada, a decade earlier. Cafés were no longer guarded as once they had been. There were plenty of other soft targets for attackers to pick without seeking out a synagogue. The place of worship can only have been chosen for its religious significance, as the Ibrahimi mosque in Hebron was in 1994.[21]

After decades of secular politics, a new religious core is being exposed at the heart of the Israeli-Palestinian conflict. Journalists have noticed the shift; those who have covered the region over a period of time understand the important role which it is coming to play. The diplomats interviewed for this book agree that faith is a factor which may have been overlooked in the past; it certainly has not been addressed. From the time they watched corpses being pulled from the rubble of the King David Hotel in 1946, and before, until they watched corpses being pulled from the rubble of bombed buildings in Gaza in the summer of 2014, international reporters have been the eyes and ears of audiences around the world. No one would pretend that they have always done their job perfectly, or even always well – but they have made a vital contribution to the understanding of a unique conflict with connections across large parts of the globe. Today, the reporting of the Israeli-Palestinian conflict has been influenced by the pressures affecting journalism everywhere: the challenge of funding expensive news operations. 'It's true that in previous times, like 2008–2009, there were more foreign journalists in Israel,' says Nitzan Chen:

> The journalism budget was cut. The death of print, and television used to send lots of people now it's just a one-man crew. And because of the Internet you can get much more material instead of spending your time and money by being here physically.

In their remarks quoted in Chapter 3, Harriet Sherwood and Simon McGregor-Wood, two correspondents formerly based in Jerusalem, also suggested that the conflict was receiving less attention than previously. That was briefly reversed in the summer of 2014 as bloodshed in Gaza increased to a level unknown in recent years, but even then, immediately prior to the outbreak of fighting, international correspondents in Jerusalem pointed to the way that their numbers had declined, and wondered which news organization might be next to scale down, or depart altogether. Yet 'being here physically' is where journalism offers its great value. As the fighting raged in Gaza during 'Operation Protective Edge', two other conflicts challenged Gaza for international editorial attention: Ukraine and the rise of ISIS in Iraq and Syria. Both of those took audiences, and governments, by surprise partly because the events leading up to their breaking out had been so sparsely covered.[22] The former Soviet Union was not considered so much of a story anymore; it was almost impossible to cover at close quarters the activities of ISIS. In the absence of news coverage – whatever its shortcomings may be – audiences and political leaders are left in the dark, and liable to be caught out. In a world where so many feel an attachment to the Israeli-Palestinian conflict for reasons of history, politics, or faith, the need for headlines from the Holy Land is greater than ever.

Notes

Introduction

1. Hass (2014).
2. Shindler (2013), p. 246.
3. Gringras (2010).

1   Reporting from the Ruins: The End of the British Mandate and the Creation of the State of Israel

1. Hobsbawm (1995), p. 32.
2. Shepherd (1999), p. 5.
3. Hollingworth (1990), p. 141.
4. Ibid.
5. Board (1946a), p. 1.
6. Hollingworth (1990), p. 141.
7. For example, Shepherd (1999), p. 225.
8. *Daily Mail*, 23 July 1946, front page. It is always interesting for foreign correspondents to see what is making the news at home: the King David Hotel report had to share that morning's *Daily Mail* front page with the story of a riot at a dog-racing track in Harringay, North London. The unrest had been caused by the disqualification of a dog which had come in second – a decision which presumably cost quite a lot of people quite a lot of money.
9. Ibid.
10. *World Pictorial News*, No. 275 (1946) Imperial War Museum Films. Available at http://jiscmediahub.ac.uk/record/display/010-00001523#sthash .BR0KoaEG.dpuf. Accessed 30 January 2015.
11. 'National Military Organization' in pre-State Israel.
12. Ibid.
13. *Daily Express*, 23 July 1946, p. 2.
14. Ibid.
15. Golani (2009), p. 4.
16. *Daily Express*, 23 July 1946, p. 2.
17. Ibid.
18. *Daily Express*, 23 July 1946, front page.
19. *The Times*, 23 July 1946, p. 4.
20. Ibid.
21. *Manchester Guardian*, 23 July 1946, p. 5.
22. The Irgun Zvai Leumi (National Military Organization), an armed group in Mandate-era Palestine fighting to establish a Jewish state.
23. Roman (2010), p. 26.
24. Ibid.
25. As noted above, other sources put the figure at 91.

26. Roman (2010), p. 27.
27. For example, in *By Blood and Fire* (1981), his dramatic and readable account of the attack, Thurston Clarke has Sir Evelyn Barker, the GOC (General Officer Commanding) British Troops in Palestine talking to his subordinates at a meeting, 'Well, we'd better be quick,' he said. 'I understand we're due to be blown up this morning.' (p. 161).
28. *Manchester Guardian*, 23 July 1946, p. 5.
29. Ibid.
30. Board (1937), preface.
31. Ibid., p. 5.
32. Even as a correspondent in the Gaza Strip in the early years of this century, I realized there were huge parts of Gazan society which were off limits to me because I was a man. I remember a rare interview with a mother whose baby had been killed taking place in the company of two or three male relatives.
33. *Daily Mirror*, 23 July 1946, back page.
34. Ibid.
35. *New York Times*, 24 July 1946, p1.
36. Ibid.
37. Ibid.
38. *Daily Mirror*, 24 July 1946, front page.
39. Ibid.
40. *World Pictorial News*, No. 275 (1946) Imperial War Museum Films. Available at http://jiscmediahub.ac.uk/record/display/010-00001523#sthash.BR0KoaEG.dpuf. Accessed 30 January 2015.
41. *Daily Mail*, 25 July 1946, front page.
42. Board (1946b).
43. Gallagher (1946).
44. *New York Times*, 27 July 1946, p. 6.
45. Carruthers (2011), p. 90.
46. Cited in BBC News 'America Widens "Crusade" on Terror', first published 16 September 2001. Available at http://news.bbc.co.uk/1/hi/world/americas/1547561.stm. Accessed 2 January 2014.
47. *Daily Mail*, 29 July 1946.
48. See, for example, Chittal (2015).
49. *Daily Express*, 1 August 1946.
50. Ibid.
51. *Daily Mail*, 1 August 1946.
52. Ibid.
53. Ibid.
54. *Daily Mirror*, 1 August 1946, p. 8.
55. *Manchester Guardian*, 24 July 1946, p. 5.
56. *Daily Mail*, 1 August 1946, p. 1.
57. *Manchester Guardian*, 6 August 1946, p. 5.
58. Golani (2009), p. 4.
59. Ibid., p. 87.
60. Ibid., p. 70.
61. Ibid.
62. Ibid.

63. Ibid.
64. *Daily Express*, Wednesday 3 December 1947.
65. *Daily Express*, Monday 1 December 1947.
66. *Daily Mirror*, Monday 1 December 1947.
67. *Daily Express*, Wednesday 3 December 1947.
68. *Daily Express*, 8 December 1947.
69. *Daily Express*, 9 December 1947.
70. Interview, London 21 March 2014.
71. Short, Magazine, Lee-Enfield.
72. Christie (2000?), p. 2.
73. Ibid., p. 48.
74. Ibid., p. 59.
75. Ibid., p. 60.
76. Ibid., p. 61.
77. *Daily Express*, Tuesday 2 December 1947.
78. The Stern Gang, a splinter group from the Irgun, dedicated to violence as a means of achieving Jewish statehood.
79. Golani (2009), p. 111.
80. Khalidi (1992), p. 290.
81. Mansfield (1992), p. 235.
82. Levin (1997), p. 57. I am grateful to Professor Tamar Liebes and Dr Zohar Kampf of the Hebrew University of Jerusalem for drawing this text to my attention.
83. *Manchester Guardian*, 16 May 1948.
84. Ibid.
85. For a fuller account of this demonstration, see Rodgers (2013), pp. 63–4.
86. Shindler (2013), p. 43.
87. Holbrooke (2008).
88. Shindler (2013), p. 39.
89. *Daily Mirror*, 14 May 1948.
90. Baram (2004), p. 70.
91. Ibid., p. 71.
92. Ibid.
93. *Observer*, 25 April 1948.
94. Ibid.
95. *Observer*, 2 May 1948.
96. *Observer*, 11 April 1948.
97. Ibid.
98. Ibid.
99. *Daily Express*, 17 May 1948.
100. *Daily Express*, 15 May 1948.
101. Ibid.
102. *Daily Mail*, 18 May 1948.
103. *Daily Express*, 20 May 1948.
104. The film *My Neighbourhood*, directed by Julia Bacha and Rebekah Wingert-Jabi (2012) tells the story of one such case, and the protests which happened in response.
105. *Daily Mail*, 15 May 1948.
106. *New York Times*, 15 May 1948.

107. Ibid.
108. *New York Times*, 17 May 1948.
109. Ibid.
110. Ibid.
111. *New York Times*, 14 May 1948.
112. *New York Times*, 15 May 1948.
113. Ibid.
114. Ibid.
115. State of Israel Government Press Office website, 2014. Available at https://forms.gov.il/globaldata/getsequence/getHtmlForm.aspx?formType=gpocardeng@pmo.gov.il. Accessed 5 May 2015.
116. I briefly mentioned this encounter in an earlier book. Rodgers (2012), p. 51.
117. *New York Times*, 16 May 1948.
118. Ibid.
119. *Observer*, 30 May 1948.
120. Ibid.
121. *Observer*, letters page, 30 May 1948.
122. *The Times*, 20 May 1948.
123. Ibid.

2 Six Days and Seventy-Three

1. Shindler (2013), p. 125.
2. Ibid., p. 124
3. Cameron (1968), p. 334.
4. Ibid., p. 328.
5. Ibid., p. 334.
6. Interview with the author, Jerusalem, 23 June 2014.
7. Churchill and Churchill, p. 74.
8. Hart, Alan (1967) 'Middle East Crisis: Israel report', ITN. Broadcast 24 May 1967. Available at http://jiscmediahub.ac.uk/record/display/042-00053220. Accessed 30 January 2015.
9. Churchill and Churchill (1967), p. 75.
10. Ibid., Introduction.
11. *News of the World*, 4 June 1967.
12. Ibid.
13. Ibid.
14. Churchill and Churchill (1967), p. 75.
15. *News of the World*, 4 June 1967.
16. Dayan (1978), p. 341.
17. Ibid., pp. 341–2.
18. Obituary, Jewish Telegraph Agency, published 7 April 1986. Available at http://www.jta.org/1986/04/07/archive/moshe-pearlman-dead-at-75. Accessed 4 July 2014.
19. Dayan (1978), p. 337.
20. *News of the World*, 29 August 2010.
21. Churchill and Churchill (1967), p. 1.
22. Ibid.

23. *New York Times*, 5 June 1967.
24. Ibid.
25. Ibid.
26. Eretz Israel Museum website.
27. *Daily Express*, 7 June 1967.
28. *Daily Mail*, 6 June 1967.
29. Ibid.
30. Ibid.
31. *Guardian*, 9 June 1967.
32. AP report published in the *Daily Express*, 7 June 1967.
33. *Guardian*, 7 June 1967.
34. *Daily Mirror*, 7 June 1967.
35. Ibid.
36. *New York Times*, 9 June 1967.
37. In the absence of any official source for this figure, it comes from my own enquiry to the Foreign Press Association in Israel. I am grateful to Glenys Sugarman of the FPA for her assistance in this, and other matters.
38. *Daily Express*, 7 June 1967.
39. *New York Times*, 6 June 1967.
40. *Guardian*, 6 June 1967.
41. Ibid.
42. Interview with the author, via Skype, between London and Saint-Julien de Briola, Ariège, France, 8 December 2014. All subsequent citations from David Hirst are taken from this interview.
43. *New York Times*, 5 June 1967.
44. Harold Jackson reports in the *Guardian*, 5 June 1967.
45. Cameron (1968), p. 336.
46. Ibid., p. 338.
47. Shindler (2013), p. 125.
48. Bowen (2004), p. 172.
49. *Guardian*, 7 June 1967.
50. Interview with the author, Jerusalem, 23 June 2014.
51. Aburish (1998), p. 11.
52. A gallery of David Rubinger's photographs, including this one, can be seen on the *Time* website http://content.time.com/time/photogallery/0,29307, 1730968_1564872,00.html. Accessed 4 July 2014.
53. Interview with the author, Jerusalem, 23 June 2014.
54. Mansfield (1992), p. 274.
55. Cameron (1968), p. 342.
56. *Guardian*, 9 June 1967.
57. Ibid.
58. *News of the World*, 11 June 1967.
59. Cameron (1968), p. 344.
60. Lindley, Richard (1967) 'Israel-Egypt War Aftermath', ITN. Broadcast 14 June 1967. Available at http://jiscmediahub.ac.uk/record/display/039-00046590. Accessed 30 January 2015. The script extract cited here paraphrases Jeremiah 31:16–17 in the King James Bible.
61. Hirst (2003), p. 345.
62. Sand (2012), p. 3.
63. Mansfield (1992), p. 295.

64. *Daily Express*, 8 October 1973.
65. *Daily Express*, 10 October 1973.
66. *Daily Mirror*, 10 October 1973.
67. Ibid.
68. *Daily Mail*, 9 October 1973.
69. *Daily Mail*, 10 October 1973.
70. Ibid.
71. *Daily Mirror*, 13 October 1973.
72. Email response, received 21 October 2014, to questions from the author. Unless otherwise indicated, all subsequent citations from John Pilger come from the same source.
73. *Daily Mail*, 10 October 1973.
74. *Daily Express*, 12 October 1973.
75. Mansfield (1992), p. 296.
76. Shindler (2013), p. 144.
77. Sandy Fawkes. Obituary. *Daily Telegraph* website. First published 30 December 2005. Available at http://www.telegraph.co.uk/news/obituaries/1506578/Sandy-Fawkes.html. Accessed 6 June 2014.
78. *Daily Express*, 20 October 1973.
79. *New York Times*, 8 October 1973.
80. Ibid.

3 Any Journalist Worth Their Salt

1. This quotation, and all subsequent ones from Crispian Balmer, come from an interview with the author in Jerusalem, 23 June 2014.
2. This quotation, and all subsequent ones from Jodi Rudoren, come from an interview with the author in Jerusalem, 7 January 2014.
3. This quotation, and all subsequent ones from Jeremy Bowen, come from an interview with the author in London, 16 December 2014.
4. This quotation, and all subsequent ones from Chris McGreal, come from an interview with the author via Skype, 9 June 2014.
5. This quotation, and all subsequent ones from Harvey Morris, come from an interview with the author in London. 1 May 2014. Yasser Arafat took over the PLO leadership in February 1969 (Aburish, p. 90).
6. Palestinian uprising against Israel.
7. For detail of the way the intifada spread in Gaza, see Hass (2000), pp. 33–50.
8. 'Two Die in Gaza Clash', *Guardian*, 10 December 1987.
9. Fisher (1987).
10. 'Israeli Paras on Patrol as Gaza Violence Continues', *Daily Telegraph*, 11 December 1987.
11. Usher (1999), p. 21.
12. This quotation, and all subsequent ones from William Booth, come from an interview with the author in Jerusalem, 24 June 2014.
13. Interview with the author, Tel Aviv, 27 June 2014.
14. This quotation, and subsequent ones from Harriet Sherwood, come from an interview with the author in London, 3 June 2014.
15. For a full account of this episode in Zionist and journalism history, see Baram, Chapter 2.

16. Baram (2004), p. 33.
17. This quotation, and all subsequent ones from Donald Macintyre, come from an interview with the author in London, 2 May 2014.
18. Shindler (2013), p. 170.
19. Shlaim (2001), p. 211.
20. Shlaim (2001), p. 479; Shindler (2013), p. 220.
21. Shindler (2013), p. 298.
22. www.aipac.org. Accessed 18 July 2014.
23. This quotation, and all subsequent ones from Matt Rees, come from an interview with the author in Jerusalem, 24 June 2014.
24. Earle, Steve (2002) *Jerusalem*, E-Squared/Artemis records.
25. This quotation, and all subsequent ones from Yolande Knell, come from an interview with the author in Beit Sahour, West Bank, 23 June 2014.
26. Sambrook (2010), p. 12.
27. Ibid.
28. BBC News (2013) 'Kerry "confident" of Israel-Palestinian Talks Progress' Available at http://www.bbc.co.uk/news/world-middle-east-24832742. Accessed 25 July 2014.

4   The Roadmap, Reporting, and Religion

1. http://www.un.org/news/dh/mideast/roadmap122002.pdf. Accessed 10 May 2013.
2. http://www.un.org/apps/news/story.asp?NewsID=6903&Cr=palestin&Cr1=#.UYz7BMpZSsG. Accessed 10 May 2013.
3. Quoted in the *Los Angeles Times*, 4 June 2003.
4. Ibid.
5. Hollis (2010), p. 141.
6. Ibid., pp. 141–2.
7. http://web.archive.org/web/20041020235150/http://www.whitehouse.gov/news/releases/2003/05/iraq/20030501-15.html. Accessed 10 May 2013.
8. Ibid.
9. The *New York Times* website, first published 5 February 1999. Available at http://www.nytimes.com/1999/02/05/news/05iht-france.t_0.html. Accessed 6 August 2014.
10. *Los Angeles Times*, 4 June 2003.
11. *New York Times*, 4 June 2003.
12. *Daily Telegraph*, 4 June 2003.
13. *Independent*, 5 June 2003.
14. *New York Times*, 4 June 2003.
15. *Guardian*, 5 June 2003.
16. See Rodgers (2013), p. 69.
17. *Daily Mail*, 5 June 2003.
18. *Independent*, 5 June 2003.
19. *New York Times*, 4 June 2003.
20. Quoted in the *Daily Mirror*, 4 June 2003.
21. *Daily Telegraph*, 4 June 2003.
22. *Daily Mail*, 5 June 2003.
23. Ibid.

24. http://news.bbc.co.uk/1/hi/world/middle_east/2965282.stm.   Accessed   10 May 2013.
25. Ibid.
26. Ibid.
27. Ibid.
28. Interview, London, 7 August 2014. All subsequent quotations from Alan Philps are from the same interview.
29. Interview, Jerusalem 24 June 2014.
30. Peters and Newman (eds) (2012), p. 1.
31. Ibid.
32. The Roadmap – see note 1, p. 1.
33. The Roadmap, p. 6.
34. *Israel: Facing the Future* (2013), BBC Television documentary broadcast on BBC2 at 9 pm on Wednesday 17 April 2013.
35. Available   at   http://news.bbc.co.uk/1/hi/in_depth/middle_east/israel_and _the_palestinians/key_documents/1682961.stm. Accessed 13 May 2013.
36. Available at http://blogs.channel4.com/paul-mason-blog/brit-gaza-fault-line -heard-lot/2094. Accessed 8 August 2014.
37. *Guardian*, 5 June 2003.
38. Ibid.
39. Cited in 'Sharon orders Gaza pullout plan', BBC News website, 2 February 2004. Available at http://news.bbc.co.uk/1/hi/world/middle_east/3451497 .stm. Accessed 13 May 2013.
40. Fisk (2005), p. 1269.
41. Sharon (2001), p. 258.
42. Haberman (1995).
43. Quoted in Rodgers (2013), p. 88.
44. UNRWA (2003).
45. Quoted in Rodgers (2013), p. 142.
46. Shlaim (2000), p. 517.
47. Interview with the author, London, 21 October 2014. All subsequent quotations from Levy are taken from this interview.
48. http://www.bitterlemons.net/, 27 August 2012. http://www.bitterlemons -international.org/inside.php?id=1552. Accessed 14 May 2013.
49. Ibid.
50. Interview conducted by Skype between London and Princeton University, 15 July 2014. All subsequent quotations from Kurtzer are taken from this interview.
51. von Clausewitz (2008), p. 32.
52. Shindler (2013), p. 246.
53. Ibid.

5   Going Back Two Thousand Years All the Time

1. Jabotinsky (1923), p. 6.
2. Abu-Amr (1994), p. 66.
3. For example, in an article in the *Guardian* on 8 September 2014, Avi Shlaim referred to Hamas as 'the Islamic resistance movement that rules Gaza'.
4. Reuters (2008).

5. Ibid.
6. BBC, 2014.
7. BBC News 'Gaza conflict: Israel PM Netanyahu vows further campaign'. Available at http://www.bbc.co.uk/news/world-middle-east-28871703. Accessed 10 September 2014.
8. Ibid.
9. Pappe (2006), pp. 278–9.
10. United Nations Office for the Coordination of Humanitarian Affairs occupied Palestinian territory factsheet, November 2013. Available at http://www.ochaopt.org/documents/ocha_opt_hebron_h2_factsheet_november_2013_english.pdf. Accessed 12 September 2014.
11. Website of the Temporary International Presence in Hebron (TIPH). Available at http://www.tiph.org/en/About_Hebron/Hebron_today/. Accessed 12 September 2014.
12. I.e., 2013.
13. I.e., at Israeli soldiers, police, and settlers.
14. 'In a West Bank Culture of Conflict, Boys Wield the Weapon at Hand' New York Times website. First published 4 August 2013 (appeared in the print edition of the New York Times on 5 August 2013). Available at http://www.nytimes.com/2013/08/05/world/middleeast/rocks-in-hand-a-boy-fights-for-his-west-bank-village.html?pagewanted=all&module=Search&mabReward=relbias%3As%2C{%222%22%3A%22RI%3A14%22}. Accessed 12 September 2014.
15. Interview with the author, via Skype between London and New York, 6 November 2014. This and all subsequent citations from Gold come from this interview.
16. When 'Arabs massacred Jewish colonists in Hebron', Mansfield (1992), p. 205.
17. From Orwell's *Nineteen Eighty-Four*.
18. OED.com. Available at http://www.oed.com/view/Entry/176872?redirectedFrom=settlement#eid. Accessed 15 September 2014.
19. Maale Adummim Living the Life. Available at https://www.facebook.com/pages/Maale-Adumim/130961380393342?sk=info&tab=page_info. Accessed 15 September 2014.
20. Pappe (2006), p. 1.
21. See Rodgers (2013), p. 121.
22. Russian: 'tochnost' i kratkost'.
23. Scott (1921).
24. CiF Watch website. Available at http://cifwatch.com/. Accessed 19 September 2014.
25. A daily supplement published with the *Guardian*.
26. At that time, the body dealing with complaints against newspapers in Britain.
27. http://www.camera.org/. Accessed 19 September 2014.
28. Cited from the 'about' section of the 'Camera' website. Available at http://www.camera.org/index.asp?x_context=24. Accessed 19 September 2014.
29. Interview with the author, Jerusalem, 26 June 2014. All subsequent quotations attributed to Nitzan Chen come from this interview.
30. BICOM website. Available at http://www.bicom.org.uk/about/. Accessed 26 September 2014.

31. Interview with the author, Ramallah, 25 June 2014. All subsequent quotations attributed to Xavier Abu Eid come from this interview.
32. For a reflection on differing Israeli and Palestinian PR resources during the second intifada, see Luyendijk (2010), pp. 146–9.
33. Cockburn, Patrick (2014b).
34. Associated Press, 11 September 2001.
35. 'AP Protests Threat to Cameraman', Associated Press Despatch, 12 September 2001.
36. See Rodgers (2012), Chapter 6.
37. Philo and Berry (2011), p. 315.
38. Ibid., p. 286.
39. See Streitmatter (1997), p. 71.

6   The Ambassador's Eyes and Ears

1. See, for example, Senator Joseph Cirincione's speech at American University, Washington DC, 23 March 2003. Available at http://carnegieendowment.org/pdf/npp/AmericanSpeech.pdf. Accessed 9 October 2014.
2. Hollis (2010), p. 139.
3. See UN OCHA (2007), p. 20.
4. Ibid., p. 15.
5. For details, see the *Jerusalem Post* website 'Fogel Family identified as victims of Itamar Terror attack'. Available at http://www.jpost.com/Diplomacy-and-Politics/Fogel-family-identified-as-victims-of-Itamar-terror-attack. Accessed 14 February 2015.
6. This quotation, and all subsequent ones attributed to Yolande Knell, are taken from an interview with the author conducted in Beit Sahour, West Bank, on 23 June 2014.
7. See, for example, 'Three killed in Gaza convoy blast' the Guardian website, first posted 15 October 2003. Available at http://www.theguardian.com/world/2003/oct/15/israel.usa. Accessed 10 October 2014.
8. This quotation, and all subsequent ones attributed to Daniel Kurtzer, are taken from an interview with the author conducted via Skype between London and Princeton University on 15 July 2014.
9. See Rodgers (2013), p. 98.
10. US Department of State website. Available at http://www.state.gov/j/ct/rls/other/des/123085.htm. Accessed 17 October 2014.
11. This quotation, and all subsequent ones attributed to Tom Fitzalan Howard, are taken from an interview with the author conducted in London on 13 November 2014.
12. See Rodgers (2012), p. 135.
13. This quotation, and all subsequent ones attributed to Lord Levy, are taken from an interview with the author conducted in London on 21 October 2014.
14. 'No 10 blocks envoy's book on Iraq', the *Observer*, first posted 17 July 2005. Available at http://www.theguardian.com/politics/2005/jul/17/uk.books. Accessed 15 November 2014.
15. This quotation, and all subsequent ones attributed to Sir Jeremy Greenstock, are taken from an interview with the author conducted in London on 7 November 2014.

16. This quotation, and all subsequent ones attributed to Sir Sherard Cowper-Coles, are taken from an interview with the author conducted in London on 27 November 2014.

17. This quotation, and all subsequent ones attributed to Matt Rees, are taken from an interview with the author conducted in Jerusalem on 24 June 2014.

18. 'Blair admits he is shocked by discrimination on the West Bank', the *Independent*, 13 October 2007. Available at http://www.independent.co.uk/news/world/middle-east/blair-admits-he-is-shocked-by-discrimination-on-the-west-bank-396733.html. Accessed 24 October 2014.

19. 'Blair admits shock at West Bank discrimination', The Office of Tony Blair website. Available at http://www.tonyblairoffice.org/news/entry/blair-admits-shock-at-west-bank-discrimination/. Accessed 24 October 2014.

20. 'Jewish group demands recall of UK envoy to Israel', the Guardian website. Available at http://www.theguardian.com/world/2002/oct/21/israel. Accessed 27 October 2014.

7 Social Media: A Real Battleground

1. Horowitz, Roth, a Weiss (2014).
2. Kershner (2014).
3. Ibid.
4. BBC News website 'Israel: Hamas "will pay price" after teenagers found dead'. First published 1 July 2014. Available at http://www.bbc.co.uk/news/world-middle-east-28102253. Accessed 4 November 2014.
5. BBC News website 'Palestinian Mohammad Abu Khdair '"was burned alive"'. First posted 5 July 2014. Available at http://www.bbc.co.uk/news/world-middle-east-28174519. Accessed 4 November 2014.
6. BBC News website 'Gaza crisis: Toll of operations in Gaza'. First posted 1 September 2014. Available at http://www.bbc.co.uk/news/world-middle-east-28439404. Accessed 4 November 2014.
7. BBC News website 'Israel kills Palestinians suspected of teenagers' murders'. First posted 23 September 2014. Available at http://www.bbc.co.uk/news/world-middle-east-29323163. Accessed 14 February 2015.
8. Isikoff (2014).
9. Baker (2014).
10. Interview with the author, London, 29 September 2014.
11. See Rodgers (2012), p. 130.
12. Tweet from Remi Kanazi (@remroum) 2 October 2013. Accessed 6 November 2014. For more on #askIDF, see also Al-Jazeera's 'The Stream': 'Israeli army hosts #AskIDF: Palestinian solidarity activists use Twitter chat to highlight alleged abuses.' Available at http://stream.aljazeera.com/story/201310021924-0023082. Accessed 6 November 2014.
13. For example, BBC News website 'Israel: Government pays students to fight internet battles', first published 14 August 2013. Available at http://www.bbc.co.uk/news/blogs-news-from-elsewhere-23695896. Accessed 26 September 2014; AP 'Israel to pay students to defend it online', USA Today website, 14 August 2013. Available at http://www.usatoday.com/story/news/world/2013/08/14/israel-students-social-media/2651715/. Accessed 26

September 2014; Jerusalem Post website 'Government to use citizens as army in social media war', first published 14 August 2013. Available at http://www.jpost.com/Diplomacy-and-Politics/Government-to-use-citizens-as-army-in-social-media-war-322972. Accessed 6 November 2014.

14. Cited from Jerusalem Post website article referred to in note 11, above.
15. Available at https://twitter.com/IDFSpokesperson/status/49349362005432 3200. Accessed 6 November 2014.
16. This was the figure at 7 November 2014.
17. Cited in Lynfield (2014).
18. Search on Twitter for 'Hamas', 7 November 2014. Results at https://twitter .com/search?q=hamas&src=typd. Accessed 7 November 2014.
19. 'US, European Airlines suspend flights to Israel', CNN website. Posted 23 July 2014. Available at http://edition.cnn.com/2014/07/22/travel/israel-flights -suspended/. Accessed 14 February 2015.
20. For details on the aftermath of the attack, see BBC News 'Hamas Militants name new leader'. Posted 26 July 2002. Available at http://news.bbc.co.uk/ 1/hi/world/middle_east/2153948.stm. Accessed 6 January 2015.
21. Cited in BBC News 'Gaza conflict: Israel to investigate school shelling'. First posted 31 July 2014. Available at http://www.bbc.co.uk/news/world-middle -east-28578633. Accessed 17 November 2014.
22. For example the Guardian website ' "The world stands disgraced" – Israeli shelling of school kills at least 15'. First posted 31 July 2014. Available at http://www.theguardian.com/world/2014/jul/30/world-disgrace-gaza-un -shelter-school-israel. Accessed 17 November 2014.
23. This, and all subsequent citations from Chris Gunness, are taken from an interview with the author conducted by Skype between London and Jerusalem on 20 October 2014.
24. For example on the Guardian website, 'UN spokesman Chris Gunness breaks down during interview on Gaza – video'. First posted 31 July 2014. Available at http://www.theguardian.com/world/video/2014/jul/31/ un-spokesman-chris-gunness-breaks-down-during-aljazeera-interview-video. Accessed 17 November 2014.
25. 'Prosor calls to suspend UNRWA's spokesperson', from the website of the Permanent Mission of Israel to the United Nations. Available at http://embassies.gov.il/un/statements/letters/Pages/UNRWA-Spokesperson-is -Biased.aspx. Accessed 1 December 2014.
26. Interview with the author, London, 29 September 2014.
27. Calderone (2014).
28. 'Four children killed by Israeli shelling in Gaza – medical officials', Reuters. Posted 16 July 2014. Available at http://uk.reuters.com/article/2014/ 07/16/uk-palestinians-israel-children-idUKKBN0FL1PS20140716. Accessed 6 January 2015.
29. Greenwald (2014).
30. Shea was speaking at a conference to mark the fifth anniversary of the academic journal *Media, War and Conflict*. His remark was tweeted by the author from the conference, and can be found at https://twitter.com/search? q=%40jmacrodgers%20shea&src=typd. Accessed 19 December 2014.
31. Israel Ministry of Foreign Affairs 'PM Netanyahu holds a press confer- ence 6 Aug 2014'. Available at http://mfa.gov.il/MFA/PressRoom/2014/

Bibliography

Aburish, Saïd (1998) *Arafat: From Defender to Dictator* (London, Bloomsbury).

Abu-Amr, Ziad (1994) *Islamic Fundamentalism in the West Bank and Gaza* (Bloomington and Indianapolis, IN, Indiana University Press).

Ahmed, Akbar S. (1999) *Islam Today: A Short Introduction to the Muslim World* (London, I.B. Tauris).

Alter, Charlotte (2014) 'Netanyahu tells world leaders "Hamas is ISIS and ISIS is Hamas"', *Time* Magazine website. Posted 29 September 2014. Available at http://time.com/3445394/netanyahu-un-general-assembly-hamas -abbas/. Accessed 7 January 2015.

Baker, Luke (2014) 'Clashes erupt as Israeli police kill Palestinian', Reuters website. First posted 31 October 2014. Available at http://uk.reuters.com/article/2014/ 10/31/uk-mideast-palestinians-israel-shooting-idUKKBN0II2JD20141031. Accessed 4 November 2014.

Baram, Daphna (2004) *Disenchantment: The Guardian and Israel* (London, Guardian Books).

BBC (2014) 'Language when reporting terrorism', from BBC Editorial Guide-lines. Available at www.bbc.co.uk/editorialguidelines/page/guidance-reporting -terrorism-full#definitions. Accessed 8 September 2014.

Board, Barbara (1937) *Newsgirl in Palestine* (London, Michael Joseph).

Board, Barbara (1946a) '50 Die as Jews Blow Up Our Palestine H.Q.: Digging Goes On', *Daily Mirror*, 23 July.

Board, Barbara (1946b) 'Army's X-ray Men Hunt Terrorists in Jewish Hospitals', *Daily Mirror*, 31 July.

Bowen, Jeremy (2004) *Six Days* (London, Pocket Books).

Calderone, Michael (2014) 'CNN removes reporter Diana Magnay from Israel-Gaza after "Scum" Tweet', The Huffington Post. Posted 18 July 2014. Avail-able at http://www.huffingtonpost.com/2014/07/18/cnn-diana-magnay-israel -gaza_n_5598866.html?1405690372. Accessed 6 January 2015.

Cameron, James (1968) *What a Way to Run the Tribe* (London, Macmillan).

Carruthers, Susan (2011) *The Media at War* (Basingstoke, Palgrave Macmillan).

Chittal, Nisha (2015) 'J.K. Rowling, Aziz Ansari respond to Rupert Murdoch's tweet about Muslims', MSNBC.com website. Posted 12 January 2015. Available at http://www.msnbc.com/msnbc/jk-rowling-aziz-ansari-respond -rupert-murdochs-criticism-muslims. Accessed 30 January 2015.

Christie, Donald (2000) 'Flashback-Haifa' (unpublished memoir lent to the author by the Christie family).

Churchill, Randolph S. and Churchill, Winston S. (1967) *The Six Day War* (London, Heinemann).

Clarke, Thurston (1981) *By Blood and Fire: The Attack on the King David Hotel* (London, Hutchinson).

Cockburn, Patrick (2014a) *The Jihadis Return: ISIS and the New Sunni Uprising* (New York, OR Books).

Cockburn, Patrick (2014b) 'The Secret Report that Helps Israel Hide Facts', Independent website. Available at http://www.independent.co.uk/voices/comment/israelgaza-conflict-the-secret-report-that-helps-israelis-to-hide-facts-9630765.html. Accessed 14 February 2015.

Cossali, Paul and Robson, Clive (1986) *Stateless in Gaza* (London, Zed Books).

Council of the European Union, The (2012) *Council Conclusions on the Middle East Peace Process*. 10 December 2012. Available at http://www.consilium.europa.eu/uedocs/cms_Data/docs/pressdata/EN/foraff/134140.pdf. Accessed 14 May 2013.

Cowper-Coles, Sherard (2013) *Ever the Diplomat: Confessions of a Foreign Office Mandarin* (London, Harper Press).

Crooke, Alastair (2009) *Resistance: The Essence of the Islamist Revolution* (London, Pluto Press).

Danahar, Paul (2013) *The New Middle East: The World After the Arab Spring* (London, Bloomsbury).

Dayan, Moshe (1978) *Story of My Life* (London, Sphere Books).

Dunsky, Marda (2008) *Pens and Swords: How the American Mainstream Media Report the Israeli-Palestinian Conflict* (New York, Columbia University Press).

Elgot, Jessica (2014) 'Mark Regev, world's best known spinner, in an unwinnable war of words', Huffington Post website. Posted 1 August 2014. Available at http://www.huffingtonpost.co.uk/2014/07/31/mark-regev-israel-gaza_n_5637328.html?utm_hp_ref=uk. Accessed 7 January 2015.

Eretz Israel Museum website 'Mandelbaum Gate'. First published 2011. Available at http://www.eretzmuseum.org.il/e/96/. Accessed 12 May 2014.

Fawcett, Louise (ed.) (2013) *International Relations of the Middle East* (3rd edition) (Oxford, Oxford University Press).

Fisher, Dan (1987) 'Youth Killed, 16 Wounded in Gaza Clash', *Los Angeles Times*, 10 December.

Fisk, Robert (1992) *Pity the Nation* (Oxford, Oxford University Press).

Fisk, Robert (2005) *The Great War for Civilization* (London, Fourth Estate).

Friedman, Thomas (1998) *From Beirut to Jerusalem: One Man's Middle Eastern Odyssey* (2nd edition) (London, Harper Collins).

Gallagher, O'Dowd (1946) '143 Jews Held in Tel Aviv Cages', *Daily Mail*, 31 July.

Golani, Motti (2009) *The End of the British Mandate for Palestine, 1948: The Diary of Sir Henry Gurney* (Basingstoke, Palgrave Macmillan).

Greenwald, Glenn (2014) 'NBC news pulls veteran reporter from Gaza after witnessing Israeli attack on children', The Intercept. First posted 17 July 2014. Available at https://firstlook.org/theintercept/2014/07/17/nbc-removes-ayman-mohyeldin-gaza-coverage-witnesses-israeli-beach-killing-four-boys/. Accessed 6 January 2015.

Gringras, Robbie (2010) 'The bottom line: An Israeli cartoonist offers a graphic challenge to American Jews', Forward: the Jewish Daily website. Posted 27 January 2010. Available at http://forward.com/articles/124445/the-bottom-line/#ixzz3pnq97yyl. Accessed 20 January 2015.

Haberman, Clyde (1995) 'Besieged settlements: Are they worth keeping?' Posted 10 April 1995. Available at http://www.nytimes.com/1995/04/10/world/besieged-settlements-are-they-worth-keeping.html. Accessed 14 May 2013.

Halliday, Fred (2005) *100 Myths about the Middle East* (London, Saqi).

Harel, Amos (2014) 'Wave of Palestinian terror starting to resemble a religious war', Ha'aretz website. Posted 18 November 2014. Available at http://www .haaretz.com/news/diplomacy-defense/1.627127. Accessed 16 January 2015.

Hass, Amira (2000) *Drinking the Sea at Gaza: Days and Nights in a Land under Siege* (New York, Owl Books).

Hass, Amira (2003) *Reporting from Ramallah: An Israeli Journalist in an Occupied Land* (Los Angeles, CA, Semiotext(e)).

Hass, Amira (2014) 'When a Haaretz journalist was asked to leave a Palestinian university', Haaretz website. Posted 28 September 2014. Available at http://www.haaretz.com/news/features/.premium-1.618007. Accessed 19 January 2015.

Hirst, David (2003) *The Gun and the Olive Branch* (3rd edition) (London, Faber & Faber).

Hobsbawm, Eric (1995) *The Age of Extremes: 1914–1991* (London, Abacus).

Holbrooke, Richard (2008) 'Washington's Battle over Israel's Birth', *Washington Post*, 7 May 2008. Available at http://www.washingtonpost.com/wp-dyn/content/article/2008/05/06/AR2008050602447.html. Accessed 29 April 2014.

Hollingworth, Clare (1990) *Front Line* (London, Jonathan Cape).

Hollis, Rosemary (2010) *Britain and the Middle East in the 9/11 Era* (Chatham House Papers, pub. Wiley-Blackwell).

Horowitz, Adam, Roth, Scott, and Weiss, Philip (2014) 'Israel maintains gag order in missing teens' case, leading to charge of media "manipulation"', Mondoweiss website. First published 23 June 2014. Available at http://mondoweiss.net/2014/06/maintains-missing-manipulation. Accessed 4 November 2014.

Isikoff, Michael (2014) In Yahoo! News interview, 'Meshaal condemns murder of journalists, admits Hamas killed Israeli teens'. Yahoo! News website. Posted 22 August 2014. Available at http://news.yahoo.com/hamas-leader -don-t-compare-us-to-isil-193125056.html. Accessed 14 February 2015.

Jabotinsky, Ze'ev (1923) *The Iron Wall*. Available at http://www.jabotinsky.org/multimedia/upl_doc/doc_191207_49117.pdf. Accessed 4 September 2014.

Karetzky, Stephen and Frankel, Norman (eds.) (1989) *The Media's Coverage of the Arab-Israeli Conflict* (New York, Shapolsky Publishers).

Kershner, Isabel (2014) 'Abduction of young Israeli hitchhikers spurs debate on conduct', *New York Times* website. First published 16 June 2014. Available at http://www.nytimes.com/2014/06/17/world/middleeast/abduction-of -young-israeli-hitchhikers-spurs-debate-on-conduct.html?module=Search& mabReward=relbias%3Aw%2C{%222%22%3A%22RI%3A18%22}. Accessed 4 November 2014.

Khalidi, Walid (ed.) (1992) *All that Remains: The Palestinian Villages Occupied and Depopulated by Israel in 1948* (Washington DC, Institute for Palestine Studies).

Kurtzer, Daniel C., Lasensky, Scott B., Quandt, William B., Spiegel, Steven L., and Telhami, Shibley Z. (2013) *The Peace Puzzle: America's Quest for Arab-Israeli Peace, 1989–2011* (Ithaca, NY, and London, Cornell University Press).

Levin, Harry (1997) *Jerusalem Embattled: A Diary of the City under Siege* (London, Cassell).

Loyn, David (2014) 'Jon Snow's Gaza appeal risks reducing reporting to propaganda', the Guardian's 'Comment is Free' website. Posted 3 August

2014. Available at http://www.theguardian.com/commentisfree/2014/aug/03/jon-snow-gaza-appeal-reporting. Accessed 7 January 2015.

Luyendik, Joris (2010) *Hello Everybody! One Journalist's Search for Truth in the Middle East*. Translated by Michele Hutchinson (London, Profile).

Lynfield, Ben (2014) 'Israel-Gaza conflict: Benjamin Netanyahu blames Hamas for civilian casualties in Gaza Strip', The Independent website. First posted 13 July 2014. Available at http://www.independent.co.uk/news/world/middle-east/israelgaza-conflict-benjamin-netanyahu-blames-hamas-for-civilian-casualties-in-gaza-strip-9603619.html. Accessed 7 November 2014.

Mansfield, Peter (1992) *A History of the Middle East* (London, Penguin).

Newman, David (2013) 'Territory and Borders' in Peters, J. and Newman, D. (eds.) *The Routledge Handbook on the Israeli-Palestinian Conflict* (Abingdon, Routledge), p. 138.

Pappe, Ilan (2006) *A History of Modern Palestine: One Land, Two Peoples* (Cambridge, Cambridge University Press).

Peters, J. and Newman, D. (eds.) (2012) *The Routledge Handbook on the Israeli-Palestinian Conflict* (Abingdon, Routledge).

Philo, Greg and Berry, Mike (2011) *More Bad News from Israel* (London, Pluto Press).

Remnick, David (2013) 'The Party Faithful', *The New Yorker*, 21 January 2013, pp. 38–49.

Reuters (2008) *Handbook of Journalism* (2nd online edition). Available at http://handbook.reuters.com/index.php?title=Main_Page. Accessed 5 September 2014.

Rodgers, James (2012) *Reporting Conflict* (Basingstoke, Palgrave Macmillan).

Rodgers, James (2013) *No Road Home: Fighting for Land and Faith in Gaza* (Bury St Edmunds, Abramis).

Rodgers, Peter (2005) *Herzl's Nightmare: One Land, Two Peoples* (London, Constable and Robinson).

Roman, Yadin (2010) *The King David* (2nd edition) (Israel, Dan Hotels publication).

Said, Edward W. (2000) *The End of the Peace Process: Oslo and After* (London, Granta).

Sambrook, Richard (2010) *Are Foreign Correspondents Redundant? The Changing Face of International News* (Oxford, Reuters Institute for the Study of Journalism).

Sand, Shlomo (2012) *The Invention of the Land of Israel: From Homeland to Holy Land* (London, Verso).

Scott, C.P. (1921) 'A hundred years'. Available at http://www.theguardian.com/commentisfree/2002/nov/29/1. Accessed 19 September 2014.

Shalev, Chemi (2014) 'Faulty lines: Netanyahu says "ISIS" but his listeners hear "Gaza, occupation" ', Ha'aretz website. Posted 14 September 2014. Available at http://www.haaretz.com/blogs/west-of-eden/.premium-1.615612. Accessed 7 January 2015.

Sharon, Ariel (2001) *Warrior* (New York, Touchstone).

Shepherd, Naomi (1999) *Ploughing Sand: British Rule in Palestine* (London, John Murray).

Shindler, Colin (2013) *A History of Modern Israel* (Cambridge, Cambridge University Press).

Shlaim, Avi (2001) *The Iron Wall: Israel and the Arab World* (London, Penguin).

Snow, Jon (2014) 'The children of Gaza – Jon Snow's experience in the Middle East', *Channel 4 News* YouTube channel. First posted 26 July 2014. Available at https://www.youtube.com/watch?v=ACgwr2Nj_GQ. Accessed 7 January 2015.

State of Israel Government Press Office (2014) 'Notice to resident and visiting foreign correspondents in Israel'. Available at http://gpo.gov.il/English/presscards/Pages/GPOPressCards.aspx. Accessed 6 May 2014.

Streitmatter, Rodger (1997) *Mightier than the Sword: How the News Media have Shaped American History* (Oxford, Westview).

Tait, Robert (2015) 'Naftali Bennett denies his conduct led to deadly 1996 Israeli shelling of UN compound', first published on the *Telegraph* website 6 January 2015. Available at http://www.telegraph.co.uk/news/worldnews/middleeast/israel/11328035/Naftali-Bennett-denies-his-conduct-led-to-deadly-1996-Israeli-shelling-of-UN-compound.html. Accessed 7 January 2015.

UN OCHA (United Nations – Office for the Coordination of Humanitarian Affairs) (2007) 'The humanitarian impact on Palestinians of Israeli settlements and other infrastructure in the West'. Available at http://www.ochaopt.org/documents/thehumanitarianimpactofisraeliinfrastructurethewestbank_full.pdf. Accessed 9 October 2014.

UNRWA (2003) 'Twenty-third progress report – October–December 2003'. 31 December 2003. Available at http://unispal.un.org/UNISPAL.NSF/0/910E3D4DBE19CB0C85256E40005199B4. Accessed 4 March 2013.

Usher, Graham (1995) *Palestine in Crisis: The Struggle for Peace and Political Independence after Oslo* (London, Pluto Press).

Usher, Graham (1999) *Dispatches from Palestine* (London, Pluto Press).

von Clausewitz, Carl (2008) *On War* (Oxford, Oxford University Press).

Walt, Stephen M. and Mearsheimer, John J. (2008) *The Israel Lobby and Foreign Policy* (London, Penguin).

Index

Printed and bound in the United States of America